T0305887

Global Economic Governance and Human Development

Traditional understandings of economic development in low- and mid-income countries have largely been influenced by the economic narrative of Western Official Development Assistance (ODA). Within this framework, compliance with macroeconomic orthodoxy and early integration in Global Economic Governance (GEG) regimes are presented as enabling conditions to reach enhanced and sustainable levels of economic growth and social betterment. Yet, this narrative often fails to answer fundamental questions surrounding relational dynamics between the economies of ODA beneficiary countries and the GEG regimes they are asked to join.

Bringing together contributions by Government officials, academics and development practitioners, this edited volume explores quantitative and qualitative approaches to socio-economic analysis in low- and mid-income countries, highlighting the conditions under which international economic policies and institutions can foster – or hinder – their socio-economic growth. In particular, contributions address the impact of both West and China-inspired international economic regimes on value-adding capacity, trade, investments, job creation and social development, thus advancing the debate on what policy and legal provisions should low- and mid-income countries adopt in order to maximize the benefits and minimize the costs deriving from joining international economic regimes.

A comprehensive investigation of both sides of the Global Economic Governance and Human Development relationship; this book will interest scholars, practitioners and graduate students working in the areas of international relations, international political economy, global governance, international economics, development studies and human security.

Simone Raudino is Visiting Professor at the Kiev School of Economics, Ukraine, and the founder of Gap Consultants, a Hong Kong-based business consultancy company exploring alternative measures to promote economic growth in low-income countries.

Arlo Poletti is Associate Professor at the University of Trento, Italy. His research interests focus on the political economy of trade, the politics of international regulatory cooperation and the political economy of international institutions.

The International Political Economy of
New Regionalisms Series
Series Editor: Timothy M. Shaw

The International Political Economy of New Regionalisms Series presents innovative analyses of a range of novel regional relations and institutions. Going beyond established, formal, interstate economic organizations, this essential series provides informed interdisciplinary and international research and debate about myriad heterogeneous intermediate-level interactions. Reflective of its cosmopolitan and creative orientation, this series is developed by an international editorial team of established and emerging scholars in both the South and North. It reinforces ongoing networks of analysts in both academia and think-tanks as well as international agencies concerned with micro-, meso- and macro-level regionalisms.

For more information about this series, please visit: www.routledge.com/ASHSER-1146

Post-Hegemonic Regionalism in the Americas
Toward a Pacific–Atlantic Divide?
Edited by José Briceño-Ruiz and Isidro Morales

From Millennium Development Goals to Sustainable Development Goals
Rethinking African Development
Edited by Kobena T. Hanson, Korbla P. Puplampu and Timothy M. Shaw

Understanding Mega-Free Trade Agreements
The Political and Economic Governance of New Cross-Regionalism
Edited by Jean-Baptiste Velut, Louise Dalingwater, Vanessa Boullet and Valérie Peyronel

Pan-Caribbean Integration
Beyond CARICOM
Edited by Patsy Lewis, Terri-Ann Gilbert-Roberts and Jessica Byron

Global Economic Governance and Human Development
Edited by Simone Raudino and Arlo Poletti

Global Economic Governance and Human Development

**Edited by Simone Raudino
and Arlo Poletti**

LONDON AND NEW YORK

First published 2019
by Routledge
2 Park Square, Milton Park, Abingdon, Oxon OX14 4RN

and by Routledge
605 Third Avenue, New York, NY 10017

First issued in paperback 2021

Routledge is an imprint of the Taylor & Francis Group, an informa business

British Library Cataloguing-in-Publication Data
A catalogue record for this book is available from the British Library

Library of Congress Cataloging-in-Publication Data
Names: Raudino, Simone, editor. | Poletti, Arlo, editor.
Title: Global economic governance and human development / edited by Simone Raudino and Arlo Poletti.
Description: Abingdon, Oxon ; New York, NY : Routledge, 2019. | Series: The international political economy of new regionalisms series | Includes bibliographical references and index.
Identifiers: LCCN 2018025624 | ISBN 9781138049130 (hardback) | ISBN 9781315169767 (e-book)
Subjects: LCSH: Developing countries–Economic policy. | Economic assistance–Developing countries. | Economic development–Developing countries. | International economic relations. | Developing countries–Foreign economic relations. | Developing countries–Economic conditions. | Developing countries–Social conditions.
Classification: LCC HC60 .G545 2019 | DDC 338.9009172/4–dc23
LC record available at https://lccn.loc.gov/2018025624

ISBN 13: 978-1-03-209435-9 (pbk)
ISBN 13: 978-1-138-04913-0 (hbk)

Typeset in Times New Roman
by Out of House Publishing

A Franca Giudice,
che con straordinaria intelligenza, generosità e
grazia ha percorso il secolo breve
con il passo lungo di una civiltà millenaria

To Franca Giudice,
who with extraordinary intelligence, generosity and
grace has crossed the short century
with the long stride of a millennial civilization

Contents

Figures

Tables

Contributors

Editors

Simone Raudino is Visiting Professor at the Kiev School of Economics, Ukraine, and the founder of Gap Consultants, a Hong Kong-based business consultancy company exploring alternative measures to promote economic growth in low-income countries.

Arlo Poletti is Associate Professor at the University of Trento, Italy. His research interests focus on the political economy of trade, the politics of international regulatory cooperation and the political economy of international institutions.

Contributors

Uzma Ashraf is a Fellow at the Law and Economics Center, George Mason University, US. She has worked in the Civil Services of Pakistan as Assistant/Deputy Commissioner (2002–2010) and advised national governments and international development organizations including the World Bank and the Asian Development Bank. She has contributed to policy and academic reports coordinated by the Atlantic Council, US, and the Research Grants Council, Hong Kong.

Emily Bakos is a Research Analyst for the US government, focusing on private sector development and economic growth in Afghanistan. She holds a MA in International Affairs and International Economics from the Johns Hopkins School of Advanced International Studies, US, and a BA in International Political Economy from Fordham University, US.

Eugenia Baroncelli is Associate Professor of Political Science at the University of Bologna, Italy. Between 2001 and 2006 she worked at the World Bank as a consultant on trade, tariff and IPR policies. In addition to global economic governance and the EU-World Bank relations, she has researched, among other, the IPE of trade, democracy and security, focusing on the peace dividend from SAFTA trade preferences between India and

Pakistan, the role of neo-Gramscian development studies and Susan Strange's thought in IPE.

Adams Bodomo is Director of the Global African Diaspora Studies (GADS) Research Centre at the University of Vienna, Austria where he is Chair Professor of African Studies (Languages and Literatures). Professor Bodomo has done pioneering work on twenty-first century Africa–Asia studies, with a particular focus on the African Diaspora in China, Africa's experiences with globalization, and on the linguistic and cultural relations between Africa and Asia.

Paul Fishstein is a Senior Analyst with the US government. He has been involved with research and project implementation in Afghanistan intermittently since 1977, and has served as Director of the Afghanistan Research and Evaluation Unit (AREU), Afghanistan, as well as manager of health care and humanitarian programmes in Afghanistan and Pakistan. He holds an MS in Agricultural and Resource Economics from the University of Maryland (College Park), US, and a BA in English Literature from Beloit College, US.

Marcel Hanegraaff is Assistant Professor of Political Science at the University of Amsterdam, the Netherlands.

Sergey Korablin is Deputy Director at the Institute for Economics and Forecasting at the National Academy of Science of Ukraine and Member of the Expert Committee of the National Bank of Ukraine. He has previously worked as Director of the Monetary and Foreign Exchange Policy Analysis Department at the National Bank of Ukraine (2005–2015); as consultant at the United Nations Development Programme (2000–2005) and; as Head of Division at Ukraine's Prime Minister Office (1996–1999).

Roberto Lampa is Full Researcher at the National Scientific and Technical Research Council (CONICET), Argentina, and Assistant Professor at the National University of General San Martin (UNSAM), Argentina.

Eunice Rendón Cárdenas currently works as a private consultant on security and safety-related matters and as a contributor for several newspapers, including Reforma, Mexico, and El País, Spain. She is a Member of the National System of Researchers (CONACYT), Mexico, and Visiting Professor of the Tecnológico de Monterrey, Mexico. She was the Director General and Undersecretary of Prevention and Citizen Participation of the Mexican Ministry of Interior (SEGOB) and Head of the Institute for Mexicans Abroad at the Mexican Ministry of Foreign Affairs (IME).

Daniela Sicurelli is Associate Professor at the University of Trento, Italy. Her research interests include the politics of international development cooperation and of the European Union external relations.

Acronyms

ACEA	European Automobile Manufacturers' Association
ACP	African Caribbean and Pacific
ADB	Asian Development Bank
ADF	Asian Development Fund
ADFIs	Asian Development Finance Institutions
AIIB	Asian Infrastructure Investment Bank
ALCS	Afghanistan Living Conditions Survey
AMF	Asian Monetary Fund
ANDS	Afghanistan National Development Strategy
APTTA	Afghanistan–Pakistan Transit Trade Agreement
ASEAN	Association of South East Asian Nations
BoP	Balance of Payments
BRI	Belt and Road Initiative
BRICS	Brazil, Russia, India, China and South Africa
CASes	Country Assistance Strategies
Cat DDO	Catastrophe Deferred Drawdown Option
CDB	China Development Bank
CEPAL	*Comisiòn Economica Para América Latina y el Caribe*
CMI	Chiang Mai Initiative
CODHES	*Consultoría para los Derechos Humanos y el Desplazamiento*
COPs	Conference of the Parties
CPEC	China–Pakistan Economic Corridor
CPI	Consumer Price Index
CSO	Central Statistics Organization (Afghanistan)
DAC	Development Assistance Committee
DDO	Deferred Drawdown Option
DFIs	Development Finance Institutions
DPF	Development Policy Financing
DPOs	Development Policy Operations
DTCs	Developing and Transitioning Countries
EC	European Commission
ECA	Europe and Central Asia

ECLAC	Economic Commission for Latin America and the Caribbean
EFF	Extended Fund Facility
ELG	Export-Led Growth
EMEs	Emerging Market Economies
EMDCs	Emerging Markets and Developing Economies
EODB	Ease of Doing Business
EPAs	Economic Partnership Agreements
ETUC	European Trade Union Confederation
EU	European Union
EUROsociAL	Program for Social Cohesion in Latin America
EXIM	Export–Import Bank of China
FARC	Revolutionary Armed Forces of Colombia
FDI	Foreign Direct Investment
FILs	Financial Intermediary Loans
FOCAC	Forum on China–Africa Cooperation
FPI	Foreign Portfolio Investment
FTAA	Free Trade Area of the Americas
FTA	Free Trade Agreements
GATT	General Agreement on Tariffs and Trade
GCFF	Global Concessional Financing Facility
GDP	Gross Domestic Product
GEG	Global Economic Governance
GFC	Global Financial Crisis
GFRP	Global Food Crisis Response Program
GNI	Gross National Income
GPA	Government Procurement Agreement
GPGs	Global Public Goods
HD	Human Development
HDI	Human Development Index
HDI+	Human Development Index Plus
HICs	High Income Countries
IADB	Inter-American Development Bank
IBRD	International Bank for Reconstruction and Development
IDA	International Development Association
IDB	Inter-American Development Bank
IDB	Islamic Development Bank
IFC	International Finance Corporation
IFIs	International Financial Institutions
IL	Investment Lending
ILO	International Labour Organization
IMF	International Monetary Fund
IOs	International Organizations
IPF	Investment Project Financing
ISDS	Investor-State Dispute Settlement

ISI	Import Substitution Industrialization
ITO	International Trade Organization
LAC	Latin America and the Caribbean
LDCs	Least Developed Countries
LICs	Low-Income Countries
MAD	Mutual Assured Destruction
MCs	Ministerial Conferences
MDBs	Multi-lateral Development Banks
MDGs	Millennium Development Goals
MENA CFF	Middle East and North Africa Concessional Financing Facility
MERCOSUR	*Mercado Comùn del Sur*
MICs	Mid-Income Countries
MIGA	Multilateral Investment Guarantee Agency
MSJ	*Mesa de Seguridad y Justicia*
NAFTA	North American Free Trade Agreement
NATO	North Atlantic Treaty Organization
NBU	National Bank of Ukraine
NDB	New Development Bank
NGOs	Non-Governmental Organizations
NRVA	National Risk and Vulnerability Assessment (Afghanistan)
NSAs	Non-State Actors
OCA	Optimum Currency Areas
ODA	Official Development Assistance
OECD	Organization for Economic Cooperation and Development
PCA	Political Cooperation Agreement
PEF	Pandemic Emergency Financing Facility
PFM	Public Finance Management
PPP	Purchasing Power Parity
PQLI	Physical Quality of Life Index
PRC	People's Republic of China
PRSPs	Poverty Reduction Strategy Papers
PTAs	Preferential Trade Agreements
RAS	Reimbursable Advisory Services
RCEP	Regional Comprehensive Economic Partnership
RETF	Recipient-Executed Trust Fund
RTAA	Reciprocal Trade Agreement Act
RTAs	Regional Trade Agreements
SAARC	South Asian Association for Regional Cooperation
SAFTA	South Asian Free Trade Agreement
SAGAR	Security and Growth for all in the Region (India)
SALs	Structural Adjustment Loans
SAPs	Structural Adjustment Programs

SBA	Stand-By Arrangement
SCO	Shanghai Cooperation Organization
SDGs	Sustainable Development Goals
SMEs	Small- and Medium-sized Enterprises
SMP	Staff Monitored Program
SOE	State Owned Enterprise
SRF	Silk Road Fund
TA	Technical Assistance
TICAD	Tokyo International Conference on African Development
TNC	Trans-National Corporation
TPP	Trans-Pacific Partnership
TTIP	Transatlantic Trade and Investment Partnership
UN	United Nations
UNCTAD	United Nations Conference on Trade and Development
UNDP	United Nations Development Programme
UNFCCC	United Nations Framework Convention on Climate Change
UNGA	United Nations General Assembly
UNODC	United Nations Office on Drugs and Crime
UNSC	United Nations Security Council
USAID	United States Agency for International Development
VPA	Violence Prevention Alliance
WB	World Bank
WBG	World Bank Group
WHO	World Health Organization
WTO	World Trade Organization

Introduction

Simone Raudino and Arlo Poletti

> *Let's agree on definitions,*
> *and we will spare the world half of its illusions*
> René Descartes

The world of *Global Governance*

Despite having gained celebrity status for more than two decades in the study of international politics and global affairs, there remains substantial confusion about the concept of *Global Governance* (Hofferberth 2015). Ambiguity surrounds the meaning of both terms *Global* and *Governance*. While not seeking to systematically do justice to this rich conceptual debate, let alone to propose a synthesis to it, we offer a working definition that provides the overarching conceptual umbrella for the contributions to this volume.

Following a lead offered by Lawrence S. Finkelstein (Finkelstein 1995), we agree that the term *Global* points to something over and beyond what is usually conveyed by the terms *international, interstate, intergovernmental* or *transnational*. Historically, the term *Global* has gained prevalence with what many have perceived as a crisis of the State-centred system, an international system gravitating around the belief that States are the only rightful political units for the establishment of legitimate and effective rule. This crisis has been largely driven by the emergence of political, economic, social and cultural processes transcending traditional State boundaries which, altogether, have fundamentally called into question the State's ability to effectively sustain the production of collective goods within its boundaries, problematizing its role both as a level playing field and as a unit (Cerny 1995).

A breaking of the exclusive link between territory and political power (Held and McGrew 2002) created the permissive condition for the increasingly significant role played by supranational and trans-national actors, including International Organizations (IOs), International Financial Institutions Trans-National Corporations (TNCs) and Non-Governmental Organizations (NGOs). The rise in number and importance of this new class of actors thus called for new theoretical frameworks and terminologies that were not associated with the inter-state system created in 1945. Against this

background, the adjective *Global* came to be associated to different political processes aiming to promote, regulate, or intervene, more or less purposefully, in the common affairs of humanity in which States could not be
recognized anymore as the only relevant political units. The term *Global*
thus describes patterns of political interconnectedness and interdepend-
ence among different classes of international actors, of which national
governments only represented one specific class, that are potentially or actually global in reach.

The term *Governance* is also beset by varying usages. Let us begin from
what would appear to be self-evident: *Governance* can safely be assumed
to signify something different from *Government*. Since the rise of the
Westphalian system in seventeenth century Europe, the international system
lacks hierarchy among sovereign States, which means that it is not possible to
talk about an international *Government*. In the passage from middle age to
modernity, European sovereigns freed themselves from the yoke of universal
institutions – the Pope and the Emperor – and established self-legitimizing and
self-referential sovereign systems which did not recognize superior authorities: *superiorem non recognoscens*. Because the term *Government* cannot be
applied to relations among sovereign States, a fuzzier and less definitive term
has come to connote any form of wilful coordination among independent
political units. Paraphrasing Carl von Clausewitz's celebre definition of war,
it could be said that *Governance* is the continuation of *Government* through
other means, in a context lacking the foundational feature of Government,
e.g. *sovereignty*.

Authors in this volume understand *Governance* as a less compelling and
more heterogeneous form of social organization than the one associated
with the term *Government*. We also agree with Finkelstein's rigour in
defining *Governance* as "an activity – that is, doing something" (Finkelstein
1995): *Governance* is an inherently active phenomenon and the institutions of
Governance should therefore be seen as *means* of exerting governance, rather
than as *ends* in themselves. Following this line of thought, he reaches the conclusion that "*Global Governance* is governing, without sovereign authority,
relationships that transcend national frontiers". We find this first part of
Finkelstein's definition well suited for the understanding used in this volume –
yet we ought to disagree with his second part of the definition, which sees
Global Governance as "doing internationally what Governments do at home",
exactly because the international system lacks the defining feature of national
governments, which base their authority upon the principle of *sovereignty* and
its key manifestations, including the monopoly of the legitimate use of violence. As Keohane (2002) fittingly puts it, "since there is no global government, global governance involves strategic interactions among entities that
are not arranged in formal hierarchies".

We therefore agree with James N. Rosenau who stresses how, contrary to
Government processes, *Governance* mechanisms are more related to "steering"
and "[trying to] control", rather than "commanding" [as in *Government*]

(Rosenau 2009). Such interpretation also finds support in the etymology of the word, deriving from the Greek "kybenan" and "kybernetes", which means "to steer" and "to pilot or helmsman". Highlighting the absence of formal hierarchies as a key defining feature of *Global Governance* does not imply a negligence of the role of power. On the contrary, power, and the struggle to exert power, are key to understand *Global Governance*. Yet, contrary to what happens for Government, the entities that wield governance power are often not formally authorized to do so by the "sovereign authority", which means that they are often not regarded as legitimate by those who are affected by them (Keohane 2002).

Global Governance naturally poses two broad sets of questions. The first is who the players are: a characterization of the "actors" participating to the shaping of *Global Governance* is necessary if we have to retain a meaningful definition of the phenomenon. The second is a definition of the mechanisms used by these actors in steering, or at least trying to steer, *Global Governance* – these mechanisms being obviously related to and dependent upon the nature of the actors we estimate being legitimate players.

Actors

The deeper international interdependency that settled-in at the end of the Cold War made international affairs the legitimate business of an increasing number of small- and mid-sized corporate and non-profit organizations, rather than the exclusive preserve of national sovereign States, inter-governmental organizations and selected trans-national corporations. Such development further complicated the theoretical differentiation existing between "Globalization shapers" (or "controllers") – actors contributing in shaping *Global Governance* – from "Globalization takers" (or "controlees") – actors adapting to international norms and regulations set by others.

While different authors rely on criteria of different natures, they mostly conclude that national governments, international organizations and networks, transnational corporations and transnational non-governmental organizations should be counted among the "Globalization shapers". Some scholars have adopted resolutely comprehensive criteria in compiling the "shapers" list. For example, in a topical article, James N. Rosenau opts for virtually leaving no one out of the "shapers/controllers" group: "*Global Governance* is conceived to include system of rules at all levels of human activity – from the family to the international organization – in which the pursuit of goals through the exercise of control has transnational repercussions" (Rosenau 2009: 14). Rosenau leverages his definition upon a decision of the Council of Rome,[1] concluding that the term should "not only encompass the activities of Governments, but also include the many other channels through which commands' flow in the form of goals framed, directives issued, and policies pursued" (Rosenau 2009: 8).

Finkelstein, on his side, is more sceptic of the usefulness of such an encompassing definition: "Does it really clarify matters, however, or facilitate the research enterprise, to toss [transnational criminal organizations] in a hopper along with States, intergovernmental organizations, nongovernmental organizations, and Moody's investors' services? Global Governance appears to be virtually anything" (Finkelstein 1995: 368). Finkelstein has a compelling point and yet his question leaves unattended the most burdening task: individuating and defining a discriminatory criterion to sift actors who can be categorized among the "shapers/controllers" from those who are to be relegated among the "takers/controlees".

This is no straightforward exercise. While everybody would agree on the functional and normative difference between national sovereign governments and single-family units, it also seems obvious that at some point the discriminant between "shapers/controllers" and "takers/controlees" needs to be drawn in an arbitrary fashion. Should the discriminant be based on the size – demographic, economic or else – of the actors? Should the source of these actors' funding – State budgets rather than private contributions or self-financing – be chosen as a stick of measurement? Could institutional or ownership structures around the world be standardized and eventually be taken as a norm criterion?

All these potential criteria present their own sets of challenges. If economic size mattered, then the legitimacy of many State actors should be questioned: with a Gross Domestic Product (GDP) of roughly USD 30 million, the Republic of Tuvalu would qualify as one of the 23 million Small- and Medium-sized Enterprises (SMEs) incorporated in the European Union (EU)[2] – yet, as a sovereign State, it is entitled to a diplomatic representation in its own right at the United Nations (UN) and at the EU. Similarly, if an international NGO with regular funding from a Government's budget should be categorized among the "shapers/controllers", it remains unclear why a think tank relying on private contributions should be relegated among the "takers/controlees". State-controlled enterprises such as Gazprom are certainly to be counted among the "shapers", along fully privately-owned companies of the calibre of Apple; yet, it would be impossible finding an objective and properly justified threshold for the dozens of millions of other private, State-owned or State-participated active companies around the world. The same goes with non-governmental organizations, interest groups, lobbies, societies and the dozens of other categories in which different national legislations have institutionally declined the natural human tendency to act via organized social action.

If an arbitrary threshold has to be established, we decide to draw such a line at a point that takes into consideration the following: i) recognition – either *de iure* or *de facto* – by players who indisputably pertain to the "shapers/controllers" group; ii) capacity to mobilize human and financial resources beyond these actors' inner social/professional circles; and iii) capacity to exert influence on a transnational scale. Any international actor complying with these criteria will be considered as a "Globalization shaper", and therefore a legitimate object of interest in the ontology of this volume.

Mechanisms

Generosity (profligacy?) in defining the group of "Globalization shapers" brings Rosenau to identify no less than a dozen control mechanisms (Rosenau 2009: 16–36). Abundance comes as a natural consequence of the number of actors Rosenau considers as influencing *Global Governance*, but also results from a certain commingling of control mechanisms and classes of actors.[3]

The exercise engaged by Rosenau is worthwhile. Yet, as Finkelstein had hinted, it seems to get enmeshed in an open, never-ending process. Rosenau is fully aware of the many obstacles lying on the path he has chosen: in his words, such exercise is destined to convey a "sense of the degree to which global governance is likely to become increasingly pervasive and disaggregated in the years ahead" (Rosenau 2009: 17), rather than an exhaustive compilation. In the interest of pragmatisms, this volume will simply recognize as control mechanisms of *Global Governance* any organized action that officially stems from one of the *Global Governance* "shapers/controllers" and that is recognized as such by other "shapers/controllers".

According to this definition, the American invasion of Afghanistan; the decision of Samsung and Apple to draw to an end their legal battles on copyright infringements and; the efforts of the Government of Saudi Arabia to diversify its economy away from oil revenues should all be considered mechanisms of *Global Governance* as much as, say, the decision of a local Nigerian NGO to wind-down activities in one specific Nigerian province. All these activities respect the above-mentioned criteria (provided that the NGO is registered, recognized and/or financed by a sovereign State, an international organization or another "Globalization shaper"). As heterogeneous, unconventional and skewed as such categorization might sound, it is somehow representative of the very essence of *Global Governance*, whereby authority and capacity to influence are diffused, interdependent and non-hierarchical.

Despite the absence of formal hierarchies, influence in *Global Governance* is also exerted through traditional paradigms of power. For example, in the most extreme forms, a dominant State can issue authoritative decisions on behalf of one or more subordinate States, such as when these subordinate States decide to formally adopt a foreign currency (Kahler and Lake 2009). In the case of supranational institutions, political authority can be shifted to a collective unit that can make binding or authoritative decisions, and is sometimes even provided with credible enforcement power (Goldstein et al. 2000). In other cases, actors such as States, NGOs and organizations representing business interests give shape to softer types of cooperation in the form of networks based on voluntary adherence to common rules, reciprocity and trust (Abbott and Snidal 2009). While in all these governance mechanisms influence is exercised in the absence of formal vertical authority, this authority appears to remain shaped and enforced via more classic mechanisms of Government.

Global Economic Governance (GEG)

Following our discussion above, it is important to note the inherent difficulty one faces in identifying clear policy boundaries within *Global Governance*. Hardly any policy area falls outside the scope of *Global Governance*. While the coveted ground of the high politics – matters that are vital to the very survival of the most important political units, the nation States – such as military security, foreign policy and fiscal matters, are predictably high on the agenda of "Globalization shapers", virtually no policy area is excluded from their range of activities.

Indeed, one of the very characteristics of *Global Governance* is the capacity of "shapers" to hold increasing sway upon "takers" by simply carrying on their daily activities. Interconnectedness works both vertically and horizontally: steering in one policy area has far-fetched political, legal and economic implications in other policy areas. This mirrors dynamics at the national level – where, for example, decisions in the fiscal area have implications in all other policy areas – but also comes as a corollary of the interdependency paradigm upon which the very concept of *Global Governance* is based. Interconnectedness also translates in the globalization of domestic policy areas and business sectors, which at its own turn implies a progressive blurring of borders between traditional governmental thematic areas. Hence, while it still makes sense to distinguish policy areas in terms of actors and control mechanisms, we are compelled to note that a clear-cut definition of the boundaries of the "economic" dimension of *Global Governance* is becoming progressively difficult.

Keeping in mind this important caveat, this volume tries nonetheless to focus on the economic sphere of *Global Governance* – e.g. *Global Economic Governance (GEG)* – by defining it as the "diffuse act of governing, without sovereign authority, economic relationships that transcend national frontiers".

Understandably, and similarly to processes around the general term of *Global Governance*, there is much disagreement around the term GEG. Not everyone agrees with an encompassing definition of the term: for example, in its *Report of the Secretary General* titled *Global Economic Governance and Development*, the United Nations General Assembly (UNGA) identifies GEG as the "role of multilateral institutions and processes in shaping global economic policies, rules and regulations" (UNGA 2011: 2). This rather restrictive understanding is reinforced by the idea that "the existing mechanisms of global economic governance were created more than 60 years ago" (UNGA 2011: 2), which implies that institutions and processes established before the Bretton Woods and Dumbarton Oaks conferences are little relevant to today's GEG.

We ought to disagree with this understanding in so far as the single GEG's most defining feature remains the market economy. Most of the key mechanisms of the market economy – including private ownership; freedom to engage in economic enterprise; freedom to move production factors; fiat currency and; legal inheritance – were all adopted well before the funding of the United Nations (or the Society of Nations for that matter), the World Bank (WB), the International Monetary Fund (IMF) and the General Agreement on Tariffs and Trade (GATT)/World Trade Organization (WTO).

In fact, national Governments based on the tenets of the market economy are the very founding fathers of the IFIs that UNGA portrays as the main "shapers/controllers" of GEG. The historical legacy of this genesis is still evident today: out of the forty-four countries which participated to the Bretton Woods conference, it was the five of them with the strongest market economies that yielded disproportionate negotiating power (USA, UK, France, Germany, Japan), as this eventually reflected in the governance systems of the new-born institutions. Although membership to global IFIs was subsequently expanded and the allocation of votes was regularly updated, countries pertaining to the G7 and, to a lesser extent, other countries pertaining to the Organization for Economic Cooperation and Development (OECD), still maintained their guiding role, with IFIs mostly acting on their behalf. This is not to say that IFIs have no room for independent action, or that the interests of OECD States and those of global IFIs are perfectly aligned; yet, the relationship between the two can largely be read as one of principal/agent.

In light of this, it should come as no surprise that an independent review of the role of ten different classes of actors in influencing global business norms across thirteen regulatory fields has found that nation States have, by far, been the most important players (Braithwaite and Drahos 2000). Among them, the USA, the UK, France and Germany have been found to be the most influential. In economic affairs, International Organizations (IOs) (systemic/intergovernmental level), and particularly IFIs, have often behaved as institutional relays of these and other powerful OECD national governments.

Human Development

The concept of *Human Development* has a somehow less encompassing and better-defined meaning than the concept of GEG. Introduced for the first time by Pakistani economist Mahbub Ul Haq in the 1990 UN Human Development Report, *Human Development* refers to the process of "enlarging people's freedoms and opportunities and improving their well-being". In line with Amartya Sen's work (Nussbaum and Sen 1993), Ul Haq operationalized life improvements through the variable of *capabilities:* a person's potential to do and become. Capabilities are considered necessary equipment that one has to pursue for a life of value; their most basic expression includes good health, access to knowledge and a decent material standard of living, while more elaborated versions may take into consideration the ability to participate in the decisions affecting one's life, to have control over one's living environment, to enjoy freedom from violence, to have societal respect, and to relax and have fun.

When introduced in 1990, the Human Development Index (HDI) represented a fairly revolutionary departure from previous statistical operationalizations of the concept "development". The HDI index chipped away the mainstream interest for economic variables and focused instead on some of the social manifestations of those economic variables, merging economic and social indicators into a single index. The process was instrumental in serving the more general cause of shifting attention away from rather theoretical operationalizations of *wellbeing* – including macroeconomic indicators and far-fetched understandings of *security* such as the military perspective that dominated the Cold War's security narrative – into a more relevant, realistic and, ultimately, truthful portray of what normative philosopher Ken Booth aptly called the interests of "real people in real places" (Booth 1996: 366).

Dissenting voices on mainstream understandings of "development" were not completely new in the 1990s, as questions on the suitability of orthodox economic measures in gauging people's wellbeing had long been asked before the work of Mahbub Ul Haq and Amyarta Sen. In particular, heterodox voices suggesting that GDP was ill-suited to accurately measure a society's overall wellbeing had already sprung right after the Bretton Woods conference had sanctioned GDP as the standard tool for sizing up a country's economy. In 1959, American economist Moses Abramovitz already suggested the need to be "skeptical of the view that long-term changes in the rate of growth of welfare can be gauged even roughly from changes in the rate of growth of output" (Abramovitz 1959: 21). In the 1970s and 80s development economists already suggested to go beyond GDP by putting greater emphasis on employment, redistributive growth and capacity to meet people's needs; such push concretely resulted in the Physical Quality of Life Index (PQLI), a precursor of the HDI. Although these ideas remained minoritarian, they were predictive of a theoretical shift to come.

The normative drive behind the theoretical shift introduced by the *Human Development* concept is based on a simple belief: betterment in people's quality of life ought to be the only true purpose of economic growth. *Human Development* is a reminder that humanity should be interested in economic growth only in so far as it can improve quality of life – or *capabilities* in Ul Haq and Sen's wording–, and not because economic output is good per se. Such a self-evident axiom had gone largely forgotten both in mainstream economics and in popular understandings of wealth, and the invention of the GDP index in the 1940s did little to address existing (mis)perceptions. On the contrary, increases in GDP per capita across the Western world, particularly after the end of the Second World War, had generally been hailed as a self-evident proof of healthy economic systems and good "developmental" processes being underway. This faith concealed doubtful assumptions and, at times, interest-driven research.

The theoretical assumption underpinning the belief of a linear relation between the national aggregate output and people's wellbeing had largely been driven by so-called "trickledown economics": the idea that everyone stands to benefit from a richer society, and that "a rising tide lifts all boats". The assumption is not inherently wrong or historically unfound: one only needs thinking at the exceptional socio-economic growth of Victorian Britain or post-Xiaoping China, to know that general economic expansion can bring improvements across the entire social spectrum of whole nations. However, the idea is just too general and unqualified to identify all the concurrent conditions that contributed in determining such outcomes. As, no doubt, there must have been concurrent conditions at work: one only needs thinking at the phenomena of GDP expansion cum middle-class income stagnation in post-Nixon America or GDP expansion cum pauperization of the lowest income quartile in Menem's Argentina to realize that economic growth does not automatically entail social betterment for everyone.

Trickle-down economics is an oversimplified reading of a set of phenomena – wealth creation, distribution and use – that remain dependent upon and correlated through extremely complex, and at time unfathomable, variables. The epistemological and empirical limits of trickle-down economics have been raised in the economic literature by many, most notably by exponents of the Historical School of Economics, and more recently by a large group of mainstream and heterodox economists, including Joseph Stiglitz and Ha-Joon Chang. These contributions strongly maintain that economic expansion as measured by value-adding indexes do not automatically translate in proportional increases in people's living standards. Further, a narrow focus on a brute measurement of economic growth eventually leads to a fetishization of a process while losing touch with the content – or to the prioritization of a *mean* over the originally-sought *end*. Eventually, as Max Horkheimer had warned in his *Critique of instrumental reason* (Horkheimer 2012), such processes risk leading to the tyranny of efficiency over meaningfulness and the forfeiting of democracy for technocracy.

The theoretical underpinnings of the *Human Development* approach are rich. In the institutional declination of the UN, *Human Development* is about "expanding the richness of human life, rather than simply the richness of the economy in which human beings live ... an approach that is focused on people and their opportunities and choices" (UNDP 2016). Yet, the corresponding statistical implications of the approach have been rather modest: the HDI simply consists in a composite index weighting i) alphabetization and ii) life expectancy variables along iii) the traditional GDP variable. Such pragmatic compromise is understandable considering the statistical predicament implied by each new variable added to a global composite index. Data needs to be retrieved from all countries before they can be standardized and compared. This is an endeavouring exercise explaining why in 1990 UNDP compromised on the HDI by only adding two social variables to the traditional GDP variable. Yet, the genie was out of the bottle: since then, dozens of development indicators privileging social and political perspectives – including *Human Security*, democracy, freedom and happiness indexes – have added their voices to and successfully competed with traditional economic measures of wellbeing.[4]

In trying to give a broader operationalization to the concept of socio-economic development, authors in this volume will at time make reference to a *theoretical* index of *Human Development*, as it would be defined by the set of variables used by some existing statistical surveys – which typically includes food security, gender equality and housing conditions on top of more granular definitions of health coverage and education.[5] The variables adopted in the Afghanistan Living Condition Survey (ALCS) developed by the Afghan Central Statistics Organization (CSO) with the support of the World Bank can be taken as an example of a modern and comprehensive operationalization of the *Human Development* concept along these lines. We will refer to this theoretical index comprehensively operationalizing *Human Development* as "HDI+".

Structure of the volume

The volume brings together contributions by Government officials, academics and development practitioners with a view to both fostering a dialogue between different communities that, despite dealing with the same subject matters, all too often remain isolated, and developing insights that can benefit a wide audience of development-focused professionals.

The first contribution by Raudino represents the conceptual building block of this collective research endeavour. This first chapter develops a framework to think systematically and comprehensively about the GEG/HDI+ nexus, thus providing a unitary and coherent conceptual reference for all contributions to the volume. More specifically, Raudino argues that, within a given community, three variables are directly and significantly involved in determining *Human Development* levels: i) the creation of wealth; ii) the distribution of wealth; and iii) the use of wealth. He considers these three variables as mutually inter-dependent and accounting, at any given point in time, for the HDI+ level in a given community, and its likely progression over the near future. After elaborating on each of these three dynamics, the chapter specifies the various causal channels through which GEG bears on the prospects of wealth creation, distribution and use. In particular, Raudino argues in favour of focusing on how globalization "shapers" affect economic growth opportunities in low- and mid-income countries by steering two key sets of policies: macroeconomic (and in particular, monetary, fiscal and business regulatory policies) and Balance of Payments (BoP) (current account and capital and financial account) policies. Moreover, this chapter systematically discusses how each contribution to the volume speaks to this conceptual framework. We defer to Raudino's chapter for an overview of how the contributions included in this volume problematize and empirically assess the relationship between GEG and HDI+.

Two distinctive and important features of the following contributions – Chapters 2 to 10 – should be stressed at this stage.

First, while the chapters focus on the roles of globalization "shapers" that have traditionally attracted scholarly attention, i.e. WTO, WB and they also expand the analytical focus of the debate to include a wider set of international institutions that are increasingly playing a major role as globalization "shapers". In particular, the analyses carried out in Chapters 2, 3 and 8 cover four sets of multilateral governance systems. Chapter 2 by Hanegraaff and Poletti, for instance, seeks to shed light on the political-economic factors that can enable a more effective representation of poorer countries' interests in GEG by carrying out an analysis of populations of Non-State Actors (NSAs) active at a traditional multilateral institution such as the WTO, but also at an increasingly important multilateral institutional venue such as the United Nations Framework Conventions on Climate Change. Chapter 3 by Baroncelli, develops an original investigation of how the World Bank has internally adapted in the face of the structural and multiple crises it has faced in the last decade. Chapter 8 by Korablin, albeit only indirectly, analyzes the challenges faced by commodity-dependent economies and their limited room for action when interacting with IMF programmes.

The volume also touches upon the increasingly important role played by regional globalization shapers. Chapter 5 by Sicurelli does so by investigating the political-economic drivers of EU trade agreements with a number of Asian countries in order to shed light on the likely impact of these EU-led trade initiatives on their development potential. Chapter 7 by Lampa considers an additional regional institution by showing how MERCOSUR, in combination with the national economic policies of MERCOSUR countries, crucially affected within-region development trajectories.

Moreover, and in line with the discussion on the critical role that States continue to play in GEG, other contributions to this volume focus on the role of national globalization "shapers". Chapter 9 by Rendón Cárdenas, and Chapter 10 by Bakos and Fishstein, for instance, analyse how US foreign aid contributed to privileging traditional security approaches to conflict prevention in Latin American countries, and achieved only modest results in fostering economic growth in Afghanistan, respectively. Moreover, Chapters 4 and 6 investigate the increasingly important role played by China. More specifically, Chapter 4 by Ashraf discusses whether the Chinese Belt and Road Initiative represents a challenge to the so-called Western International Economic Order, while Chapter 6 by Bodomo sheds light on the implications of Chinese Foreign Direct Investments (FDI) in Africa for broader patterns of country-to-region cooperation, and African development prospects more generally.

The second important distinctive feature of this collective volume consists of the broad coverage of its field perspectives, ensuring a global geographical scope when it comes to analyzing the globalization "takers". For instance, Chapter 7 by Lampa and Chapter 9 by Rendón Cárdenas cover the Latin American continent, developing field perspectives on Colombia and Mexico, and some MERCOSUR countries respectively. Chapter 6 by Bodomo covers the African continent through an analysis of Chinese FDI flows in a number of African economies. The Asian continent is also widely represented in the volume through the analyses developed in Chapter 5 by Sicurelli, who investigates the politics generated by EU trade agreements with South Korea, Vietnam and Singapore, in Chapter 4 by Ashraf, who offers insights on the likely effects of the Chinese Belt and Road Initiative for Pakistan's economy, and in Chapter 10 by Bakos and Fishstein, who develop an in-depth assessment of the many remaining challenges that the international community still faces in supporting HDI+ in Afghanistan. Finally, Chapter 8 by Korablin touches upon Ukraine, a former Soviet Republic that is located in the EU's East neighbourhood region and that, despite possessing a strong industrial base, still faces significant development challenges.

Ultimately, the volume offers a comprehensive investigation of both sides of the GEG–HDI+ relationship, not only considering a wide-ranging set of globalization "shapers", but also collecting field perspectives from a diversified set of globalization "takers".

Notes

1 Such decision notices how "the concept of governance should not be restricted to the national and international systems but should be used in relation to regional, provincial and local governments as well as to other social systems".
2 According to the European Commission's definition, a company needs to either have a turnover below EUR 50 million or a balance sheet total below EUR 43 million and less than 250 staff to be considered a medium-sized company.
3 The heterogeneous group thus created includes transnational nascent control mechanisms (including private volunteer and profit-making organizations), social movements, sub-national nascent control mechanisms (including cities and microregions), State-sponsored mechanisms, jointly sponsored mechanisms, cross-border coalitions, transnational institutionalized control mechanisms (such as credit rating agencies), subnational institutionalized mechanisms (such as crime syndicates), State-sponsored mechanism, jointly-sponsored institutionalized mechanisms. Rosenau individuates two macro-groups to which all these mechanisms can trace their root to: either resulting from State-driven, top-down processes or; from indirect, bottom-up processes of organizational activities that eventually get transformed into institutionalized control mechanisms (Rosenau 2009).
4 A list that is by no means exhaustive include: the *Corruption Perception Index* (first launched in 1995) by Transparency International; the *Democracy Index* (2006) by the Economist; the *Human Freedom Index* (2008) by the Fraser and Cato Institutes; the *Worldwide Press Freedom Index* (2002) by Reporters without Borders; the *World Happiness Report* (2012) by the UN Sustainable Development Solutions Network; the *Social Progress Index* (2013) by the Social Progress Imperatives; the *Human Rights Data Project* (1994) of the University of Connecticut.
   These add-up to indexes that were already available before the HDI was developed, including *Freedom in the World* (1972) and *Freedom of the Press* (1980) indexes by Freedom House, the *Physical Quality of Life Index* by the Overseas development Council (1975).

5 A good example of social survey providing a granular portray of *Human Development* is provided by the Afghanistan Living Condition Survey (ALCS) elaborated by the Afghan Central Statistic Organization with the support of the international donor community. Obviously, it would be impossible having a general index taking in consideration all these variables for all countries. See http://cso.gov. af/Content/files/01.pdf

References

Abbott, K. W. and Snidal, D. (2009), 'The governance triangle: regulatory standards institutions and the shadow of the state', in W. Mattli and N. Woods (Eds.), *The politics of global regulation*, Princeton: Princeton University Press.

Abramovitz, M. (1959), *The allocation of economic resources*, Stanford: Stanford University Press.

Booth, K. (1996), '75 years on: rewriting the subject's past–reinventing its future', in S. Smith, K. Booth and M. Zalewski (Eds.), *Positivism and beyond*, Cambridge: Cambridge University Press.

Braithwaite, J. and Drahos, P. (2007), *Theory of world security*, Cambridge: Cambridge University Press.

Cerny, P. (1995), 'Globalization and the changing logic of collective action', *International Organization*, 49(4): 595–625.

Finkelstein, S. L. (1995), 'What is global governance?', *Global Governance*, 1: 367–372.

Goldstein, J., Kahler, M., Keohane, R. and Slaughter, A. M. (2000), 'Introduction: legalization and world politics', *International Organization*, 5: 385–399.

Held, D. and McGrew, A. (2002), 'Introduction', in A. McGrew and D. Held (Eds.), *Governing globalization: power, authority, and global governance*, Cambridge: Polity Press.

Hofferbeth, M. (2015), 'Mapping the meanings of global governance: a conceptual reconstruction of a floating signifier', *Millennium*, 43(2): 598–617.

Horkheimer, M. (2012), *Critique of instrumental reason*, London: Verso.

Kahler, M. and Lake, D. A. (2009), 'Economic integration and global governance: why so little supranationalism?', in W. Mattli and N. Woods (Eds.), *The politics of global regulation*, Princeton: Princeton University Press.

Keohane, R. (2002), Global governance and democratic accountability', in D. Held and M. Koenig-Archibugi (Eds.), *Taming globalization: frontiers of governance*, Cambridge: Polity Press.

Nussbaum, M. and Sen, A. (1993), *The quality of life*, Oxford: Oxford University Press.

Rosenau, J. N. (2009), Governance in the twenty-first century. In J. Whitman (Ed.), *Palgrave advances in global governance*, Basingstoke and New York: Palgrave MacMillan.

United Nations General Assembly (UNGA) (2011), *Global economic governance and development. Report of the Secretary General.*

United Nations Development Programme (UNDP) (2016), *What is human development?*, Human Development Report 2016.

1 The Global Economic Governance – Human Development nexus

Simone Raudino

The determinants of Human Development

Several *Human Development* indexes capture, more or less precisely, comprehensively and meaningfully, how many opportunities people are granted in life and how much freedom they have in deciding what to do out of these opportunities. Both variables ultimately account for people's chances to become who they want to be in their lives. As different indexes measure different aspects of *Human Development*, this article considers a hypothetic weighted basket of the most common Human Development Indexes and defines it as *HDI+*.[1]

In light of the above, this chapter sets to answer the question of what contributes to positive changes in *Human Development*. What budges HDI+, or other development indexes for that matter, in one direction or another? I argue that, within a given community, three variables are directly and significantly involved in determining *Human Development* levels: i) the creation of wealth; ii) the distribution of wealth; and iii) the use of wealth. These three variables are mutually inter-dependent and account, at any given point in time, for the state of *Human Development* in a given community and its likely progression over the near future.

A positive economic conjuncture given by an optimal interplay between these three variables is a necessary, and yet not sufficient, condition for progress. Economic variables are not sufficient because *Human Development* is not an exclusively economic affair: cultures detrimental to people's dignity and physiological aspirations, legislations restricting freedoms and rights, natural and man-made disasters, are some examples of how non-economic variables can prevent high *Human Development* despite the existence of an economic governance environment conducive to steady and inclusive economic growth.

While *Human Development* is not an exclusively economic affair, economic variables remain major determinants of HDI+. Economic growth is a *conditio sine qua non* for positive societal changes to happen: without economic output there can be no "development" in general and no *Human Development* in particular. Improved living standards, social betterment and enhanced freedom of choice result from relational exchanges where the counter-parties providing the goods and services necessary for such progresses to happen need to be compensated. The few exceptions to this basic law can be found in economies based on slavery, indentured labour, colonialism, altruism or voluntarism, all of which represent marginal phenomena in contemporary societies.

Human Development is better understood as a flow contributing towards a growing stock. A community benefiting from increasing flows of *Human Development* has to cover the increasing marginal costs associated to such acceleration in the process. Similarly, a community's stock of *Human Development* needs being serviced along the years because stocks are not automatically maintained, and because maintenance does not come free of cost. These costs are almost always born by the communities benefiting from *Human Development*: the households, companies and public entities producing wealth and investing (part of) that wealth into their own well-being. On the other side, communities depending upon exogenous financial injections with little endogenous capacity to add value, to generate their own revenues and to create their own sources of *Human Development*, are ultimately destined to fail in the maintenance or further expansion of their *Human Development* stock.

There are countless historical examples of this basic law. While external financial injections in many Sub-Saharan African countries after decolonization and, more recently, in Afghanistan and Iraq after the NATO interventions of 2001 and 2003 respectively, have allowed improvements in social indicators, these have also left any *Human Development* progress at the mercy of external dependency. Societies that have undertaken a reshuffling in the ownership of their national assets without producing additional economic expansion, such as Cuba after the Castro revolution of 1959, or Zimbabwe after the Mugabe revolution of 1980, have initially improved HDI+ levels, but subsequently failed to maintain such trends. Enhanced *Human Development* metrics accompanied by stagnant or even negative economic expansion – a phenomenon that is fairly common in Least Developed Countries (LDCs) engaged by the Millennium Development Goals (MDGs) and the Sustainable Development Goals (SDGs) initiatives – typically point to a reliance upon externally subsidized welfare systems, a model that, from an economic and developmental perspective, has proven over and again as both self-defeating and unsustainable.

The creation of wealth

The wealth of national communities is standardly measured as Gross Domestic Product (GDP) or Gross National Income (GNI). Both are rather weak indexes of the capacity of a given community to create wealth. Most notably, they have been criticized on the account of: i) ignoring the centrality of human difference and psychology in defining the meaning and significance of wealth to different individuals and to different cultures worldwide; ii) failing to account for public goods and scarce resources such as clean air, fresh water or parental care; and iii) falling short of providing a faithful portray of how resources are truly distributed among and within political units (Stiglitz et al. 2009).

Yet, GDP has the undisputable merit of creating a standard, a norm against which the wealth of different communities and their evolutions over time can be compared. Without a norm it is difficult to compare; without comparison it is difficult to analyse and; without analyses there would be limited scope for normative action. As the different attempts at substituting GDP/GNI with other accounting measures have so far gone barren, GDP/GNI represents the standard departing point for any inquiry into the wealth of local, regional, national and international communities.

How is wealth created? Because wealth is normally understood as the value of all the assets – whether owned by a person, household, company, organization, municipality or country – the question boils down to what is considered as an asset and how assets are produced. Assets can have intrinsic (drinkable water) or instrumental (fiat money) value, but ultimately value is given by social consent: the inter-social agreement of considering something valuable. What is valuable for one person is not necessarily valuable for another and this despite the fact that, given certain environmental or structural circumstances, certain assets are valuable to everyone. For albeit some biological elements give intrinsic value to certain asset classes – we all need eating and sleeping and we all prefer clean and spacious environments to cramped and dirty spaces – assets are ultimately inter-socially defined. The value of an asset is therefore defined on the basis of how much other people are willing to trade or provide labour, psychic effort, capacity and time in exchange for it, and how many people are willing to do so. Unsurprisingly, this definition is close to many definitions of money: because wealth and assets are rather intangible concepts, we use money as a quantifiable proxy.[2]

The mechanisms allowing a society to add value in goods and services and to exchange such value in the international system at "fair" prices represent the *conditio sine qua non* of any "development" – whether this is understood in purely economic fashion (as captured by GDP/GNI) or in the more comprehensive understandings portrayed by HDI+. It is not the scope of this chapter to discuss the mechanisms that allow a country to create wealth; yet, in establishing a conceptual umbrella for a volume that systemically touches on aspects of wealth creation without explicitly addressing them, two interesting elements should be noticed here.

The first is about the ontology of one of the leading themes throughout the volume: the mechanisms that allow a community to create value – i.e. to grow wealthy. While these topics have been debated in economics for centuries, economic theory has reached no consensus on the topic. At the same time, the history of economic practices seems to suggest that some communities, at any given point in history, have indeed mastered this practice – from ancient Egyptian and Greek civilizations to Renaissance Europe to countries pertaining to the Organization for Economic Cooperation and Development (OECD) today. Logically, we shall conclude that the "objective mechanisms of wealth creation" must be "somewhere out there". Suffice here to say that the creation of wealth is a process involving, among others, issues relating to capital formation, resource allocation, application of the principles of increasing marginal returns and economies of scale, balancing between capital-intensive and labour-intensive sectors, public interventions, market imperfections, trade, foreign investments, local content rules, provisions on repatriation of profits and reinvested earnings, corporate governance, human resources, migration and social policies. Most of these issues are more or less directly discussed throughout the book.

The second element relates to the prevailing epistemology used in understanding and conceptualizing wealth. The accounting methodologies that are currently used to measure wealth worldwide are far from perfect, and yet their limits should not divert attention away from the worthy task of measuring, assessing and intervening upon wealth creation processes. Most notably, the prevailing accounting methodologies allow for useful differentiations between the absolute and relative value of assets: while the production capacity of the world economy has been estimated in 2016 at a nominal value of USD 75.2 trillion (IMF 2016), its Purchasing Power Parity (PPP) value has been estimated at USD 127 trillion (IMF 2016). This difference, with the PPP value representing almost the double of the nominal value, is accounted by price differences across countries: PPP is what allows the most faithful comparison between different people's capacity to access the goods and services that contribute to *Human Development* in the communities they live in.[3] Other economic coefficients, including the Gini coefficient or the social expenditure to budget ratio help in making sense of how easy or difficult is for different economic strata of the population to access these goods and services at their relative prices.

Hence, while common practices of reifying wealth with money and national wellbeing with GDP/GNI both represent gross simplifications of complex concepts and phenomena, such concepts do not necessarily hinder the pursuance of normative action; on the contrary, they are necessary tools in investigating, assessing and intervening upon policies affecting *Human Development*.

The distribution of wealth

Wealth distribution can be understood in many different ways; none of them, however, can be taken as a safe port of entry for a discussion around Global Economic Governance (GEG). Yet all issues of wealth distribution are foundational to *Human Development* both because of their direct effects upon people's wellbeing (for example, via direct forms of wealth redistribution such as the financing of fiscal expansionary measures or the creation of decently paid public jobs), and because of their indirect effects on the other two variables analyzed here (wealth creation and wealth use): an optimal distribution of income creates the necessary incentives to stimulate an optimal use of resources and optimal levels of economic demand and, therefore, optimal levels of economic activities.

A standard and nonetheless partially misleading understanding of the topic comes from the question of how wealth is distributed across different units of account – be these nations; economic sectors (primary, secondary and tertiary); industries within each sector (as classified, for example, by the United Nations Conference on Trade and Development (UNCTAD)); social classes (which, for simplicity, are often divided into capital owners, entrepreneurs and workers) or classes of workers.

Undoubtedly, such approach provides some useful insights into distributive (one economic party obliges other parties to surrender some of their wealth: for example, by creating a monopoly, a cartel or by introducing new trade protection or fiscal measures) and re-distributive (one economic party wilfully surrender some of its wealth to the benefit of other economic parties: for example, by offering public procurements, introducing social security nets, promoting remittances or foreign aid) mechanisms. On the basis of these understandings, many economists cry injustice when noticing that wealth inequality, measured by the share of the wealthiest 1% and 10% of adults compared to the rest of the world's adult population, is continuously on the rise. The increasing financialization of OECD economies since the 1970s has accelerated the phenomenon, inaugurating an era of exponential capital returns against stagnant labour returns, even within "wealthy" countries. In 2016, we reached the point in which the bottom half of the world's population collectively owned less than 1% of total wealth, while the wealthiest top 10% owned almost 90% of that wealth.

These observations are fair and yet of limited utility as they fail to consider the causal relations between the processes of wealth production, distribution and use. In fact, they even fail to consider that, very next to the concept of wealth distribution, lie the concepts of wealth creation and use. This obviously limits the usefulness of the "distribution" concept: the three processes are intrinsically entangled, and judging one independently from the others can only give partial and skewed understandings of the overall phenomenon being analysed.

Independently from the classes of subjects being considered, we naturally expect wealth to be mostly present where it is created – no one would object to that. Yet, history shows the persistent tendency of the "wealth creators" in shaping socio-economic structures and rules in such a way that the reiteration of wealth creation processes becomes increasingly easier for them, while the first iteration of wealth creation processes for other subjects remains equally difficult or even becomes increasingly harder. Hence, discussions around injustices of wealth distribution are better framed in terms of fairness in the distribution of those conditions that are necessary and sufficient to create wealth, rather than in terms of distribution of "finite" wealth in absolute terms.

A key *Human Development* issue relates to how wealth distribution can optimize results in terms of maximization of advantages for the largest possible number of people. I argue that this question can most fruitfully be declined via two sub-questions: i) how should wealth be distributed among public entities on the one side, and physical and private legal persons on the other and; ii) how should wealth be distributed among different institutional/ corporate sub-groups within each of these two separate macro-groups.

Concerning the first, it should be noted that public budgets (at all levels: federal, state and sub-national) can represent anything between the almost totality of a country's GDP (Zimbabwe reports 98% of its national aggregate demand as being government-driven) and less than 20% (Hong Kong and Singapore are among the economies depending the least upon Government's spending). On average, OECD countries have a Government spending/GDP ratio of 45.6%, with Ireland (29.4%) and France (57%) marking the opposite ends of the spectrum (OECD 2015). Supra-national public budgets have also come to play an important role in some countries, particularly in tightly-integrated political entities such as the EU, where the communitarian budget can add several percentage points to the public budget/GDP ratio.[4]

The decision of how much of the national income should be supplied by publicly controlled activities (or how much of the national aggregate demand should come from publicly controlled activities) is fundamentally political. This decision also answers the long debated question of how much State there should be into the economy. Economic schools around the world have long contended the relative advantages of theoretical positions dispersed along the spectrum comprised between two diagonally-opposed models: socialism and market fundamentalism. History shows how Governments inspired by both models have at times been successful in promoting *Human Development*, while also showing how other Governments, equally influenced by both models, have been incapable of doing so.

While history has proven the unviability of the socialist systems adopted by the Soviet Union and its Eastern European allies until 1989 (Campbell 1992; Roeder 1993), social-democratic systems along the Scandinavian model are largely regarded as successful (Giddens 1998; Einhorn and Logue 2003). Similarly, while the highly liberist policies of selected Latin American and Sub-Saharan African countries in the 1980s and 1990s have generally been recognized as unsuccessful, the liberal economic reforms initiated by Deng Xiaoping in China in 1979 and Lee Kuan Yew in Singapore earlier in the 1970s are universally perceived as a success (Naughton 1995; Lall 1996).

The point of many authors in this volume is not about establishing a hierarchy between these different models, if not about individuating those relative strengths and weaknesses, which could ideally contribute to improve *Human Development*. Just as no one would debate today that John Maynard Keynes, a staunch believer in the virtues of free market, was wrong when he famously noted that the market needs "rules of the road and governmental actions" (Samuelson 1946: 43) in order to function – a contention that builds on liberist assumptions while abjuring the fundamentalist credo that markets are self-regulating and self-sustainable –, so no one in this volume would question the necessity of both socialist and market fundamentalist elements in finding an optimal GEG recipe: the point is, which of these elements, in which quantities and in which sequence.

The question of how resources should be divided between public and private stakeholders needs to be complemented with the question of how resources should be allocated among the different groups populating these two constituencies. The "expenditure side" of the imperfect science dealing with the use of public resources, Public Finance Management (PFM), has long grappled with the question of how much public resources should be dedicated to the production and distribution of which public goods – and how that should be done. According to the law of diminishing marginal utility, increasing the consumption of a "product" (goods or services) while keeping the consumption of other products constant, leads to a decline in the marginal utility derived from each additional unit of the "product". If we consider public goods – security, infrastructures, literacy, university education, vocational trainings, security, access to finance and the alike – as "products" that are necessary or at least conducive towards entrepreneurship and increased productivity, then it becomes clear that a society is bound to gain much more from distributing USD 1 million among 10 underprivileged undergraduate students than by investing that same amount in guaranteeing luxurious living conditions for one student only. A society is better off when it optimizes the consumption and investment of its public resources by finding the right balance between the nature and the quantity of the benefits on the one side, and number of beneficiaries on the other.

The underlying logic governing the private sector is not too different. While any society must guarantee the principle of the private enjoyment of private wealth, this principle cannot be applied at the cost of the sustainability of the economy at large, for history has shown over and again how economically unsustainable societies eventually turn against the wealthiest among them – either in Parliament or in the streets. From the ontological perspective, well before the normative perspective, the economic sustainability of a society has therefore logical priority over the enjoyment of private riches. In societies where this priority was not given due consideration – developing countries with extreme wealth differences such as Brazil and South Africa – the "haves" live in the constant fear of the "have-nots", and this obviously impact their very own *Human Development* levels.

Because economies are not self-regulating, what appears as a logical priority still needs to be consciously enforced. Independently from what one person or one family or one business group have done to secure their stock of wealth and independently from how large that stock of wealth is, there are limited opportunities for those actors to spend their wealth in such a way to benefit the society at large. There is only a limited amount of lunches, haircuts, shoes and entertainment events that millionaires or billionaires can purchase. The fact that they purchase more expensive goods and services is of limited utility, as this typically increases the profit margins of niche industries in an exponential fashion, replicating the problem of limited distribution. This means that a society with an excessively high Gini coefficient is bound to have a number of structural impediments to growth due to limitations in its national aggregate demand, unless there is a conscious effort at addressing such imbalances.

While income inequality is intrinsic to all economies, it is proved that an excess of income inequality creates disincentives to the optimal functioning of an economy and a democratic society (Ostry et al., 2014). Therefore, the question is how much inequality is physiological to a system, and how to avoid excessive inequality hampering growth. This question has long been studied in the US economy. In 1978 a typical American worker was earning USD 48,000 per year, while an income in the top 1% was in the range of USD 390,000 per year, both adjusted for 2010 inflation; in 2010, these figures had gone down to USD 33,000 and up to USD 1.1 million respectively. Thomas Piketty shows that the highest peaks in the percentage of national wealth owned by the top 1% US earners were reached in 1928 and 2007, when they owned more than 23% of the total US national income, and he argues that these disparities were the underlying causes of the two major financial crises of the twenty-first century (Piketty 2014). Piketty's argument suggests that wealth distribution is not only related to the optimal and suboptimal functioning of an economy, understood as the optimization of its output, if not to its capacity to self-regulate. The creation of unsustainable wealth disparities can eventually lead to a breakdown of the financial system, with dire repercussions in the real economy, both nationally and internationally.

Similarly, empirical research shows that economic growth in the most successful economies in the 1950s–1980s period (most OECD countries) and the 1980s–2010s period (BRICS and other emerging economies in Asia, Latin America and Africa) is fundamentally related to the expansion of their middle classes (Easterly 1999; Kharas 2010, 2017). Such expansion could also be obtained because of deliberate policies aiming at avoiding an excessively high concentration of wealth in the top 1, 5 and 10 percentiles of these societies, while pulling people out of poverty to firmly place them into the lower echelons of the middle class.

The use of wealth

The use of wealth is defined by mainstream economics as the channelling of resources into consumption, investments or savings: it relates to what we do with the wealth we create. Yet, to properly look at the matter, these are largely fictitious categories. Part of today's consumption, for example, could be categorized as investments to create tomorrow's savings: in order to preserve the stock of human resources of a family, a company or an entire country, their individuals are bound to a certain number of fixed expenses, including lodging, boarding, education and healthcare, which could all be factored into the development equation as investments rather than final consumption.

Independently from the formal distinctions run by mainstream economics, the use of wealth is closely correlated and partially consequential to its creation and distribution: households, companies and governments can only spend the wealth they have created, been assigned or borrowed, the latter case being a function of what markets deem them worth having. At the same time, the modality in which existing wealth is being used, contributes to determining the pace and modality in which new wealth is being created and distributed; for example, a company using part of its profits to invest in staff education and meritocratic bonuses has high chances of outperforming a company distributing the totality of its surplus via dividends to its shareholders.

Governments and central banks also have the powerful prerogative of setting legislative and policy frameworks capable of influencing the use that private actors make of their own money. Fiscal and monetary policies create a system of incentives and disincentives which bear enormous responsibility in moulding the private sector's economic behaviour. As a whole, these policies also define the conditions under which a society, understood as the sum of its human resources, capital goods and financial assets, can optimize its output.

Fiscal, monetary and PFM decisions contribute in defining economic governance in the public sector, which chiefly concerns itself with the collection and allocation of public resources. In those countries where the State directly oversees a large share of the economy, the Government is in the privileged position of directly controlling the country's economic behaviour, and particularly its marginal propensity to consume, save or invest. Public wealth can be used for plain redistributive policies, via social welfare measures, but also to stimulate the economy via public intervention programmes, which can privilege the role and position of capital holders (for example by injecting public money in an ailing private bank or by nationalizing a large private company struggling with debt) or the role and position of labour (for example by promoting Keynesian fiscal expansionism). While consumption usually guarantees high political returns, this cannot be done indefinitely or in disregard of the size and international credibility of the concerned economy without incurring in BoP disequilibria, high debt-servicing costs and default risks.

For example, since the 2000s, Southern European countries (Greece, Italy, Spain, Portugal and France to a certain extent) have balanced the lukewarm results of their sluggish private sector by maintaining high employment opportunities in the public sector and by continuing subsidizing generous welfare systems. This allowed them to maintain relatively high standards of living, but also created unsustainable deficits resulting in disproportionally-high debt/ GDP ratios and lingering default risks. Conversely, Eastern Asian economies, and particularly China and South Korea, have long used high saving rates as a growth strategy, wilfully accepting to postpone the enjoyment of the profits they were accumulating. Protracted investments have allowed them to raise the international economic ladder at exceptionally sustained rates – yet, this strategy also came at the price of people's renouncement to the much higher living standards and better life conditions they could have afforded. A regime of ever-expanding domestic and international investments has also meant an increased propensity to accept risk, which has resulted in higher losses along the years, as it has become evident in the increasing number of Chinese deals gone sour in Africa and Latin America.[5]

Governments and central banks hold a strong sway upon the general economy even in those countries where they do not have direct control upon national economic asset. In particular, fiscal and monetary policies can create incentives for physical and legal persons to invest their disposable income rather than to consume or save; to do so in the real economy (rather than in speculative financial sectors); and to choose national economic ventures (rather than foreign investment opportunities). Furthermore, legal provisions can also create strong incentives in pushing national asset-holders to comply with existing fiscal policy provisions, to favour the repatriation of capitals and/or to stem capital flight. Similarly, these same legal provisions can attract qualified overseas investments – both as Foreign Direct Investments (FDIs) and as Foreign Portfolio Investments (FPIs) – leave the country open to international short-term speculative capital or even isolate the country from international investment flows altogether.

Hong Kong and Singapore are perhaps the best examples of hyper-liberal economies in which the Government, in coordination with the central bank and key commercial banks, manages nonetheless to maintain a strong grip on the economy by intervening on fiscal policies, business regulatory frameworks, central interest rates, and, in the case of Singapore, currency rates. The US, which contrary to popular perceptions has a large percentage of its GDP depending upon public spending, lies in a peculiar spot, as, on top of controlling the traditional monetary and fiscal leverages, can also access its role of issuer of the currency of ultimate resort, allowing its Government to run a growing deficit for as long as US creditors will have faith in Washington's hegemony.

All in all, the distribution and use of public and private wealth are instrumental in allowing a country to reach its optimal output potential and even in expanding it.

The influence of GEG on wealth variables

The contention that economic policies adopted by the Government of a given community have a fundamental responsibility in determining *Human Development* among the subjects of that same community is a fairly obvious proposition. Economic policies are devised with the precise intention of affecting a more or less comprehensive part of the people living in the very national and sub-national communities that chose, adopt and implement such policies. For example, the Korean labour policy; the Californian social security policy or; the Ouagadougou Municipality energy tariff policy are all examples of measures that directly affect *Human Development* in the national and/or subnational communities taking and implementing these decisions – respectively, the residents of Korea, California and Ouagadougou Municipality. Sometimes, these policies are adopted at a supranational level, as it is the case for the EU in those policy areas where EU institutions have exclusive competency, including trade.[6]

It is by looking at the relationship between the communities setting the economic policies on the one side, and the communities affected by them on the other, that the overall concept of *Global Economic Governance* gains in interest and centrality. For, as it should be suspected, if certain policies: i) only apply to the communities that promote them, other policies; ii) influence, either directly or indirectly, communities well beyond the group that originally took and enforced them. Let us call the first group *shapers-to-shapers-only* policies and divide the second group into *shapers-to-all* and *shapers-to-takers-only* policies.

Both these groups of economic policies (*shapers-to-shapers-only* on the one side and *shapers-to-all* and *shapers-to-takers-only* on the other) are the preserves of GEG: "the diffuse act of governing, without sovereign authority, economic relationships that transcend national frontiers".[7] Yet, while both groups of policies affect *Human Development* among sub-national, national and supra-national communities worldwide, the second group of policies has the singular feature of applying, either directly or indirectly, to subjects (households, companies and public entities) that not only did not participate in choosing and adopting them, but in most cases are also foreigner to the very political jurisdictions adopting them.

As a matter of example, a UN Security Council (UNSC) decision on the extension of embargo measures against Iraq; a European Union decision on the adoption of anti-dumping measures against China; an Australian decision to finance asylum seeker turnback missions on its coastline are all examples of decisions affecting *Human Development* among foreign subjects that did not participate to the decision-making processes that led to these policies. Some other decisions imply a formal acceptance from the subjects that are on the receiving end of these economic and financial policies – yet, considering the imbalance in negotiating power, these can hardly be seen as decisions fully owned by the subjects to whom they apply. This is arguably the case when a Least Developed Country (LDC) or a Low-Income Country (LIC) signs up to a comprehensive investment agreement with China; when it restructures its debt with the London club or; when it negotiates a Regional Trade Agreement (RTA) with partners that have far more clout and resources to influence the negotiation process.

Interestingly, this same mechanism is also at work when the receivers of economic policies are not even meant to be a subject of the adopted policies. For example, the US monetary policy and the Chinese fiscal policy affect the economic opportunities of hundreds of thousands of companies and the livelihood of hundreds of millions of households outside the US and China – yet, these subjects not only are not part of the decision-making process, they are not even among the subjects to which these policies were originally addressed. In all likelihood, they did not even figure in the standard stakeholder analyses attached to these decision-making processes. One of these examples occurred during the quantitative easing policies adopted by core economies (US and EU) after the 2008 financial crisis, with increased liquidity and zero-bound interest rates contributing in exporting inflationary pressure and speculative capital to emerging economies, eventually resulting in rising commodity prices and food crises. Other relevant examples are given by the many cases of trade diversion occurring every time a new RTA is signed, which typically prompts trade losses for non-RTA members.

The GEG system and the volume's developmental focus

Just like for *shapers-to-shapers-only* policies, the national governments of OECD countries (and at times of Brazil, Russia, India, China and South Africa (BRICS)) countries; International Organizations (IOs) and; International Financial Institutions (IFIs) are mostly responsible for *shapers-to-all* and *shapers-to-takers-only* policies. Crucially, in all typologies of policies, the distinction between "shapers" and "takers" lies in the fact that the shapers' economic policies are related to the GEG system in a reciprocal fashion (e.g. they influence the system and are influenced by it), whereas the takers' policies are related to that same GEG system in an unidirectional fashion (they are influenced by the system without getting a chance of influencing it).

The shapers' policies at the sub-national, national and supranational level affect the creation of a GEG system which, at its own turn, affects these variables. In particular, the political, economic and social forces represented in the national Governments of OECD (and at times BRICS) countries have the capacity to shape most of the GEG rules – including through trade, investment, monetary and financial regulations resulting from bilateral agreements and multilateral treaties and institutions – which will ultimately influence them by hampering or facilitating the adoption and implementation of certain economic policies within their own borders.

On the other side, the relation between the economic policies of GEG "takers" and the GEG system is not reciprocal. GEG "takers", e.g. most non-OECD, non-BRICS countries, are influenced in a unidirectional fashion, which means that, while they have no opportunity or limited opportunities to influence the GEG system, they still have to abide by its pervading rules. When these actors join the ranks of, or negotiate deals with, OECD/BRICS groups of Governments, IOs and IFIs, their comparatively limited negotiating power and leverage means that they mostly have to accept the conditions imposed upon them.

It is important noting that dynamics of creation, distribution and use of wealth in OECD and BRICS countries shape, at their own turn, the GEG system. Because economic actors and interests in GEG "shapers" are in a reciprocal relation with the GEG system, the relation between processes of wealth production, distribution and use within GEG "shapers" on the one side and the setting of the GEG system (rules, institutions and agenda) on the other is best described as "reflexive", e.g. the two terms are mutually interdependent because bound in a circular relation of cause and effect.[8] This means that, from the perspective of the GEG "shapers", the GEG system is not an independent variable, as it relies upon dynamics of creation, distribution and use of wealth within the same "shapers". As the list of shapers changes continuously – most notably in the last thirty years with the exponential growth of BRICS countries – and as policy priorities within these polities are fluid, it is normal to expect that the rules and institutions defining the GEG system are also continuously changing.

Nonetheless, most of the authors in this collection treat the current GEG system (widely identified with the broad and somehow fuzzy concept of

"Bretton Woods system") as a medium-term independent variable or a given, because these rules have remained relatively stable since the end of the Second World War. Yet, if observed over longer time horizons, the GEG system is every-thing but static: one only needs thinking at the imperial and colonial systems in place until the 1960s and at the different hegemonic powers throughout modern history to realize that GEG is constantly reforming itself. Significantly, several authors in the volume discuss the perceived crisis of the Bretton Woods system while stressing the rise of competing systems, and most notably the growing "Beijing Consensus" in Asia and Africa.

As suggested in the introduction, while *Human Development* is a relevant concept worldwide, this has its maximum potential for normative impact in developing countries, where the lowest hanging development fruits can most usefully be reaped. This is evident throughout the book, whose most recur-rent analytical questions include how GEG affects the processes of creation, distribution and use of wealth in Least Developed Countries (LDCs), Low-Income Countries (LICs) and Mid-Income Countries (MICs), and how these processes, at their own turn, influence *Human Development* dynamics in these same countries. Several authors subsequently move into normative territory, questioning how LDCs, LICs and MICs can shape their interactions with the GEG in such a way that their processes of creation, distribution and use of wealth can benefit the most.

The GEG > Wealth > Human Development transmission chain

Human Development depends upon the three variables of wealth creation, distribution and use; in LDCs, LICs and MICs, these three variables are, at their own turn, heavily influenced by the GEG system. In a more structured form:

1. Over the medium term, (GEG) is taken as an independent variable (X1) holding sway upon the (creation, distribution and use of wealth in LDCs, LICs and MICs), considered a dependent variable (X2);
2. (The creation, distribution and use of wealth in LDCs, LICs and MICs) is subsequently assumed to be an independent variable (X2) holding sway upon HDI+ levels in these same countries, considered a second order dependent variable (X3).

One part of the international practitioner community active in economics, finance, diplomacy, international civil service and international civil advocacy tends to identify the manifestations of the GEG system in LDCs, LICs and MICs with "development" policy areas, normally covered by the work of the United Nations (UN), IFIs, national development agencies and Non-Governmental Organizations (NGOs). Similarly, one part of the economic and international relations literature concurs in ascribing to "development" disciplines, usu-ally sub-divided into "development politics", "development economics" and "development cooperation", the core responsibility of dealing with the impact of GEG upon the socio-economic outlook of developing countries.

I argue that such narrow characterization is due to the traditional understanding of "development" promoted by the world of Official Development Assistance (ODA). By and large, the ODA conceptual framework has been shaped by OECD governments and their institutional appendixes, which have portrayed abidance to macroeconomic orthodoxy and proactive efforts at integrating the GEG system as the neutral, teleological, long-term goal of any "development" policy.

The theory behind the practice of ODA itself focuses on a sort of preparatory phase in which beneficiary countries are taken up to the minimum economic requirements necessary to meaningfully integrate the GEG system. In practice, most ODA work focuses on the distribution of services and consumer goods, strengthening of public institutions and development of physical infrastructures, while setting aside some of the most relevant policy questions prioritized in High-Income Countries (HICs), including issues relating to technology transfer, corporate, industrial, investment, export and research and development policies.

This collection disagrees with such a narrow categorization of "development" and takes a radically different approach. It sees traditional ODA understandings of "development" as superficial as they hide fundamental questions regarding the nature of the functional relation between the economies of ODA beneficiary countries and the GEG system (rules, institutions and agenda) they are asked to join and/or adapt to. By looking at the GEG > Wealth > *Human Development* relay chain, this volume considers "development" as a much larger policy area, covering all GEG and HICs policy decisions that ultimately influence HDI+ in LDCs, LICs and MICs. In other words, this book sees "development" as being fully and legitimately part of Harold Lasswell's famous understanding of politics in terms of "who gets what, when and how", in a system in which the liberal credo of international economic relations as a positive sum game does not necessarily hold true. By scrutinizing different bits of the relay chain, authors show how GEG, and therefore globalization "shapers" – including OECD Governments, OECD-based Multi-National Corporations, OECD-based Civil Society Organizations, global International Organizations and IFIs – affect economic growth opportunities in LDCs, LICs and MICs by influencing their processes of wealth creation, distribution and use.

What emerges is the description of two broad mechanisms through which globalization "shapers" influence HDI+ levels among globalization "takers": macroeconomic (fiscal, monetary and business regulatory) and Balance of Payments (BoP) (current account and capital and financial account) policies.[9] While macroeconomic policies are typically understood by globalization "shapers" as part of their domestic political realm, these often end up being *shapers-to-all* policies. On the other side, BoP policies are purposefully designed to impact the globalization "shapers" relations with the

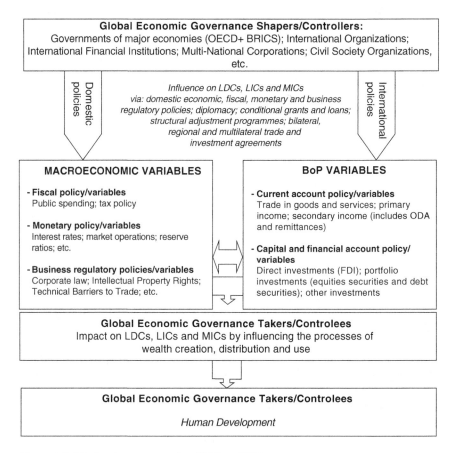

Figure 1.1 Mechanisms connecting GEG to HDI+

world economy and therefore typically fall under either the *shapers-to-all* or the *shapers-to-takers-only* policy categories.[10]

The two sets of policies are inextricably linked and any change in one of the two necessarily entails a change in the other. The relay mechanism connecting the GEG "shapers" to the GEG "takers" and the GEG system to HDI+ in LDCs, LICs and MICs via their processes of wealth creation, distribution and use is illustrated in Figure 1.1.

How authors in this volume interpret the GEG/HDI+ nexus

While dealing with a broad set of research themes and methodologies, authors contributing to this volume relate their chapters to two common questions: i) whether Globalization "shapers" promoting policies and institutional reforms directly or indirectly affecting Least Developed Countries (LDCs),

Low Income Countries (LICs) and Medium Income Countries (MICs) are favouring *Human Development* among the population of these countries and; ii) what could be done to improve the GEG impact upon HDI+ in these countries. In order to link GEG to HDI+, all chapters deal, in a more or less direct and explicit fashion, with mechanisms of creation, distribution and use of wealth.

Some chapters look at the GEG/HDI+ relation from an institutional perspective. Hanegraaff and Poletti (Chapter 2) investigate the degree of representation that civil society organizations from countries pertaining to different income groups have in some International Organizations (World Trade Organization and United Nations Framework Convention on Climate Change), concluding that non-state actors from both the least developed and high income groups are disproportionally represented compared to mid-income countries. The prima facie evidence of this interesting finding would suggest that representation processes in international democratic institutions allow LDCs and LICs to find adequate representation in GEG institutions, a seemingly necessary condition for guaranteeing balanced and inclusive GEG policies. Yet, the authors' suggestion that the reason for the over-representation of LDCs and LICs lies in their global advocacy and lobbying capacity being heavily subsidized by the financial support given by High Income Countries (HICs) also raises questions as to the true independency and real finality of these representations.

Sicurelli (Chapter 5) indirectly tackles some of these questions when looking at the real drivers of the international trade negotiation strategies of a GEG "shaper" (the EU) renowned for its normative discourse in international economic relations. The chapter does so by looking at trade negotiation dynamics between the EU and GEG "shapers" (Singapore and South Korea, both pertaining to the HICs group) on the one side and a GEG "taker", Vietnam, on the other. The result suggests that, independently from the normative discourse wrapping most EU negotiations around Regional Trade Agreements (RTAs), the "shapers" tend to put stronger pressures upon the "takers" – particularly with reference to adjustments to international regulatory standards – while using softer measures of norm promotion in their negotiations with fellow "shapers".

While Baroncelli (Chapter 3) focuses on the role and institutional developments of the World Bank Group (WBG) since the 2000s, many of this chapter's conclusions could be extended to the larger group of multilateral institutions framing the current GEG system, e.g. the Bretton Woods system as composed by Washington-based institutions and regional IFIs controlled by OECD Governments. Baroncelli convincingly argues that, despite the magnitude of structural challenges faced by these institutions in the 2000s (the "multi-complex crisis" given by the 2007 food crisis, the 2008 spike in energy prices and the 2008–2009 financial crisis), despite the shrinking pool of WBG's perspective clients (given by the progressive economic graduation of LDCs and LICs into MICs and HICs), and despite growing competition from BRICS countries (and including their IFIs offshoots in the form of the New Development Bank and the Asian Infrastructure Investment Bank), the WBG has been able to provide apt, sizeable and pertinent responses, also thanks to its adapting culture, decisive internal reforms and exceptional levels of technical expertise. This, in turns, suggests that the WBG – and its sister IFIs – still have a strong role to play for a long time to come.

The chapters providing field perspectives are those that, most prominently, underline the increasing hiatus between the limited scope of ODA policies and budgets on the one side and the real drivers of wealth creation, distribution and use, and therefore of HDI+ developments in LDCs, LICs and MICs, on the other. Looking at post-independency economic reforms in Ukraine, the second-largest economy of the former Soviet Union, Korablin (Chapter 8) concludes that the resources invested by the international community so far have contributed in stabilizing the macroeconomic scenario against endemic fragility and wild economic swings caused by de-industrialization, lack of investments and a vastly kleptocratic public administration. This, in turn, has avoided major humanitarian risks across the country, particularly since the beginning of the war with Russia in 2014. Yet, internationally-sponsored reforms have essentially turned Ukraine into an open commodity economy, leaving it highly dependent upon exports in the primary sector and the international conjunctures governing these markets. In particular, Korablin notices that despite its wealth of productive factors, the Ukrainian economy has proved incapable to implement counter-cyclical economic policies, to diversify, to climb the value-adding ladder, to scale production, to re-industrialize and to acquire the best foreign technology and capital goods without relying on foreign investors alone.

Bakos and Fishstein's reading of externally-financed economic policies in Afghanistan since 2001, and Rendón Cárdenas' interpretation of externally-financed security and military policies in Latin America in the 2000s, equally portray ODA policies as partially useful and yet controversial and limited in scope. The former (Chapter 10) underlines the exceptionality of the Afghan case, where a "cash splash" of almost USD 1 trillion in 15 years has allowed vast HDI+ improvements – with particular attention to health, alphabetization, human rights and access to amenities – while nonetheless leaving untouched the country's traditional economic insecurity and dependency upon external financial support, thus failing to jump-start the economic processes leading to fit dynamics of creation, distribution and use of wealth. The latter (Chapter 9) shows how international military assistance to violence-prone areas controlled by narco-traffickers in Colombia and Mexico has achieved some results with reference to the curbing of drug production and smuggling and the neutralization of drug cartels, and yet has failed in the essential mission of integrating large portions of the society in fairer and more comprehensive processes of wealth creation and distribution. Instead, external military assistance has contributed in defining such societal sectors as "enemies" of the society, and therefore heightened social tensions and human rights' violations.

Bakos and Fishstein are careful in pointing out how modern Afghanistan has never been capable of creating a viable economy – they notice, for example, that in 1975, which is considered the height of the country's development trajectory, Afghanistan's per capita GDP was still the thirteenth lowest in the world and that, historically, "Afghans were unaccustomed to paying taxes". This creates a sort of buffer zone for any judgement on the impact of Western international assistance since 2001, to the extent that GEG standards on macroeconomic policy and trade cannot be seen as fundamental drivers of HDI+ developments in a failed state. On the other side, Rendón Cárdenas, dealing with Colombia and Mexico, two countries whose socio-economic indicators firmly place them in the group of MICs, underlines critical elements in the role played by international security assistance to these countries (*Plan Colombia* and *Plan Mérida*), arguing that non-abidance to key principles of *Human Security* has likely caused more harm than good. These international and largely fallimentary policies are juxtaposed to some of the two countries' own initiatives, based on endogenous, tailor-made interventions, which successfully promoted socio-economic integration as a key driver of HDI+ growth. Ultimately, both articles underline how logics of external assistance need to be better integrated in local contexts and how the concept of "sustainability" needs to turn from a buzzword into a real practice.

Lampa's analysis (Chapter 7) of the GEG's impact upon the economies of three MERCOSUR countries (Argentina, Brazil and Uruguay) hinges on the interplay between national and regional economic policies in Latin America. The article suggests that the MERCOSUR downturn that begun in 2013 – entailing GDP recession or stagnation, fiscal adjustments, rising unemployment, capital flight and sharp devaluations – was given by a short circuit between some of the MERCOSUR member countries' domestic redistributive policies on the one side and the regional commercial policies promoted by MERCOSUR itself, commonly known as "open regionalism", on the other. Lampa argues that the economic openness introduced under the GEG lobby in the 1990s resulted in an increased economic financialization and trans-nationalization of the Latin American industries while national governments were implementing redistributive and fiscal stimulus policies, which expanded consumption. Such consumption could be maintained as long as the terms of trade were favourable for MERCOSUR economies and the out-regional demand (mainly Chinese) was robust; when the external scenario worsened, both sharp increases in outwards portfolio investments and sharp decreases in inwards FDI implied severe external constraints on the BoP of MERCOSUR member countries. Ultimately, Lampa's article underlines the persistent fragilities of MERCOSUR economies due to their strong reliance upon exogenous demand and exposure to short-term financial capital movements, showing how mismatches between GEG-sponsored policies and national economic policies adopted in response to domestic political consultations can result in painful losses on HDI+, as it happened in these three countries in the 2000s.

Most contributors share the feeling that the current GEG system is facing strong headwinds in a context of increasing global fragility. The 1970s opposition to what would have later been defined as "Washington Consensus" was directed against a solid, confident, self-centred GEG system. Even when the anti-globalization movement formalized in the 1990s, surging to world notoriety during the first anti-globalization protest in Seattle in 1999, the GEG was still perceived as a formidable institutional complex supported by countries representing the vast majority of the world GDP and dominating the market of economic theories. Judged through any metric, the prevailing 1990s GEG system was an institutional Leviathan. This same system is now seen from many quarters as "becoming increasingly fragmented while losing its vigor … suffering through internal rifts and a loss of confidence in multilateralism and international institutions" in Ashraf's words.

New competitors are rising from several corners and most prominently from the East: this is most poignantly underlined in the contributions of Ashraf (Chapter 4) and Bodomo (Chapter 6), underlying how China has been able to conquer increasingly larger business deals, diplomatic favours, cultural influence and political clout in Asia and Africa respectively. The extent of such global revolution cannot be under-estimated: China's vision for the Belt and Road Initiative (BRI) is to turn the whole of the Eurasian continent in an immense market for its goods and services and, perhaps more importantly, for its currency and high-risk investment appetite. The pervasiveness of Chinese economic, political and, increasingly, social and demographic interests in Africa is such that it has spurred scholars to talk about a new colonialism or neo-colonialism. The same efforts of HICs pictured by Baroncelli through the WBG reforms that limited vote redistribution within its Board, are assessed in these two articles from the other end, looking at the BRICS dissatisfaction with the current GEG system, and at the reasoning and strategic planning behind their efforts to establish an alternative GEG system centred upon South–South multilateralism and the internationalization of their financial assets and monetary systems. It is no coincidence that these perspectives come from scholars who have a professional focus on GEG "takers": despite the fact that both Sub-Saharan Africa and South-Asia were co-opted in the prevailing GEG system of alliances and support networks, they have both manifested frustration with many of its elements, including a manifest incapacity to promote fast economic catch-ups among LDCs and LICs, and to explain or institutionalize the economic reforms that have proved to be so successful in Eastern and South-Eastern Asia.

Does this volume suggest a negative correlation between the policies of the current GEG system and HDI+ in LDCs, LICs and MICs? Not on its manifest linkages: if there is one thing on which every author agrees, is that the current GEG system has been able to dedicate sizeable resources – estimated by the OECD in an average of USD 180 billion a year since the 2010s – to advancing spending and policy reforms in these countries. Several authors have underlined how the current GEG system has been able to give representation to usually silent, under-represented stakeholders (Hanegraaff and Poletti, Chapter 2); to provide emergency assistance in countries unable to meet their basic and post-war recovery needs (Bakos and Fishstein, Chapter 10), to deal alone with endemic economic fragility and political kleptocracy (Chapter 8), to control violence and narco-trafficking (Rendón Cárdenas, Chapter 9). Key GEG institutions are described as competent, well-resourced, ready to take up new challenges (Baroncelli, Chapter 3) and their factual proactiveness, independently from their normative discourse, remains at the basis of much of the trade and economic expansion the world has witnessed since 1945 (Sicurelli, Chapter 5).

Yet, there is also both an underlying and manifest sense of GEG shortcomings and inadequacy in respect to the promotion of sustainable HDI+ in LDCs, LICs and MICs, due both to what are at times perceived as GEG hidden agendas (Lampa, Chapter 7); cleavages between ontological reality and narrative discourse (Sicurelli, Chapter 5); adoption of traditional and convenient understandings of "support", including on security policies (Rendón Cárdenas, Chapter 9); unwillingness to make room for new players who, having followed GEG rules and being still unable to find their spaces in an ever-adapting environment, are now ready to set-up an alternative GEG system (Ashraf, Chapter 4). Tellingly, in some regions of the world this new system is already taken as a given, so much so that scholars worry more about the implications and cost-effectiveness of *this* new system rather than the prevailing one (Bodomo, Chapter 6).

Most significantly, what emerges across the spectrum of this heterogeneous set of contributions is a clear sense that Government officials, academics and development practitioners need to engage in a wider, deeper and more comprehensive effort at understanding the real drivers of HDI+.

Notes

1 Referring to the discussion in the Introduction, this could be ideally given by joining different sets of variables given by the UN *Human Development Index*; the *Corruption Perception Index*; the *Democracy Index*; the *Human Freedom Index*; the *Worldwide Press Freedom Index*; the *World Happiness Report*; the *Social Progress Index*; the *Human Rights Data Project*; the *Freedom in the World* and *Freedom of the Press* indexes and; the *Physical Quality of Life Index*.

2 The standard definition of money includes the capacity of an asset to be: i) a medium of exchange; ii) a unit of account and; iii) a store of value.

3 This difference suggests that, on average, the world minus the US (the reference economy) yearly income (through rents, interests, profits and wages) could afford spending (through consumption, investments, imports and spending in government services) outside the US almost the double of what it could afford spending inside the US (or any country having a nominal GDP per capital similar to that of the US). Another way to look at it, is that the US average citizen (or the average citizen of any country having a nominal GDP per capital similar to that of the US) could, on a global average, afford spending outside the US almost the double

of what she can afford spending within the US. This is because the GDP can be calculated both from the expenditure end (Y = consumption + investment + government spending +export – imports) and from the income end (Y = rents + interests + profits + wages).

4 In 2016, Estonia, Slovakia, Greece, Lithuania, Hungary, Romania and Bulgaria all received more than 2% of their GDP in public transfers from the EU. Bulgaria's share accounted for almost 4% of its GDP. Source: www.money-go-round.eu/.

5 This is best exemplified by the increasing number of over-indebted Chinese State Owned Enterprises (SOEs) and Municipalities on the domestic front (Lo 2017), and the increasing number of non-performing sovereign loans extended on the international market, particularly to Venezuela, Zimbabwe and Sudan (*Financial Times* 2016).

6 While the typology of domestic institutions and the structure of domestic decision-making mechanisms bear responsibility in influencing domestic economic policies, the level of representation that economic interests are given in domestic politics is a complex variable that cannot be disentangled through simple binary options, such as those referring to the dichotomous split between the categories of "democracy" and "authoritarianism".

7 This is the GEG definition used in the book's introduction, mediated by Finkelstein's definition of *Global Governance* as "governing, without sovereign authority, relationships that transcend national frontiers" (Finkelstein 1995).

8 For a thorough description of the concept of *reflexivity* and its workings upon economic and financial dynamics, see Soros (1987).

9 BoP transactions include trade, primary income and secondary income under the current account part and; Foreign Direct Investments, Foreign Portfolio Investments and other financial operations, including central bank reserve operations, under the capital and financial account part.

10 GEG "shapers" steer these policies via a number of tools, including diplomatic influence on budget (fiscal) and central bank (monetary) decisions; political conditionalities attached to ODA grants and loans (offered via national development agencies, national development banks or IFIs); requests to enrol into international adjustment programmes (including IMF Staff Monitored Programmes) and; requests to join bilateral, regional and multilateral trade regimes.

References

Campbell, R. W. (1992), *The Failure of Soviet Economic Planning*, Bloomington: Indiana University Press.

Easterly, W. (1999), *The Middle Class Consensus and Economic Development*, Washington, DC: The World Bank.

Einhorn E. S. and Logue, J. (2003), *Modern Welfare States*, London: Praeger.

Finkelstein, S. L. (1995), 'What is Global Governance?', *Global Governance*, 1: 367–372.

Financial Times (October 13th, 2016), '*China rethinks developing world largesse as deals sour*'.

Giddens, A. (1998), *The Third Way*, Cambridge: Polity Press.

IMF (2016), *World Economic Outlook Database*. Online document www.imf.org/external/pubs/ft/weo/2016/02/weodata/index.aspx.

Kharas, H. (2010), *The Emerging Middle Class in Developing Countries*, OECD Working Paper No. 285, Paris: OECD.

Kharas, H. (2017), *The Unprecedented Expansion of the Global Middle Class: An Update*, Global Economy and Development Working Paper 100, Washington, DC: The Brookings Institution.

Lall, S. (1996), *Learning From the Asian Tigers: Studies in Technology and Industrial Policy*, New York: St. Martin's Press.

Lo, Chi (April 17th, 2017), 'Why China's Debt Bomb has not Exploded', *Barron's*.

Naughton, B. (1995), *Growing Out of the Plan*, Cambridge: Cambridge University Press.

OECD (2015), *General Government Spending as a Percentage of GDP*, OECD Data.

Ostry, J. D., Berg, A. and Tsangarides, C. G. (2014), 'Redistribution, inequality and growth', IMF Staff Discussion Notes, Washington, DC: IMF.

Piketty, T. (2014), *Capital in the Twenty-First Century*, Cambridge: Harvard University Press.

Roeder, P. G. (1993), *Red Sunset*, Princeton: Princeton University Press.

Samuelson, P. A. (1946), 'Lord Keynes and the general theory', *Econometrica, Journal of the Econometric Society*, 14: 187–200.

Soros, G. (1987), *The Alchemy of Finance*, Hoboken: John Wiley.

Stiglitz, J. E., Sen, A. and Fitoussi, J. P. (2009), *Measurement of Economic Performance and Social Progress*. Online document http://bit/ly/JTwmG accessed 26 June 2012.

2 Wealth and the democratization of Global Economic Governance

Marcel Hanegraaff and Arlo Poletti

Introduction

As the global governance system has become increasingly relevant in contemporary policymaking, the number and scope of organized interests mobilizing beyond national borders has also risen dramatically (Hanegraaff et al. 2015). This trend is not surprising. On the one hand, the nesting of states within increasingly influential sets of global governance systems created obvious incentives for various kinds of organized interests to mobilize on a transnational basis (Barnett and Finnemore 2004; Beckfield 2003; Meyer 1980; Tallberg et al. 2013). As some observers have noted, this process largely mirrors the growth of contentious politics during the rise of the nation state (Tarrow 2001). On the other hand, this observed expansion of transnational advocacy was further stimulated by a systematic shift towards greater involvement of civil society actors in global governance (Hanegraaff et al. 2017). While there is significant variation in how much access different International Organizations (IOs) grant to societal actors, empirical evidence confirms the existence of a far-reaching institutional transformation happening among these IOs. This process has taken place in the last few decades and has pervaded all issue areas, policy functions, and world regions (Tallberg et al. 2014).

Yet, what are the characteristics of the populations of interest groups active in these international venues? And what explains their evolution over time? This paper addresses these issues, analyzing the extent to which the organizational development of these interest groups reflects differences in economic development among countries operating within the global governance system.

Noting that the population of interest groups mobilizing on a transnational basis has steadily increased over time tells us little about the nature of these communities. Any meaningful assessment of the normative implications of this observed growth requires a systematic mapping of the structure of these communities, tracing how they evolve over time, and then identifying the potential determinants of skewed participation within them. Does this growth of transnational interest groups populations mean that global governance is becoming more representative of, and accessible to, world's citizens? Or, is it telling of ever-growing patterns of inequality and exclusion? And if patterns of inequality do exist, is there something we can do about it? Any sensible answer to these questions must be grounded into an investigation of how these populations of interest groups are constructed and how they develop (Hanegraaff and Poletti 2017; Lowery and Gray 1995).

Central to all existing discussions about the normative implications of the quantitative growth of transnational interest groups is the question of how the countries' level of economic development, i.e. the economic resources they dispose of, affects these countries' representation within such interest groups populations. Existing arguments about the relationship between countries' levels of economic development and patterns of transnational advocacy can be categorized into three broad views.

According to the first, Non-State Actors' (NSAs) participation in global governance contributes towards greater equality. For instance, world polity theorists believe that due to the growing number of international access opportunities, greater parity in the breadth of NSAs' participation in global governance will emerge across the world (Barnett and Finnemore 2004; Beckfield 2003; Boli and Thomas 1997). From a different perspective, neopluralists believe that there are inherent balancing mechanisms within interest communities, ensuring that, over time, representational participation in such communities will become less skewed (Hanegraaff 2015; Lowery and Gray 2004).

A second view suggests that existing cross-country representational differences in globally active interest groups' communities should remain fairly constant over time, reflecting existing differences in economic development among these countries. A direct proportionality between the capacity of organized interests to be active globally and their capacity to obtain resources from the environment in which they operate is perhaps the oldest and most widely accepted assumption in interest group research (Gray and Lowery 1996; Hanegraaff et al. 2015). Thus, according to this view there is a linear relationship between the availability of resources and the amount of non-state actors representing a country in global governance organizations, with different levels of income and economic development translating into roughly proportional levels of transnationally active interest groups.

A third view posits that patterns of NSAs' participation in global governance are characterized by systematic inequalities and, if anything, are destined to grow even more unequal over time. This view is shared by world system scholars who conceive of global governance structures as hierarchical systems established by hegemons to perpetuate and further their domination over peripheral states (Boswell and Chase-Dunn 2000; Chase-Dunn et al. 2000), but also by standard collective action arguments showing how interest groups that mobilize earlier in the development of an interest group community can institutionalize key advantages and further strengthen their position within such communities (Braun 2012; Carpertner 2004; Hanegraaff 2015).

In this paper we propose an alternative view about the relationship between countries' wealth and their representation within global interest communities. More specifically, we show that the relationship between countries' wealth and global advocacy is best characterized as a curvilinear u-shaped slope. We find that NSAs from both the richest *and* poorest countries' (low-income and high-income countries) are disproportionally represented at the global level, while advocates representing countries lying in the middle of the development scale, i.e. low–middle- and high–middle-income countries, are vastly underrepresented. The reason is that global advocacy and lobbying for Least Developed Countries (LDCs) is highly subsidized. Such support includes Official Development Aid (ODA), which is a big endorser of NGO and Small and Medium Enterprises (SMEs) advocacy, as well as private and corporate sponsorships. Yet, once countries become wealthier these cash flows decrease dramatically and reduce these subsidized forms of global advocacy.

To illustrate the plausibility of our hypothesis, we rely on two datasources: all interest groups that were active during WTO ministerial conferences between1995–2012 (N=1,962) and all groups active at UN climate summits between1997–2012 (N=6,665). All groups were coded based on the websites to see which type of interests they defend and for which country they advocate. The combination of these data-sources allows us to compare global advocacy across countries falling in different income groups, as well as to trace variations in interest representation among specific countries moving across different income categories over time. Our results suggest the plausibility of the hypothesis that development aid has a strong effect on countries' representation in global advocacy communities.

Our findings have important implications. On the other hand, our study speaks to the debate on the relationship between global economic governance and *Human Development*. Existing research suggests a strong positive correlation between domestic institutions and policy outcomes that support *Human Development* (Besley and Kudamatsu 2006), and a strong case has been made for the operation of similar dynamics linking democracy to *Human Development* at the global level. More specifically, some argue that global governance structures can be responsive to *Human Development* needs only insofar as they ensure the fair representation of the interests of the world's poorest countries (Jayadev 2010; Woodward 2010). Our findings about the composition of interest group communities at the global level suggest that transfers of resources from rich countries to support stakeholder involvement in global governance can be effective in increasing voice and participation of more vulnerable and marginalized states within existing international institutions. Of course, this does not necessarily mean that these global economic fora will actually be more responsive to *Human Development* needs. Precisely because a transfer of resources from richer to poorer countries largely influences greater NSAs involvement in these governance systems, there is a risk that these organizations end up implementing policy agendas of the richer countries that subsidize them (Edwards and Hulme 1998). More modestly, our analysis points out that ODA can be effective in making sure that a necessary condition for a more *Human Development*-friendly global economic governance is met, namely that these institutions ensure fair representation of NSAs from poorer countries. Whether greater representation actually translates in influence and more responsiveness to *Human Development* needs is another important question that remain outside the scope of our analysis.

On the one hand, we speak to the debate about the potential of a stakeholder strategy of democratization of global governance. The normative assumption underlying these alternative positions, particularly the so-called stakeholder model of global democracy, is that the actors affected by particular political decisions should be given the opportunity to meaningfully participate and make their voice heard in the making of such decisions (Macdonald 2008; Macdonald and Macdonald 2006; Scholte 2004; Steffeck et al. 2008; Tallberg and Uhlin 2011). While empirical research shows that growing opportunities for stakeholder involvement have not yet generated greater democratic legitimacy of IOs, at least as perceived by the stakeholder organizations operating within them (Agné et al. 2015; Dellmuth and Tallberg 2015), our findings suggest that there is room for optimism. Top-down strategies aimed at supporting greater stakeholder involvement, such as foreign aid, can be effective in shaping the development of interest groups' communities at the global level, potentially bringing about greater perceived legitimacy in the longer term. As mentioned above, whether these developments will bring about greater legitimacy is also likely to critically depend on the extent to which representation then translates into influence.

Wealth and global interest group communities

What is the relation between countries' wealth and global advocacy? This question is central to both political science scholars interested in uncovering the conditions that promote the proliferation of global advocacy, and normative scholars advancing the debate on the merits of different strategies of democratization of global governance. Political scientists interested in explaining cross-country variations in global advocacy participation have long noted, in line with classical studies on interest group communities at the domestic level, that a country's socio-economic condition is a crucial factor in influencing its societal groups' ability to mobilize politically and make their voice heard in global governance fora (Hanefraaff et al. 2015; Lee 2010; Nordang Uhre 2014; Ron et al. 2005; Smith and Weist 2005).

Normative scholars questioning how global governance can be made more democratically legitimate are also crucially interested in understanding whether, and eventually in what ways, a country's wealth influences its ability to be effectively represented in global advocacy. Given the assumption of much of this literature that a move towards a more democratic global governance requires ensuring that all relevant stakeholders are given the opportunity to meaningfully participate and make their voice heard in global policymaking (Macdonald 2008; Macdonald and Macdonald 2006; Scholte 2004; Steffeck et al. 2008; Tallberg and Uhlin 2011), investigating whether differentials in countries' levels of socio-economic development promote or hinder in systematic ways different countries' representation in global advocacy is critical to assess the long-term viability of, and the potential correctives for, a stakeholder strategy of democratization of global governance.

Many authors have looked into the mechanisms linking the wealth of different countries with their representation in global interest groups, eventually suggesting three possible types of relationship. The first suggests that a number of mechanisms contribute to ensuring that differentials in countries' levels of socio-economic development should not reflect in how countries are represented in global advocacy. Two such arguments suggest that the population of interest groups active at the global level should have a more equitable character than the distribution of global wealth. The so-called world polity theory, for instance, argues that both governmental and nongovernmental organizations embedded in the world polity receive and transmit global models of legitimate state action. According to this view, membership in international organizations has increasingly become a social imperative transmitted to other relevant actors, feeding back into the political process and leading to even greater world polity ties (Boli and Thomas 1999). The dynamics of integration in the world polity thus generate a positive dynamic that further strengthens such processes of integration. This means that world polity ties have the potential to even out existing differentials in countries' levels of socio-economic development and, ultimately, that the growing number of international access opportunities can be expected to lead to greater parity in NSAs' participation in global governance among countries (Barnett and Finnemore 2004; Beckfield 2003; Boli and Thomas 1997).

From a different angle, scholars in the so-called neopluralist tradition reach similar conclusions. Neopluralism shares with the classical collective action perspective (Olson 1965) the view that some interests can mobilize more easily than others. Yet, this strand of literature highlights a number of balancing mechanisms that are inherent to the development of interest communities which ensure that, over time, representational participation in such communities become less skewed (Lowery and Gray 2004). For instance, initially disadvantaged groups may find ways to overcome collective action problems thanks to creative leadership, selective incentives, wealthy patrons or sponsors, public subsidies, etc. (Hanegraaff 2015). A second balancing mechanism is the "density dependency effect", which dampens the mobilization potential of individual interests as interest communities grow denser (Gray and Lowery 1996; Halpin and Thomas 2012). In the context of the study of transnational advocacy, this means that interest groups from wealthier countries may have dominated global interest communities at the early stages of their development, but the balancing mechanisms outlined above have subsequently contributed to evening out skewed patterns of representational participation in favour of less wealthy countries.

A second view suggests that existing cross-country differences in terms of their representation in globally active interest groups' communities should remain fairly constant over time. The connection between organized interests' capacity to be active globally and their capacity to obtain resources from the direct environment in which they operate is perhaps the oldest and most widely accepted assumption in interest group research (Gray and Lowery 1996; Hanegraaff et al. 2015). In exploring the dynamics of evolution of interest group communities at the domestic level, scholars have pointed out how their density and diversity are crucially affected by the nature of state economies (Lowery and Gray 1995). Because this relationship holds true in the national context, it can reasonably be assumed to equally hold in the international context (Nordang Uhre 2014: 63). If it is true that more economically and socially developed states will have more extensive and diversified interest group communities at the domestic level, this should be particularly true in international contexts where costs of collective action are even higher than in the national context. Thus, according to this view there is a roughly linear relationship between the availability of resources and the amount of non-state actors representing a country in global governance, with different levels of income and economic development among countries translating roughly proportionally into different levels of transnationally active interest groups.

A third view posits that patterns of NSAs' participation in global governance are characterized by systematic inequalities which, if anything, are going to grow even more unequal over time. Again, two different theoretical perspectives can substantiate this view. On the one hand, such a view is shared by scholars who conceive of the world system as a hierarchical network of nation states bound by competitive and unequal relations (Boswell and Chase-Dunn 2000; Chase-Dunn et al. 2000). This tradition sees the world system and global governance structures as hierarchical systems established by hegemons who, having a material interest in maintaining a capitalist order, create and diffuse policy scripts which are ultimately instrumental to perpetuating and furthering their domination over peripheral states. Because IOs should be conceived as "boards of directors for ruling states" (Chase-Dunn 2000: 238), the world system theory highlights the power and inequality in NSAs' participation among core and periphery states (Beckfield 2003; Nordang Uhre 2014).

Scholars analyzing patterns of transnational advocacy through the lenses of standard collective action theory reach similar conclusions (Braun 2012; Carpertner 2004). Focusing on the incentives and constraints that interest groups face when deciding to mobilize politically, these scholars also suggest that patterns of interest representation at the international level should be characterized by growing inequalities. Indeed, the collective action perspective holds that not only some interest groups can more easily mobilize as the interest community starts developing, but also that these groups will continue to profit from these advantages throughout time. This is so because interest groups that mobilize earlier can institutionalize key advantages, i.e. achieve control over resources, gain experience, and create contacts with key policy makers and other stakeholders, and further strengthen their position within such communities (Hanegraaff 2015; Heinz et al. 1993).

While these three broad perspectives all provide plausible accounts of the relationship between countries' wealth and their representation within global interest communities, we contend they overlook the extent to which a country's representation in global advocacy communities is affected by foreign, in addition to domestic, flows of resources. Existing accounts largely overlook the extent to which poor countries' global advocacy and lobbying is highly subsidized. Foreign aid represents an important element in determining low-income countries' ability to develop economically and politically (Goldsmith 2001). Foreign aid, particularly from political entities such as the EU and the US, explicitly aims to promote the development of civil society and civic organizations, leading to the creation of thousands of interest groups with a global scope of action (Lee 2010; Ottaway and Carothers 2001). This means that foreign actors, be they international organizations, single donor governments, civil society organizations, or any other type of actor engaging in such activities, can significantly modify the material resources that NSAs operating in LDCs countries can rely on to organize politically and to make their voices heard at the global level. By increasing the amount of available resources, these foreign actors can significantly expand poor countries' opportunities to be represented in global advocacy fora. To be sure, we are not the first to consider foreign aid as a potential determinant of countries' representation in global advocacy communities. Existing research points to mixed results, suggesting the need to explore further and in more systematic ways these causal links. For instance, Smith and Wiest (2005), consider ODA as a possible determinant of cross-country differences in their representation in global interest communities, considering ODA inflows as a measure of a country's ties to the global economy, and finding that aid has a limited positive effect on proliferation of global advocacy. However, Lee (2010), who equally investigates how foreign aid affects the proliferation of global advocacy, does not find any significant statistical effect. In addition to being characterized by mixed results, existing research misses a significant amount of potentially relevant observations because of the way in which the dependent variable, i.e. global advocacy, is operationalized. Indeed, by relying on the *Yearbook of International Organizations* database these studies only considers "transnational or global" groups, overlooking a large number of national groups that are active at the global level (Beyers and Hanegraaff 2014). This selection bias is particularly important when it comes to the analysis of how foreign resources affect the character of global interest communities, since these resources can affect both national and international groups operating in poor countries.

Taking into account foreign aid as a potential support to the proliferation of global advocacy groups in poor countries allows us to develop a fourth alternative characterization of the relationship between countries' wealth and their representation in global advocacy. Such a relationship could be described as one in which poorer countries, i.e. the recipients of the largest ODA flows, are vastly overrepresented relative to their socio-economic weight, and richer countries are also overrepresented in global interest communities, while countries in the middle of the development scale are underrepresented because the twofold effect of decreasing ODA flows and a relatively low level of socio-economic development hinders the emergence of a vibrant community of interest groups active at the global level.

Research design

The data is drawn from a large-scale project (see Hanegraaff 2014) that maps all interest group participation at two international venues: the World Trade Organizations (WTO) Ministerial Conferences (between 1995–2012) and the United Nations Climate Summits (1997–2011). Both IOs play key roles in how the international economic system is structured. While multilateral negotiations in the so-called Doha Round have not lived up to the initial ambitions, decisions at this level are still being made, such as on Government Procurement, Telecommunication, etc. Moreover, the judicial system of the WTO is one of the cornerstones in global economic politics. In addition, while not directly an economic institution, the United Nations Framework Convention on Climate Change (UNFCCC) is crucial for economic development. That is, decisions made at this venue have enormous ramifications for economies in all shapes and forms. To illustrate the economic importance of this conference, most organizations active at this venue are not NGOs, but business organizations.

How is the data gathered? About the first, the interest population of the *WTO MCs*, we coded all interest organizations that were registered by the WTO-secretariat as eligible to attend and/or attended in one of the seven ministerial conferences the WTO organized since 1996. In total we identified 1962 different organizations that were eligible and/or attended at least one of the seven Ministerial Conferences. All these organizations were coded on the basis of a limited number of variables which were identified by systematically coding all the websites. For 1,409 organizations we could identify a website which offers more elaborate data on the organization; for 360 organizations we were not able to find a website, but information stored on other websites enabled us to code at least some basic features of these organizations. Only 24 organizations could not be traced. This dataset with web-based information gives us a comprehensive insight into the type of organizations interested in WTO policies, the regions or the countries where they come from, their respective areas of interest, how they are organized and so on. In addition, because we rely on all Ministerial Conferences between 1995 (Singapore) and 2012 (Geneva), we can account for density, diversity and stability changes over time.

The second data source is the *UN climate summits* interest group population (see Hanegraaff 2015). To assess the development of the Conference of the Parties (COPs) interest group community we mapped all interest organizations that attended COPs between 1997 and 2011. The dataset includes 6,655 organizations which all attended one or more of the COPs since 1995. Note that this number substantially differs from some earlier accounts of the COP interest group community (see Muñoz Cabré 2011; Nordang Uhre 2014). The reason is that previous studies included only organizations which had official UNFCCC observers. One important accreditation requirement to become an observer at a climate conference is that the organization is a non-profit establishment, which excludes for profit firms from registering. This, however, does not mean that firms do not attend these conferences. Quite the contrary, firms, and other ineligible organizations for that matter, often cope with these official requirements by registering as a member of an official observer delegation. For instance, Shell and the Dow Chemical Company attend as members of the World Business Council for Sustainable Development, while Siemens and Google attend as part of the Alliance to Save Energy. As the UNFCCC lists each individual participant and its affiliated organization on its website, we were able to identify all the organizations that attended the COP's meetings. This makes our overview of attendance much more encompassing than those provided in earlier accounts (e.g. Muñoz Cabré 2011; Nordang Uhre 2014). That is, where the former analysis identifies 1,322 organizational entities attending COPs, this dataset consists of 6,655 unique organizations. Moreover, it is also one of the main reasons that the interest group population of the UN climate summits is considerable larger than the dataset of the WTO.

Similar as for the WTO research strategy, the next step included a website-search for all these organizations. For most organizations a website was identified, providing more elaborate data on the organization. For about 20% we were not able to find a website, but information stored on other websites (for instance, from other interest groups who refer to the organization in question) enabled us to code some basic features of these organizations. Only for a small number of organizations no information at all could be found (less than 5%). This dataset with web-based information gives a comprehensive insight into the types of organizations attending COP meetings, the region or countries from which they stem from, the issue areas in which they are active, their constituency base, and how they are organized. In addition, because there is data on almost all COPs from 1995 (COP3-Japan) to 2011 (COP17-Durban), we can account for density, diversity and stability changes over a substantial period of time.

In analyzing whether or not certain countries are over- or underrepresented in global governance, we first need to establish some sort of a *benchmark* for proportional representation. We follow Gray and Lowery (1996) who argue that the number of active NSAs coming from a geographical area is roughly proportional to the size of the economy of that area. Gray and Lowery developed this argument based on the US context, in which they find that the number of groups active at the federal level from a given state is highly correlated with the size of the economy of that state. To put it differently, California has a GDP roughly five times as high as Virginia and therefore the number of active groups from California can also be expected to be around five times over the number of active groups from Virginia. The logic underlying this principle is straightforward and rather similar for different types of NSAs. Both business groups and NGOs are funded by private and public funds, hence, all things being equal, the more of these funds available, the more groups can be funded and survive. Over time, this leads to a strong correlation between the GDP of a state and the number of NSAs active within and outside these states. This mechanism has since been confirmed outside the US as well, including in the EU, and in many other countries worldwide (see Berkhout et al. 2017 for an overview). We build on these findings and start from the assumption that the number of groups from a certain country active at the UNFCC or the WTO should bear a rough proportionality, other things being equal, with the size of that country's GDP. To give an example, Sweden has a GDP twice that of Finland; hence we would expect roughly twice as many NSAs active from Sweden at the UNFCCC and WTO than from Finland. If we, however, see more NSAs from a certain country than their GDP would predict, we label this "overrepresentation". Likewise, if observe less groups from a country than their GDP would predict, we label this "underrepresentation" as their potential has apparently not been reached. This provides us a list of countries at both venues whereby some are better represented than we should expect, while others are not in line with their GDP.

To test whether or not *wealth* is a strong predictor for NSA representation in global governance we link the proportional representation to the wealth of countries. We hereby make a distinction between four income groups, as defined by the World Bank. As of 1 July 2016, low-income economies (or least developed countries – LDCs) are defined as those with a GNI per capita, calculated using the World Bank Atlas method, of USD 1,025 or less in 2015; lower middle-income economies are those with a GNI per capita between USD 1,026 and USD 4,035; upper middle-income economies are those with a GNI per capita between USD 4,036 and USD 12,475; high-income economies are those with a GNI per capita of USD 12,476 or more. We subsequently analyze how each of these income groups are represented at the UNFCCC and the WTO compared to their projected attendance based on their GDP (e.g. overrepresented, proportionally represented, or underrepresented). We discuss these trends and provide some explanation for observed variations, including development aid and other types of financial assistance to LDCs and low-income countries.

Empirical illustration

Many scholars have pointed to the fact that wealthy countries have profited most from the opening up of IOs. To see whether our data is in line with these observations we first plotted the number of NSAs per income group. Figure 2.1 portrays the number of NSAs per income group at the WTO (white bars) and the UNFCCC (dotted bars). The data confirm that wealth has a

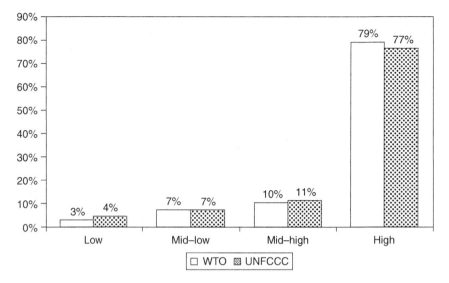

Figure 2.1 Share of NSAs active at WTO and UNFCCC per income group

strong and positive effect on the number of NSA active in global governance. Almost 80% of the organizations represented in both venues come from
a developed country (79% at WTO and 77% at UNFCCC). On the other
end, only 3% at the WTO and 4% at the UNFCCC come from LDCs. The
middle-income countries fall in the middle, whereby NSAs from middle–high
income countries are somewhat more active than NSAs from lower–middle
income countries. Looking at these numbers, it is not surprising that so many
observers cast doubts as to the equal opportunities that IOs would allegedly
provide to non-state participation from countries lying in the lower-income
echelons. Rather, one would be tempted to conclude that wealthy countries
are much better represented.

However, we argue that this is not a "fair" comparison because wealth as
a single indicator does not take into account the size of a country. To circum-
vent this problem, we compare the share of groups stemming from the four
income groups with the share of the world economy these countries represent.
In other words, LDCs combined have a 1% share in the world economy, while
3% of the groups active at the WTO represent LDCs. We consider this an
overrepresentation of 2%, etc. Figure 2.2 includes the variable GDP per
income group (black bar), which changes the picture considerably. Observe,
for instance, the share of NSAs active at the two IOs of LDCs and their share
in the economy: while there are indeed few groups active from these countries
(3% and 4% respectively), the share of these countries in the world economy
is substantially lower (1%). This means that the share of NSAs active at the
WTO and the UNFCCC coming from LDCs exceeds the expected number

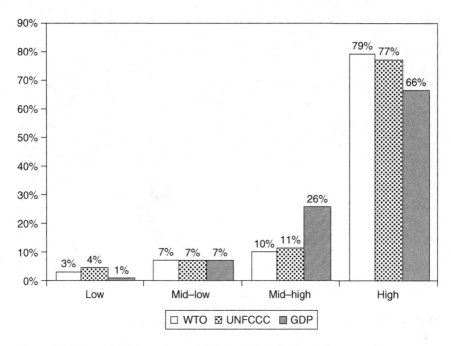

Figure 2.2 Share of NSAs active at WTO and UNFCCC per income group

from these countries. The same applies to high income groups: while three-quarters (75%) of the representation comes from these regions, they collectively account for only two-thirds (66%) of the world economy. These countries are thus also overrepresented. For middle–low-income groups, the share of NSAs representation is equal to their share in the world economy. Yet, for middle-income groups, the share of NSAs is considerably lower than the share these groups have in the world economy. While, based on their GDP, we would predict that one quarter of the groups active at the WTO and UNFCCC would come from these countries, their share is much lower (10% at the WTO and 11% at the UNFCCC).

Figure 2.3 provides a clearer illustration of this trend. In this figure we subtracted the share of the income groups in the world economy from the share of NSAs active at either the WTO (white bars) or the UNFCCC (dotted bars). A positive score thus means that more NSAs attend the conferences (either WTO or UNFCCC) than the size of the economy of these countries would predict. In contrast, a negative score indicates that countries in a certain income group are underrepresented compared to their share in the world economy, or, in other words, that the share of representation at the conferences is lower than their share in the world economy. This figure clearly illustrates the *curvilinear relation* we hypothesized between wealth and representation of NSAs at the WTO and UNFCCC conferences. Low- and high-income groups

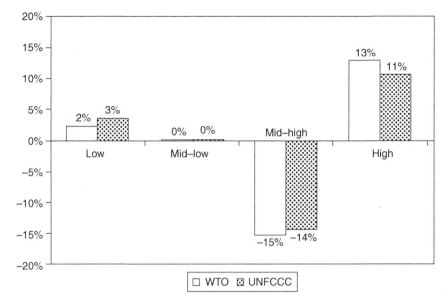

Figure 2.3 Share of NSAs active at WTO and UNFCCC per income group

are overrepresented compared to our benchmark, while high–middle-income groups are underrepresented compared to the expected number of groups we hypothesized based on their GDP share in the world economy.

Overall, there is a clear curvilinear relation between wealth and advocacy when controlling for the size of the economy. To see how robust these findings are, we dissect the results further in the next sections. We first make a distinction over time in three time periods (1997–2001; 2002–2006; 2007–2012) to see whether this relationship is consistent over time. Thereafter, we make a distinction between different types of NSAs. We begin with providing figures over time. Figures 2.4 and 2.5 are the same as Figure 2.3, i.e. highlighting over- or underrepresentation per income group, but now for three time periods. For clarity we provide separate figures for both venues: one for the UNFCCC (Figure 2.4) and one for the WTO (Figure 2.5). Both figures confirm Figure 2.3 whereby low income and high income groups are overrepresented, while middle income groups are underrepresented. We do see some variation, i.e. over time the differences become somewhat smaller, but overall the curvilinear trend remains consistent over the entire 15 year period.

Furthermore, we make a distinction between different types of NSAs, namely business groups and NGOs (Figure 2.6 for UNFCCC; Figure 2.7 for WTO). Again, we plotted over time whether these group types are over- or underrepresented at the UNFCCC and the WTO. Here something interesting can be noted. While for business groups the curvilinear relation

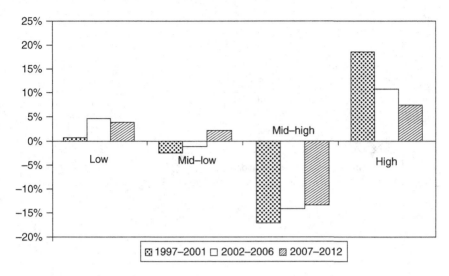

Figure 2.4 Share of NSA over time per income group – UNFCCC

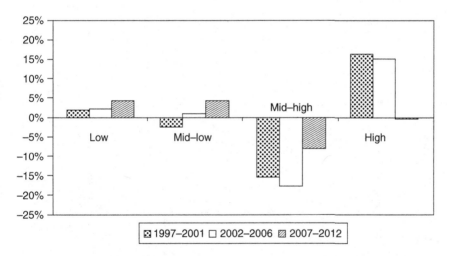

Figure 2.5 Share of NSA over time per income group – WTO

between representation by NSAs and wealth is confirmed (see polynomial trend line added), for citizen groups we see a negative linear relation indicating that wealth has a *negative* effect on the number of citizen groups active at the conferences (see also polynomial trend line added). This means that the wealthier a country becomes, the more NGOs are underrepresented compared to the size of a country. For instance, low income groups score 22% higher in

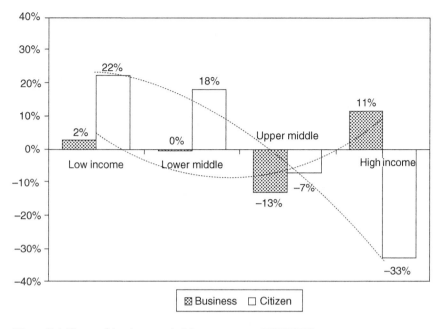

Figure 2.6 Share of business and citizen groups at UNFCCC

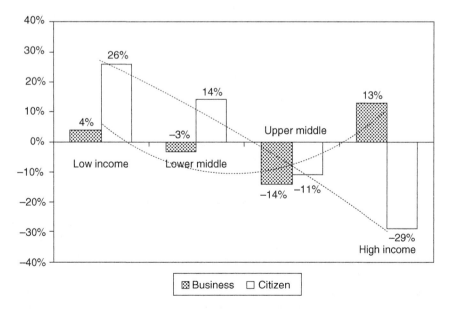

Figure 2.7 Share of business and citizen groups at WTO

the share of NSAs active at the UNFCCC than the size of their economy would predict. High income groups, in contrast, score 33% lower. We observe similar trends at both conferences.

What could explain these trends? As discussed, we expected LDC to be overrepresented because donor countries fund NSAs in these countries. This means that NSAs in these countries are not only dependent on domestic funding and can therefore expect financial support from foreign donors. To see whether this could be a viable hypothesis, we plotted the relative share of Official Development Aid (ODA) across the three recipient income groups. More precisely, we calculate how much more development aid countries in the income groups receive compared to the average. In numbers, low-income countries get 8% *more* ODA than the average across all ODA recipient countries; middle–low-income countries receive 3% more than the average ODA distributed across developing countries; high–middle-income countries receive 11% *less* ODA compared to the average ODA per country (see World Bank statistical division). This measure serves as a relative share of development aid across the income groups. If countries score a plus this means they get more ODA than average, while a negative score means they get less ODA than average. Also, by calculating average scores, we can compare the data to NSA attendance at the UNFCCC and the WTO (see Figure 2.8). The results mirror the attendance rates by NSAs: low-income groups receive most ODA, and have the highest overrepresentation. Middle–low-income economies receive average ODA levels and are fairly proportionally represented. The real drop off starts with the middle–high-income countries, which receive much

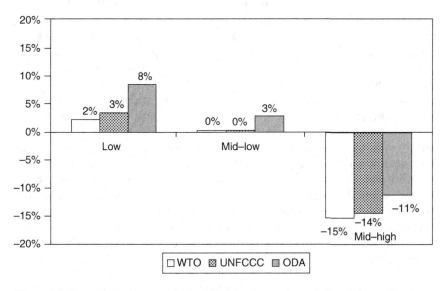

Figure 2.8 Proportional representation at IOs compared to relative ODA received, per income group

less ODA and are, to a similar extent, underrepresented at the conferences. While tentative given the descriptive nature of the data, these figures do confirm that the "development aid hypothesis" is at least plausible and deserves further attention.

Conclusion

In this chapter we problematize the notion that wealthier countries have profited the most from the opening up of IOs to civil society actors participation at these venues. This might seem true at first glance, particularly if we exclusively focus on absolute numbers. However, if we compare their attendance rates to expected values, a somewhat different story emerges. Our paper shows that both poorer and wealthier countries are overrepresented relative to their socio-economic weight in global interest group communities, while countries in the middle of the development scale tend to be underrepresented. In addition, we make a plausible case that resource transfers from richer to poorer countries, in the form of ODA, might be critical in shaping the composition of these global interest group communities.

Our empirical findings suggesting that the relationship between countries' wealth and their representation within global interest group communities should be characterized as curvilinear has important normative implications. For one, we contribute to the debate on the potential of a stakeholder strategy of democratization to generate greater democratic legitimacy in global governance. Many believe that global governance structures can be made more democratic only if poorer countries can meaningfully participate and make their voice heard within these institutional fora (Macdonald 2008; Macdonald and Macdonald 2006; Scholte 2004; Steffeck et al. 2008). If it is true that foreign aid can be effective in fostering a greater involvement of stakeholders representing the interest of societies and governments of poorer countries, then perhaps there are good reasons to expect that global governance will be perceived as more democratically legitimate than it currently is.

Second, and perhaps more importantly, our findings have important implications for the debate on how effective global governance structures can be in addressing *Human Development* needs. Amartya Sen (1999: 153) had first put forward the idea that democracy is key to defining developmental goals because it is only through discussion, exchange and public deliberation that a proper understanding of the economic needs, their content, and their force can be achieved. Extending this argument to policymaking processes at the global level, many argue that, in the absence of mechanisms fostering the participation of stakeholders from poorer countries, global governance may end up dealing inadequately with the challenges of poverty and sustainability faced by poorer countries (Woodward 2010). As Jayadev (2010: 9–10) nicely puts it,

> democracy is key to defining specific developmental goals ... there must
> be reform of existing global arrangements to better serve the needs of

representativeness and accountability ... Roughly speaking, this requires increasing voice and participation of more vulnerable and marginalized states in setting the global rules and in deliberation about those rules and their effect on capabilities.

Again, our findings seem to suggest that there is some room for optimism. Foreign aid, by contributing to increase the representation of poorer countries' in global interest communities, may end up contributing to making such institutional fora more responsive to the priorities of *Human Development*.

References

Agné, H., Dellmuth, L. and Tallberg, J. (2015), 'Does Stakeholder Involvement Foster Democratic Legitimacy in International Organizations? An Empirical Assessment of a Normative Theory', *Review of International Organizations*, 10 (4): 465–488.

Barnett, M. and Finnemore, M. (2004), *Rules for the World: International Organization in Global Politics*, Ithaca: Cornell University Press.

Beckfield, J. (2003), 'Inequality in the World Polity: The Structure of International Organization', *American Sociological Review*, 68 (3): 401–424.

Besley, T. and Kudamatsu, M. (2006), 'Health and Democracy', *American Economic Review*, 96 (22): 313–318.

Beyers, J. and Hanegraaff, M. C. (2014), 'Towards a population ecology approach of trans-national advocacy? Reviewing and exploring an emerging research field', in V. Gray, D. Lowery and D. Halpin (Eds.), *The Organization Ecology of Interest Communities: An Assessment and An Agenda*, Basingstoke: Palgrave MacMillan.

Boli, J. and Thomas, G. M. (1997), 'World Culture in the World Polity: A Century of Non-Governmental Organization', *American Sociological Review*, 62 (2): 171–190.

Boli, J. and Thomas, G. M. (1999), *Constructing World Culture: International Nongovernmental Organizations Since 1875*, Stanford: Stanford University Press.

Boswell, T. and Chase-Dunn, C. (2000), *The Spiral of Capitalism and Socialism: Toward Global Democracy*, Boulder: Lynne Rienner.

Braun, C. (2012), 'The Captive or the Broker? Explaining Public Agency-Interest Group Interactions', *Governance*, 25 (2): 291–314.

Carpenter, D. (2004), 'Protection Without Capture: Product Approval by a Politically Responsive, Learning Regulator', *American Political Science Review*, 98 (4): 613–631.

Chase-Dunn, C., Kawano, Y., and Brewer, B. (2000), 'Trade Globalization Since 1795: Waves of Integration in the World-System', *American Sociological Review*, 65 (1), 77–95.

Dellmuth, L. and Tallberg, J. (2015), 'The Social Legitimacy of International Organizations: Interest Representation, Institutional Performance, and Confidence Extrapolation in the United Nations', *Review of International Studies*, 41 (3): 451–475.

Edwards, M. and Hulme, D. (1998), 'Too Close for Comfort? The Impact of Official Aid on Nongovernmental Organizations', *Current Issues in Comparative Education*, 1 (1): 1–21.

Goldsmith, A. (2001), 'Foreign Aid and Statehood in Africa', *International Organization*, 55 (1), 123–148.

Gray, V. and Lowery, D. (1996), 'A Niche Theory of Interest Representation', *The Journal of Politics*, 58 (1): 91–111.

Halpin, D. and Thomas, H. (2012), 'Evaluating the Breadth of Policy Engagement by Organized Interests, *Public Administration*, 90 (3): 582–599.

Hanegraaff, M. (2014), *All the World's a Stage. Interest Group Politics in Global Climate and Trade Governance*, Belgium: University of Antwerp.

Hanegraaff, M. (2015), 'Transnational Advocacy Over Time: Business and NGO Mobilization at UN Climate Summits', *Global Environmental Politics*, 15 (1): 83–103.

Hanegraaff, M., Braun, C., Beyers, J. and De Bièvre, D. (2015), 'The Domestic Origins of Transnational Advocacy: Explaining Lobbying Presence During WTO Ministerial Conferences', *Comparative Political Studies*, 48 (12): 1591–1621.

Hanegraaff, M. and Poletti, A. (2017), 'The Stakeholder Model Paradox: How the Globalization of Politics Fuels Domestic Advocacy', *Review of International Studies*. https://doi.org/10.1017/S0260210517000419.

Hanegraaff, M., Poletti, A. and Beyers, J. (2017), 'Explaining Lobbying Styles Across the Atlantic: An Empirical Assessment of the Cultural And Institutional Hypotheses', *Journal of Public Policy*, 37 (4): 459–486.

Heinz, J., Laumann, E., Nelson, R. and Salisbury, R. (1993), *The Hollow Core: Private Interests in National Policy Making*, Cambridge: Harvard University Press.

Jayadev, A. (2010), 'Global governance and human development: promoting democratic accountability and institutional experimentation', Human Development Research Paper, 2010/06, United National Development Programme.

Lee, T. (2010), 'The Rise of International Nongovernmental Organizations: A Top-down or Bottom-up Explanation?', *Voluntas*, 21: 393–416.

Lowery, D. and Gray, V. (1995), 'The Population Ecology of Gucci Gulch, or the Natural Regulation of Interest Group Numbers in the American States'. *American Journal of Political Science*, 39 (1): 1–29.

Lowery, D. and Gray, V. (2004). 'A Neopluralistic Perspective on Research on Organized Interest', *Political Research Quarterly*, 57 (1): 163–175.

Macdonald, K. and Macdonald, T. (2006), 'Non-Electoral Accountability in Global Politics: Strengthening Democratic Control within the Global Garment Industry', *European Journal of International Law*, 17 (1): 89–119.

Macdonald, T. (2008), *Global Stakeholder Democracy: Power and Representation Beyond Liberal States*, Oxford: Oxford University Press.

Meyer, J. (1980), 'The world polity and the authority of the nation state', in A. Bergesen (Ed.), *Studies of the Modern World System*, New York: Academic Press.

Muñoz Cabré, M. (2011), 'Issue-linkages to Climate Change Measured through NGO Participation in the UNFCCC', *Global Environmental Politics*, 11 (3): 10–22.

Nordang Uhre, A. (2014), 'Exploring the Diversity of Transnational Actors in Global Environmental Governance', *Interest Groups and Advocacy*, 3 (1):59–78.

Olson, M. (1965), *The Logic of Collective Action: Public Goods and the Theory of Groups*, Cambridge: Harvard University Press.

Ottaway, M. and Carothers, T. (2001), *Funding Virtue: Civil Society Aid and Democracy Promotion*, Washington: Carnegie Endowment for International Peace.

Ron, J., Ramos, H. and Rodgers, K. (2005), 'Transnational Information Politics. NGO Human Rights Reporting, 1986–2000', *International Studies Quarterly*, 49, 557–587.

Scholte, J. A. (2004), 'Civil Society and Democratically Accountable Global Governance', *Government and Opposition*, 39 (2): 211–233.

Sen, A. (1999), *Development as Freedom*, Oxford: Oxford University Press.

Smith, J. and Wiest, D. (2005), 'The Uneven Geography of Global Civil Society: National and Global Influences on Transnational Association', *Social Forces*, 84 (2): 621–652.

Steffeck, J., Kissling, C. and Nanz, P. (Eds.) (2008), *Civil Society Participation in European and Global Governance: A Cure for the Democratic Deficit?*, Basingstoke: Palgrave Macmillan.

Tallberg, J. and Uhlin, A. (2011), 'Civil society and global democracy. An assessment', in D. Archibugi, M. Koenig Archibugi and R. Marchetti (Eds.), *Global Democracy. Normative and Empirical Perspectives*, Cambridge: Cambridge University Press.

Tallberg, J., Sommerer, T., Squatrito, T. and Jönsson, C. (2013), *The Opening Up of International Organizations: Transnational Access in Global Governance*, Cambridge: Cambridge University Press.

Tallberg, J., Thomas, T., Squatrito, T. and Jönsson, C. (2014), 'Explaining the Transnational Design of International Organizations', *International Organization*, 68 (4): 741–774.

Tarrow, S. (2001), 'Transnational Politics: Contention and Institutions in International Politics', *Annual Review of Political Science*, 4 (1): 1–20.

Woodward, D. (2010), 'Democratizing Global Governance for Sustainable Human Development', *Development*, 53 (1): 43–47.

3 The World Bank in the post-crisis landscape

Stasis and change after the post-Washington Consensus

Eugenia Baroncelli

Introduction

Since the second half of the 2000s, the post-Washington Consensus world has witnessed a round of crises of systemic proportions (food, fuel, financial), which have prompted the World Bank (WB)[1] to undertake reforms at multiple levels (governance, policies/programmes, organizational). In some cases, these changes have been the continuation of ongoing processes. In other, they have responded to, and have been subsequently influenced by, the challenges posed by those exogenous shocks.

While positive results have been achieved in some areas, critics have argued that the World Bank has lost grip on Global Economic Governance (GEG) (Gilbert et al 1999; Kapur 2015). Based on a theoretically informed review of grey literature, this chapter provides a structured framework to discuss these contentions. The chapter builds on previous and ongoing research on WB's reforms (Baroncelli 2011, 2013, 2018) conceptualizing policy and institutional changes in light of the 2008–2010 International Bank for Reconstruction and Development's voice and participation reform, arguing that stasis in the Bank's constituent politics (i.e. the absence of a major redistribution in shareholding rights) was instrumental to preserving the role of traditional donors while at the same time increasing the power of some Emerging Market Economies (EMEs) without touching the delicate IBRD Board equilibrium between developing and developed countries. The article also discusses post-2008 changes in lending, policy and programme practices of the whole World Bank Group (WBG), arguing that these have occurred along multiple mechanisms, with the organization's learning from past experiences, and adapting with remarkable speed to evolutions in the external environment.

On the one side, the Bank has proceeded along the path initiated in the post-Washington Consensus era, by further incorporating inputs from interested stakeholders, that have through time gained a stake in the policies and programmes of the organization, without retaining formal shareholding rights. On the other side, in responding to the 2008 crisis, and to the calls by the G-20, the organization has explicitly privileged the requests of some among its middle-income largest shareholders, to the immediate disadvantage of low income borrowers. Since 2013, the WBG has also undergone a major organizational reshaping under the presidency of Jim Yong Kim. The extent to which the three sets of change processes outlined above (governance, policy/programmes, organizational) have produced radical transformations in the politics and practice of the organization is still subject to evaluation, and an overall assessment of their shape and results will have to wait for fuller developments. Their early impacts are however discussed in the chapter, which also analyzes the key implications that have emerged so far, for both the WB's repositioning in the market for development knowledge and finance, and for the broader practice of multilateral development.

Overall, the chapter argues in favour of recalibrating bold claims about the organization's decreasing ability to contribute to its mission: many strategic and operational problems notwithstanding, the WB was able to provide a timely and relevant response to support low- and middle-income countries efforts during the 2007–2008 crisis. In turn, the WBG has devised new programmes and reorganized internal structure to strengthen its role in the provision of global public goods (most notably food security, health and cross-sector support to fragile and conflict-affected countries).

The Chapter is organized as follows: section 2 offers a synthesis of the redefinition in the WB's mission since the 1990s, and contextualizes its role in responding to the food and fuel price crises first, and of the financial crisis in the 2000s. Section 3 deepens the focus on the nature and direction of the International Bank for Reconstruction and Development (IBRD) and the International Development Association (IDA) lending as a response to the 2008 financial crisis, while section 4 addresses the development impact of such increased financial effort in the areas of development policy lending, investment lending and social protection lending. Section 5 traces the essentials of the IBRD voice and participation reform of 2008–2009, while Section 6 reconstructs the launch of the 2013 new WBG strategy. Section 7 connects the changes discussed in the previous parts, arguing about causality and impact, for both the organization and the broader cause of development. Section 8 concludes, outlining key policy implications and suggestions for future research.

A changing landscape and multiple crises: the role of the World Bank

Since the second half of the 2000s the WB has experienced multiple transformations, to adapt to the post-Washington Consensus, MDG-shaped, and poverty oriented context of development policies. In addition to the poverty and good governance envelopes, pursued through the shift from the Structural Adjustment Loans approach to the Comprehensive Development Framework, through the Poverty Reduction Strategy Papers (PRSPs) for low-income countries and the emphasis on a matrix approach to development lending, the Bank also embarked on a greener path, attaching safeguard clauses to its loans to respond to claims expressed by concerned NGOs and selected shareholders about environmental sustainability of its sponsored projects in client countries (Baroncelli 2018). Following the militarization of conflicts in Afghanistan (2001) and Iraq (2003), the Bank also supported post-crisis, reconstruction and anti-corruption efforts. It also sought a more conscious approach to trade and investment integration, supporting client countries efforts to adapt to increasingly competitive markets at the global level and providing policy advice to that effect. Along came a renewed effort in partnering with other players, national governments, other multilaterals and the private sector, to increase resources for development, effectiveness of aid coordination and donor harmonization along the Accra Agenda (2005). It is amidst these developments that the Bank faced the system-wide global shock of 2008, in fact the culmination of a seamless stream of crises, in food, fuel prices and, eventually, finance and the global economy.

From the perspective of low-income countries, the 2007 food crisis, the 2008 spike in energy prices and the 2008–2009 financial crisis constituted a veritable "crisis complex". Rising prices of staple commodities and growing energy costs had a particularly heavy impact on poor households. The then WB's President, Robert Zoellick, seized the moment to advocate a wider role for the institution as the supplier of emergency resources to help the poorest countries to cushion the downturn. These external shocks generated a consensus on the idea that action was needed to boost the WB's ability to act in support of poorer countries.

The Bank's response materialized in May 2008 with the launch of the Global Food Crisis Response Program (GFRP), a fast track initiative of loans and grants worth USD 1.2 billion in lending, primarily targeted to low-income countries (60% to Africa), raised to 2 billion in April 2009. Although the response and disbursements were fast, the strategy was far from perfect.[2] However, the GFRP experience also spurred the launch of other Programs targeted at low-income countries, such as the IDA Crisis Response Window and the IDA Immediate Response Mechanism that ameliorated the Group's ability to prepare and support countries responses to system-wide shocks.

The food and fuel price crisis had primarily affected poor households in low-income countries, including rural communities hit by bad harvests and spikes in staple and energy prices, despite the fact that the most secluded among these communities had benefitted from relative insulation from the transmission of price shocks, and the cushions provided by informal sectors, a regular source of income for most of the rural poor. The financial crisis of 2008, on the contrary, hit primarily formal sectors and the countries that were most connected with world markets. Through time, the combination of the three crises has impacted the poor with particularly severe effects. First, the most open among low-income countries have seen their food imports decline steeply as the main exporting countries were increasing the price of their products, not rarely as a result of explicit export restrictions imposed to ensure enough domestic food supplies. Second, high energy costs had further raised trade costs and reduced imports of basic commodities with heavy ratios of weight to value. Third, the shift to biofuels had further reduced the availability of basic food commodities, thus putting upward pressure on their price. Fourth, the financial crisis constrained investment and import capacity in most advanced and several developing countries. ODA levels also declined, as industrialized OECD Development Assistance Committee (DAC) countries focused their efforts largely on coping with the internal effects of the global crisis. Fifth, the financial crisis widened the number of poor people, with transition of households across poverty thresholds – and particularly retrogression towards the poverty end. According to Chen and Ravallion (2009), 53 million people fell into poverty in 2009 as a result of the financial crisis, due to the contraction in demand, jobs and related income and remittances. In turn, lower social expenditures and contraction in the utilization of basic social services have had lasting impacts on household welfare, further depressing consumption and broader labour and economic conditions.

Countering critical views and the argument that it would be an obsolete organization in GEG, analyses of the Bank's role across the 2008 crisis have highlighted how the institution has on the contrary been able to step in and provide a substantial boost to the global recovery through enhanced lending (Winters 2011). However, a non-trivial qualifier has been that the Bank's crisis lending was primarily allocated to selected middle-income economies. Critiques have been levied against the Bank's supposedly lame approach to lending to low income shareholders, which remained to pre-crisis levels for the whole Group (i.e. IBRD, IDA and IFC lending) (Woods 2010). In light of the poverty-eradicating mission of the Bank, and more so after the ambition voiced for the organization by President Jim Yong Kim at the World Bank-IMF Spring Meetings of 2013 to reach the goals of "Ending extreme poverty and boosting shared prosperity" by 2030,[3] such evidence appears somewhat problematic.

The next four sections provide a nuanced assessment of the "obsolescence argument", through the analysis of IBRD crisis lending patterns and performance, an exploration of the IBRD voice and participation reform and, last of the WBG internal reorganization.

Crisis lending and beyond

The first evidence of the WB's relevancy still passes from its financial weight. In the wake of the financial crisis, the WBG provided a record of USD 63.7 billion in new yearly commitments for countercyclical lending (fiscal year 2009–2010) to respond to clients' demands, more than doubling commitments in the period 2005–2007 (IEG 2012 – II, xii). The IBRD alone raised its gross commitments from USD 32.9 billion in 2009 to USD 44.2 billion in 2010 (Figure 3.1), which placed it above any of the other IFIs in the provision of crisis support (IEG 2012 – II, 27).[4] Since 2013, the Group has followed a continuous upward trend, moving from USD 50.2 billion in that year to 64.2 billion in 2016.[5]

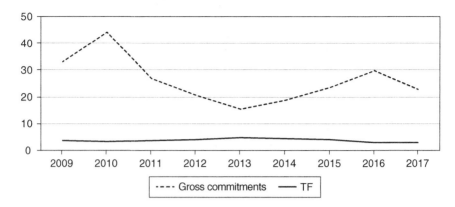

Figure 3.1 IBRD Lending and Trust Funds, 2009–2017 (USD billions)

Source: Fiscal Year Data, The World Bank, worldbank.org/financial results, accessed March–December 2017

Additionally, the Bank was able to provide loans more swiftly than other donors, with longer maturity terms, advantageous conditions for borrowers irrespective of their income level, and at comparatively competitive rates, most markedly until early 2010, but with continuing competitive conditions also after that date, particularly if compared to lending from alternative sources. (IEG 2012 – II).[6]

As noted above, the largest increase in crisis-related Bank lending went to middle-income countries, while resources for low-income countries were maintained at existing levels. The income-group targeting of WB post-crisis support is, however, less biased than it would appear at face value, as between 2007 and 2009, several major recipients have transitioned from low-income to middle-income status.[7] A more benevolent reading of the Bank's performance as a crisis manager is further premised on the consideration that its lending to emerging economies has served the broader purpose of helping precisely those countries out of the crisis, to restore their path toward becoming future engines for global growth (Winters 2011). A longer term perspective also suggests that the four IDA replenishments occurred between 2007 and 2016 have increased lending to low income countries by 78.6%, shifting from USD 42 billion (15th Replenishment 2007), to USD 49.3 billion (16th Replenishment 2010, particularly notable in the midst of the crisis), to USD 52 billion (2013 17th Replenishment), to USD 75 billion in 2016, on the occasion of the 18th Replenishment.

Compared to other major donors, however, the Bank did not strictly target its supplemental lending to countries that were hit hardest by the 2008 crisis, nor did it scale its incremental lending capacity in response to the severity of conditions of afflicted clients (IEG 2012 – II: 12). To some extent, the choice reflected a substitutive financing by the Bank, to cover needs in countries not

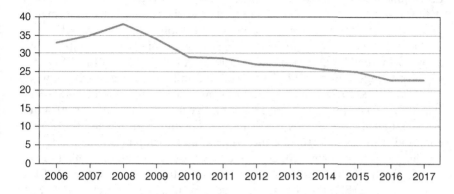

Figure 3.2 IBRD equity-to-loans ratio (%)
Source: Elaborated by Author, from WBG Annual Reports, various years

supported by IMF programmes. The evidence has also been linked to the comparatively higher risk aversion of the Bank, vis-à-vis other Multi-lateral Development Banks (MDBs), and to its longer-term approach to development financing. Tension between crisis support and risk aversion, thus, compounded with pre-existing engagement in client countries to explain this seemingly paradoxical outcome. In retrospect, the strategy has paid off, as the impact of the crisis in low-income countries has been more moderate than in the aftermaths of past crises.

On the other side, even if the WB entered the crisis with a competitive financial situation compared to other MDBs, particularly due to its conservative investment decisions in previous times, its expansive lending to middle-income countries during the crisis eroded part of its safety buffers, and eventually led the management to revise the organization's general lending terms after 2010. This, along with the Bank's particularly low interest rates (IEG 2012 – I), have led some to question the medium-term sustainability of its very lending model in times of crisis.

As Figure 3.2 shows, between 2008 and 2011, the IBRD's equity-to-loan ratio declined from 38% to 28.6%, reaching 22.7% in 2016.[8] As a result, the IBRD has subsequently reduced its lending until 2013, when it committed USD 15.25 billion. Under the presidency of Jim Yong Kim, the Group as a whole has also undergone an expenditure review (2012–2015), that has identified potential savings worth USD 404 million, from reduction in costs of general service and administrative expenses (WBG Annual Report 2015).

Investment lending products, the Bank's original core business, have accounted for the largest absolute amounts of efforts from pre- to post-crisis levels, with IBRD and IDA's commitments doubling from USD 16.8 billion to USD 32.1 billion between fiscal years 2005–2007 and 2009–2010, respectively (IEG 2012 – II). In relative terms, the most marked rise has concerned development policy lending to provide budget support to client countries. The datum is consistent with changes related to crisis lending behaviour, mainly targeted to short term macroeconomic stabilization.[9]

After the reduced pace of lending that followed the new prudential limits adopted by the IBRD, a new surge in lending occurred in 2014 (USD 18.6 billion), rising in 2015 (USD 23.52 billion), and culminating in 2016, when IBRD allocated 29.73 billion in commitments to its borrowers (see Figure 3.1). Plausibly, two major factors have played a role in the new surge: the 2014 fuel crisis and related trade crisis, particularly in commodity trade and the drop in commodity prices of 2016, and the Millennium Development Goals (MDGs) deadline and subsequent launch of the new Sustainable Development Goals (SDGs) by the UN in 2015. Sectoral lending patterns over the period 2013–2017 reflect the IBRD refocusing on large infrastructural projects with energy intensive components, with a spike of almost 400% in lending for Energy and Extractives (from USD 1.21 billion in 2013 up to USD 4.4 billion in 2017). Second, the 2015 launch of the SDGs has prompted the Group to enhance its relations with the UN, creating a dedicated Vice President (VP) to manage the WBG-UN partnership in the context of supporting the implementation of the 2030 Agenda. The emphasis on a different scale of needed resources ("trillions, not billions") and the learning from the MDGs experience (when the launch preceded the allocation of resources) have pushed the WBG to engage in a sustained financial effort to allocate development resources a few months before the launch of the SDGs.

Lending performance and development impact

Allegedly, as articulated in the previous section, enhanced lending during and immediately after the 2008 crisis occurred in a timely manner, both in absolute and comparative terms (IEG 2012 – II). The Bank's established country dialogue, and familiarity with local conditions, helped to that effect (*idem*). However, according to early evaluation reports on the WBG responses to the crisis (IEG 2012 – I) speed and timeliness did not always match development outcomes. The targets were mostly middle-income countries, and, in some sectors, not necessarily those that were most hardly hit by the crisis. *Ex post*, other issues have been identified with the outcomes of financed projects on the ground.

The objectives of IBRD post-crisis development policy operations were only partially met. In some instances, less-than-satisfactory results have been directly attributed to poor Development Policy Operations (DPOs) design. Examples of ill-conceived measures of fiscal stimulus have been the cases of El Salvador and Costarica, in Latin America, and of Serbia, Poland and Romania in the ECA region, where apparently the Bank underestimated the fiscal impact of the crisis and provided for only limited measures to consolidate the fiscal deficits. Countercyclical policies, the norm of fiscal approaches to crisis management in high-income countries, have been supported by Bank

DPOs in a range of developing clients – yet, the results have often been unsatisfactory, with further fiscal deterioration happening after the crisis. Constraints were due to multiple reasons, including the impossibility of cutting subsidies or investments during the crisis and the absence of fiscal targets in the DPOs of some countries under high fiscal stress.

Here as well, weak performances of fiscal management-focused DPOs have to be put in context. First, as for other crisis-related measures the absence of a reliable counterfactual (what would have happened had the Bank not stepped in?) makes evaluation at best tentative, particularly compared to evaluation of lending performance for projects during "regular" times, for which benchmarking is easier and more reliable. Additionally, the joint presence of WB, IMF and/or other MDBs – programmes has laden performance evaluation exercises with the burden of correct attribution. Furthermore, time consistency problems (short-term needs of crisis-impacted countries versus medium–long-term templates of pre-crisis existing DPOs) have also affected the performance of crisis-related DPOs, as well as the relevance of their evaluation by independent agencies (IEG 2012 – II).

As seen in the previous section, investment lending (64% of IBRD lending between 2000 and 2013) experienced the highest rise. Impacts, however, have been spread across years, as maturities span from 5–10 years or longer, which makes crisis-related evaluation a work in progress.[10] These difficulties notwithstanding, and with particular reference to investment lending (IL) components of public sector and social protection investment, several sources have praised the the guarantee powers that the World Bank Group, along with other MDBs, has been able to wield during the crisis years (Chelsky et al 2013; IEG World Bank Group 2014). With the crisis-induced meltdown in the private sector, one option for borrowers was to rely on government budgets for long-term financing. Yet, public finances were soon hit by the crisis too and subsequently by tighter regulations and expenditure caps, particularly in Europe, with little room to support long-term fiscal expansionary measures. Coupled with the absence of public sector guarantees, heightened risks and shorter horizons in private financing turned into a major hindrance for social and infrastructural investments during the crisis.

Lending for social protection was mostly devoted to projects in the Europe and Central Asia (ECA) and Latin America and the Caribbean (LAC) regional groupings, the areas where the worst post-crisis social consequences had been experienced. As for the general post-crisis lending pattern, the Bank's support to social protection largely privileged middle-income countries in those two regions (72% of projects and 85% of lending), and only a small group of countries among them. Most social lending privileged mildly affected countries (53%, as opposed to 47%, allocated to severely affected), and relied on existing programmes, most of which had been in place since the food crisis of 2007–2008. The Bank has subsequently worked to improve its targeting by launching a new social protection strategy with clearer focus on low-income and fragile states, particularly in the context of its initiative targeted at prioritizing fragile, conflict- and violence-affected countries (FCV), the majority of which are low-income countries. In contexts where the informal economy accounts for large parts of a country's GDP, though, the Bank's attempt at reforming existing social protection systems through flexible risk management programmes has attracted several criticisms.

Overall, any evaluation should factor in the nature of the WBG (development bank), the relation between the Bank and its shareholders and the exceptional character of development lending under systemic crises. The IEG-contested low correlation between the Bank's allocations and the crisis' severity at the country-level does not consider that loans are negotiated, and potentially approved, based on demands from client countries, rather than along predetermined allocation matrices, even though the Group strives to ensure cross-country proportionality and development effectiveness (IEG 2012 – I). Budget support to face fiscal imbalances during the crisis was at times questioned for being insufficient to achieve the desired targets, but, in other cases, so were programmes aimed at fiscal consolidation for lacking mandatory fiscal targets. Differentiation in this case has played well to respond to earlier criticism of "one size fits all" and hyper-conditioned IBRD approaches to crisis management adopted during the years of the Washington Consensus. The paradox here is that with milder conditionality and tailor-made support packages the WB was still criticized for not having achieved the desired development and poverty results. As several lending products supplied by the Bank aim at supporting medium-term development, including public goods and infrastructure, a primary focus on the short term macroeconomic performances of beneficiary countries has added more than one bias to the above IEG evaluations. The IBRD privileging of middle-income countries was, as seen above, counterbalanced by a major IDA replenishment in 2010, the creation of the Crisis Response Fast Track Facility in 2008 and of the Crisis Response Window in 2009. Furthermore, it was precisely those middle-income countries that were most suffering from the drying up of credit in private markets. By stepping in, alongside other multilaterals, yet with unequalled financial weight and robust convening and guarantee authorities, the WB may have been the key player in ramping up resources and confidence. Absent a counterfactual (the usual suspect in post-crises analyses) the role of global confidence builders that are at once able to provide swift and scalable support based on clients' demands should not be underestimated.

The "Voice and participation" reform and its aftermath

Lending patterns, and sustained support to middle-income emerging markets, should be read in conjunction with the Group's evolving organizational vision and longer-term strategies. In turn, both longer term expectations over future growth drivers and graduation issues have to be balanced with strategic considerations over shareholders' equilibria in the redefinition of the IBRD internal governance.[11]

The WB "voice and participation reform" of 2008–2010, a two-phase reform of rules guiding the re-allocation of shareholding rights and voting powers at the IBRD Board, initiated between April and November 2008, was the culmination of a longer process of change that had originated in the context of the Monterrey Consensus of 2002, to enhance the voice of Developing and Transitioning Countries (DTCs) in the decision-making of the World Bank. While a target was to give equal voice to both the group of high-income, on the one side, and middle- and low-income countries, on the other ("voting power parity"), the main result has been to reduce that divergence only in part.[12] According to the usual WB classification by income groups, post-voice reform high-income shareholders still controlled 61.6% of voting power (down from previous 65.3%), while middle- and low-income countries were commanding 38.38% (up from previous 34.67%). As of 2017, with its current 16.39% voting powers, the US still retains its veto privilege in "constituent politics" (changes in the Articles of Agreement that require an 85% majority).

Compared to 2008–2010, the US-led block of transatlantic and US-friendly shareholders has been recently put to a test. The Europeans were then particularly careful to respect Washington's desiderata in the voice reform negotiations, and abstained from "rocking the boat" even when it was clear that the negotiated redistributions still fell short from enhancing the voice of the poorest shareholder, let alone promoting equitable representation at the Board (Baroncelli 2018). Into the second year of the presidency of Donald Trump, its "America first" unilateralist approach to US foreign policy has created multiple frictions and exacerbated lingering fears of abandonment in the European allies. Harshly criticizing the EU, withering the Transatlantic Trade and Investment Partnership (TTIP) with Europe, but also stepping out of the Paris Agreement on Climate Change, demeaning the relevance of the North Atlantic Treaty Organization (NATO) in transatlantic defense and deterrence have ostensibly shaken the boat of transatlantic ties. In turn, the launch of the AIIB by China, the prompt joining by the major European countries, and the official support expressed by IMF and WB apexes, has raised eyebrows in Washington.[13] While it would be advisable that conflict mediation among top shareholders occurred at the political level – until a serious reform of the IBRD leadership selection is undertaken, effort by the management to smooth frictions – and secure budgets – via corporate diplomacy will remain the standard practice.

Into the second decade of the new millennium, several fast-growing shareholders have graduated to donor status ("recent graduates") while still keeping their status of borrowers (China, India, Brazil, Nigeria among others). While the double status ("blend countries") and the flexibility that comes with that may appear as a bonus to these countries, and a hindrance to the IBRD – which would benefit from higher subscriptions altogether, both these shareholders, and the whole organization, are likely to derive mutual gains. For the IBRD to operate smoothly, the consensus of fast growing emerging market economies (EMEs) that are also highly and densely populated, is absolutely necessary. Among them, India and China still host the higher (absolute) number of poor people in the world. They still are target countries for poverty eradication, one of the twin goals that the WBG has identified as its core objectives for the year 2030.[14] Currently, it is estimated that middle-income countries host 73% of the world's poor. Additionally, the fact that blend countries both borrow and lend from the IBRD may bode well for their representatives to support balanced positions at its Board. In turn, the Chinese, Indian, Brazilian and Nigerian governments need the IBRD for the expertise and knowledge that come with its loans, as repeatedly voiced by their leaderships, who have in time come to appreciate the benefits of its policy and investment technical assistance. China, in particular, has expressed its favour for continued support and policy advice by the Bank. Being the third subscriber to the IBRD, with 4.56% in voting powers after the US and Japan (that in 2017 wielded 16.39% and 7.07%, respectively), with an economy projected to grow, even if at a reduced pace, above 6% in the next few years, its proactive involvement in the Washington-based system of multilateral lending appears of paramount relevance.

The Chinese model of development has been at times contrasted with the "Washington Consensus", and the "Beijing Consensus" – giving a stronger role to the State, in the context of market-based controlled opening – has been quoted as winning favours with the Group President.[15] To be true, as noted by many, China has benefitted from constant support by the Washington-based IFIs (and is currently one of the largest IBRD borrower in absolute terms),[16] it has applied austerity templates not dissimilar from the IMF-mandated rigour on monetary and fiscal policies during the Asian crisis; it has pursued a steady path of integration in global markets largely consistent with the Washington Consensus advice of that day. Yet, Chinese leaders have followed that path on their own terms, manipulating austerity narratives along the needs of China's domestic system – both political and economic. The main differences with the "Washington Consensus" have been in the country's state-led approach to economic reforms, ranging from winner-picking policies to promote innovators and identifying national champions, to subsidizing and rescuing State owned enterprises and Banks when needed. The jury on the sustainability of Beijing's growth model, on economic, political and social grounds, is still out. Overall, however, China's current economic weight and position in the IBRD Board make it imperative for its management to work towards finding a compromise between Beijing and Washington's stances. While recapitalization seems to be attracting much of the current interest, that issue is only a reflection of the deeper cleavage between the leaders of the two major economies of the world on how to drive the Bank across the challenges of an increasingly multipolar global system.

Internal reorganization and the new WBG strategy

Quarrels among shareholders have been matched by the explicit reform proactiveness of President Jim Yong Kim, who has aligned the WBG with the

UN-mandated development goals by setting two specific objectives – ending extreme poverty of people living with less than USD 1.25 per day, and boosting shared prosperity for the bottom 40% in developing countries, through providing them with sustainable support – to be attained by 2030. Yet, contrary to previous policy changes (such as the "poverty turn" under the presidency of Jim Wolfenshon), the launching of the 2013 Strategy also initiated a sweeping group-wide reorganization ("One World Bank Group"), with radical resizing and organizational transformations. First, the predominantly country-based organizational structure has been reshaped with a substantial component of matrix elements, built around shared group-wide "global practices", thematic/sectoral horizontal groupings more strategically focused compared to the pre-existing networks and "anchors". The claimed rationale behind that change has been one of reflecting "the Bank's Group comparative advantages and better complement the existing strengths of its regional units and country offices", via the pervasive diffusion of existing specialized expertise across all regional units (World Bank Annual Report 2014: 12). Second, a further horizontal component has been introduced through the creation of the "Cross-cutting Solution Areas".[17]

The reform also widened the range of products available to partner countries, integrating guarantees (offered by the Multilateral Investment Guarantee Agency – MIGA) into its investment (Investment Project Financing – IPF) and policy frameworks (Development Policy Financing – DPF), upgrading risk-assessment tools (Systematic Operations Risk-rating Tool) and making loans more responsive to countries' needs during crises through the Deferred Drawdown Option (DDO), enhanced with the CatDDO (Catastrophe DDO). The WB approach to country counterparts has also been renewed through Systematic Country Diagnostics and Country Partnership Frameworks – replacing previous Country Assistance Strategies (CASes), and aimed at a "more selective" yet hopefully better targeted engagement with partners to reach development goals.[18] Joint IBRD work with the International Financial Corporation (IFC) and MIGA serves the purpose of maximizing group-wide synergies to involve the private sector in the attainment of the twin goals.

Upon the call of the Development Committee, the same rationale – sharing bank-wide expertise to identify appropriate responses to either global needs or specific client's demand in the midst of major sudden changes – has led to the launch of the Crisis Response Platform in 2016, an umbrella that regroups the full set of WBG "crisis response toolkits". In addition to the IDA Crisis Response Window developed in 2008–2009 on the occasion of the 16th Replenishment, the Group has devised new initiatives such as the Middle East and North Africa Concessional Financing Facility (MENA CFF), the Global Concessional Financing Facility (GCFF), the Pandemic Emergency Financing Facility (PEF), and a multiplicity of specific crisis-dedicated trust funds. Convened under the joint aegis of the UN, the WBG and the Islamic Development Bank (IDB) to initially support Syrian refugees along with

Jordanian and Lebanese host communities in addressing the emergency-cum-development needs stemming from the massive and protracted influx of forcibly displaced people, the MENA CFF combines contributions from eight different donors into a single facility that pools together grants and loans, but extends the modality of concessional financing to the full amount of disbursements. In addition to housing the coordination unit for the MENA CFF, the WBG is also the facility's trustee, as well as the financial intermediator between donors and implementing agencies on the ground.

A similar logic informs the concept behind the creation of the Global Concessional Finance Facility (GCFF), aimed at extending the geographical scope beyond the MENA region to support other middle-income countries that face simultaneous humanitarian and development challenges due to extensive refugee inflows from fragile and conflict-affected countries. Based on previous Bank experience in dealing with health threats, and drawing on the lessons learned from cooperating with the World Health Organization (WHO) to tackle the spread of the Ebola virus in 2014, the PEF was launched in 2016. To its usual convening power, fund pooling and expenditure capacity, as well as guarantee authority, the WBG has added the concept of pandemics insurance bonds, basically transferring to the market the risk of health outbreaks through the creation of insurance and bond products to support ex-ante hedging against health outbreaks – and, if needed, immediate financing of early remedies. The move is part of a broader evolution in development financing, that has targeted disaster-risk financing (any disaster) as a key feature of the evolving landscape of development needs in the new, crisis-affected global system. Along the model of the disaster-risk bonds launched by the WBG in 2014 to support partner countries in the Caribbean to hedge against earthquake and cyclone risks, the insurance and bond components of PEF are thought as inducements to private funds and investors to support development-related health concerns with their resources. Complemented with more traditional un-tied cash components contributed by governments and other IFIs, that would be used in case of unforeseen – new – health outbreaks (new diseases, new modalities of transmission, etc), insurance and Catastrophe (CAT) bonds should support faster and more effective intervention when needed, and serve the broader purpose of alerting potential borrowers of the need to monitor the current status of their respective health systems.

Different from stasis in governance reforms, these changes in the policies, organizational structure and structure reflect the Group's responsiveness to evolutions in its external context. On the one side, these moves have plausibly responded to the need of revamping the core WBG lending volumes after the post-crisis ebb of 2013–2014 (Sandefur and Patel 2016). On the other side, they have fulfilled the basic requirement of redefining the Group's mission in light of more frequent, diverse and intense system-wide shocks against the backdrop of ongoing notable graduations.

The WB in the new environment

The major, unrivalled surge in WB lending in 2010 has responded to the food and fuel crisis first, and to the global 2008–2009 crisis then. While the majority of that effort has been sustained by high-income shareholders, several emerging donors have substantially increased their support to affected low-income partners, through a multiplicity of initiatives both bilateral and multilateral in nature.[19] While still a fraction of the support provided by DAC donors, the relative growth in the aid effort incurred by emerging donors has legitimately raised their demands for a stronger voice in the boards of Washington-based IFIs. Change in constituent politics, however, has not materialized, as the rules of the game have preserved the US veto power at the IBRD Board, with the country's ability to singlehandedly block changes to the Articles of Agreement requiring an 85% quorum. Outcomes for developing countries as a group have been limited – and only for some major emerging economies have tangible gains materialized. Developed countries have incurred costs, but, inexplicably, they have to date (2017) managed to reverse their losses to regain previous shares (Vestergaard and Wade 2015).

Simultaneously, however, those external transformations have triggered changes in the structure of the organization and in the products it offered. Stasis in governance rules has been matched by efforts by the management to modify the Bank's structure and business to adapt to the changing environment: agile, nimble and other similar words recur in post-2008 Bank Reports, to describe the Group adaptation to a fast-changing environment, where shocks – economic, social, environmental – prompt "resilient" responses, from both affected countries/populations and the institutions that seek to provide support to them. Through the 2013 new Strategy, the Group has adapted to the fact that some EMEs have become "blend countries", implying that their need for development financing was changing, both in volume and nature. As borrowing on private markets was becoming a feasible option for a growing number of its clients – the WBG was gearing up to fiercer infra-sectoral competition in the business of development financing.[20] Compared to pre-2010, when the IBRD's share in total MDBs capital reached 50%, after 2010 that figure declined to 39% (Gleave and Morris 2015: 7). The WBG reshaping of the nature and target of its products has responded precisely to these changes, to stay in the business of multilateral financing for development.

To date, post-reorganization performance has been assessed to a limited extent, as only three years have elapsed since the reform implementation started (fiscal year 2013–2014). Prima facie evidence suggests that the reform has already produced some repercussions on the Group's internal adjustments, as well as and on its external development impact (Sandefur and Patel 2016). An early sign was a string of departures by senior management positions.[21] Internal repercussions in the post-reform years have reportedly been severe on the staff's morale, spurring rounds of complaints and further layoffs. The major bones of contention have revolved around the depth, speed and size of organizational changes and cuts in administrative costs (USD 400 million in 3-year time), triggering a reaction against the decisions of a politically appointed 4-year term President by 20-year plus trained staff with high-level diversified sector specific expertise.

To be true, the lack of appropriate incentives for staff had been identified as an early potential risk (Bretton Woods Project 2013a). Promised cuts in administrative expenditures did not bode well for providing stimulus to employees, who were in most cases forced to transition virtually overnight from the Group's country-based model to the new horizontal template. Global practices have certainly added value to the Group's work in supporting the provision of Global Public Goods (GPGs) and in responding to systemic crises. Both endeavours are cross-country in nature and require global approaches that are normally intensive in analytic and advisory content. Several voices have however mentioned the tension between the traditional Group's country and sector-based work on the one side, and the new focus on broader development goals pursued with the creation of the Global Practices (Ravallion 2015).

While the quality of knowledge production, GPGs provision and crisis prevention and response have depended largely on the Group's ability to capitalize on sharing its knowledge stock, the Group delivery remains firmly connected to the work done by country managers and team leaders, who control project budgets, and are to date the starting point of engagement to respond to country demands. It is on country management units to identify priority needs through the Country Diagnostic Studies and, subsequently, priority interventions via the Country Partnership Frameworks, with Global Practices selecting field experts only at a later stage. Often though, the transfer of premium input knowledge from Global Practices to country units much depends on the will and ability of apexes in each GP to share her or his knowledge and fine-tune it to the country-region needs.[22] The lack of institutional incentives for Global Practice VPs and employees, who often end up in fighting to maximize their budgets, to engage with country units, and the opposite need of the latter to deal with the day-to-day constraints of operational work, have at times hindered collaboration, thus reducing the gains expected from restructuring for knowledge-sharing purposes.

Weaknesses in expected synergies between country units and Global Practices have magnified the gap between the Strategy's emphasis on delivery ("deliverology") (and particularly the envisaged evolution to a "Solutions Bank", through the creation of new Cross-cutting Solutions Areas), and results on the ground (Bretton Woods Project 2013b).

While ineludible, as conducive to much needed broader vision and multisectoral approaches, the post-reorganization Bank drive to follow a "consultant firm model" in providing knowledge-based country programmes has at times resulted in the fragmentation of its products (particularly Reimbursable Advisory Services (RAS)), prioritizing shorter-term needs over medium and longer term relevant issues (IEG World Bank Group 2016). Out of 48

Technical Assistance (TA), RAS and Economic Policy Projects (nine mid- and high-income countries), targets were met for 47% of knowledge services, only for 25% of economic policy and public sector governance work, and for 30% of work in private sector development (*idem*; Bretton Woods Project 2013b). The previous datum raises some concern if seen in light of another major goal of the 2013 WBG new Strategy, i.e. that of leveraging the partnerships of the private sector, to maximize the impact of the Group's development effort in alignment of the twin goals. A similar concern applies to Financial Intermediary Loans (FILs) intermediated by the Bank to borrowers suffering from liquidity gaps in commercial banks after the 2008 crisis. Apparently, the majority of crisis-related FILs did not reach those most in need, or were not disbursed fast enough to provide support for recovery. In addition, some network elements have been reintroduced to the new structure, as coordinating between 14 different practices with only two dedicated GP VPs has proven more challenging than expected for President Jim Yong Kim. Particularly, the Senior VP for the 2030 Development Agenda, United Nations Relations and Partnerships has been created, and the VP for Sustainable Development, previously eliminated, has been reintroduced.

Overall, while emphasis on problem-solving has grown across decades in the Bank's practices and narratives (result-based management and the knowledge bank in the 1990s, the "effectiveness turn" in the 2000s), the 2013 "solutions bank" has only in part fulfilled its mission. Major improvements have been made in data accessibility and transparency, key elements in the process of enhanced knowledge sharing both internal and external to the Group sought under Jim Yong Kim's Presidency. Yet the difference between the products offered by global consulting firms and those supplied by the WBG may pose major hurdles to further organizational change in that direction.[23]

Conclusion

While the WB has undergone several changes in mission, organizational, policy and programme practices across the last 70 years, the evolutions of the past 15 years have occurred in the context (and partly as a result) of two major unprecedented transformations: i) a radical reduction in the number of existing and prospective borrowers, due to the diffusion of growth benefits to a larger number of people, and ii) an increased frequency and intensity of systemic shocks.

Since the 2000s, the WB had to adapt to structural economic changes, including unparalleled and more diffuse growth supporting the rise of middle classes in many emerging markets. Growth has however increased inequality within these countries, and to some extent, between them and the poorest among low-income partners. The higher incidence of systemic shocks has been influenced by both sustained growth and increased globalism in economic, financial and health-related transactions. The diffusion of growth based on consumption patterns dependent upon carbon systems with little cushioning mechanisms for environmental consequences have continued expanding the volume of "dirty" investments. The intensive financialization of an already global trade and service economy has in turn brought increased instability and intensified the severity of financial crises at both the regional and global levels.

As a multilateral development institution, the WBG has lost (and will inevitably continue losing) market as growth spreads across and within countries, with its clients graduating from the status of borrowers to that of lenders. At the same time, the quality of such growth patterns and their uneven distribution is having adverse consequences on social inequality, as well as on environmental and health conditions of the poorest. The dwindling in and out of poverty by the nearly poor in mid- and high-income countries is in turn a consequence of increased financial instability and related economic insecurity. The nexuses between differential growth and inequality, on the one side, and between inequality and poverty, on the other, are particularly complex (Milanovic 2011; Deaton 2013; Piketty 2014; Atkinson 2015). What is not disputed is that the development consequences of those interactions often require responses beyond the national level and most often above the competence of regional institutions.

The Bank has navigated these changes by reshaping its mission from a "poverty bank", since the late 1990s and into the 2000s, to a "knowledge bank", to the current "crisis bank" and "solutions bank", coming full circle with the IBRD original mission as a "reconstruction bank" (a war-devastated continent requiring rebuilding then; systemic economic, health, environmental, security and migratory shocks now). The medium–long-term nature of structural support to development projects, mostly relying on investment lending, has been coupled with development policy loans, that provide contingent budget support to governments of countries in immediate need of development financing. Such repositioning from an investment bank to a governance bank has occurred slowly, across the 1990s and the 2000s. Equally, the move to a global bank, providing solutions and funds to deal with global threats (environmental, health, security) has occurred gradually since the new millennium. Earlier concerns for environmentally clean projects have entered the Bank's policies in the late 1990s, with safeguards being implemented gradually across the first decade of the new millennium into WB projects. The shift to an agile, nimble and resilient holistic "crisis bank" that is able to respond swiftly to rapidly changing conditions during crises is the latest evolution, and has occurred on the basis of a review of the Bank's strengths in responding to the food and fuel crises of the late 2000s first, to the 2008 economic crisis, and, last, to the health, climate and migration crises of the 2010s.

Adaptation to these challenges has occurred relatively rapidly, both at the level of organizational practices and programmes (non-constituent or "everyday" politics), but it has failed to produce meaningful change in constituent politics, i.e. in the governance rules of the organization, which remain largely determined by competitive dynamics among large shareholders. The outcome of the Bank's early responses to the 2007–2009 crisis suggests that the organization has travelled a long way since the days of the Structural Adjustment Loans (SALs) and Structural Adjustment Programs (SAPs), escaping the strictures of the "austerian" and hyper-conditionated provisions that were transposed from the prescriptions of the Washington Consensus – directed to LAC countries in the years of the debt crisis – to most crisis response templates in the 1990s and early 2000s. Ironically, the tailor-made responses by the Bank to meet country demands during the 2008 financial crisis have been among the aspects that were explicitly criticized in the first ex-post evaluations. Too much lenience, in essence, was seen as a weakness in the Bank's approach, which was allegedly unable to scale assistance optimally, while lending too much to middle-income clients to the detriment of low-income borrowers.

While further research will have to elucidate the point, there may be a link between the privileging of middle-income borrowers in the 2008 crisis response and stasis in constituent policymaking (governance reform) to the advantage of high-income shareholders. On the one side there may be substitution (compensating) effects at play: left with contained gains in governance reforms, the requests of middle-income countries have been generously met with increased lending (and ongoing undifferentiated pricing of the Bank's lending products, vis-à-vis low-income countries). On the other side, however, the creative "reclassification" of the whole DTCs group has blurred the distributional outcomes of the reform. Selected middle-income countries have been the sole recipient of benefits from the voice reform in the whole DTCs group, so that, in the end, both lending trends and governance reforms point to the direction of open privileging of large middle-income shareholders by the organization.

The current vocal uneasiness of the US towards sustained Bank's lending to China, as well as the response by the Bank, provide further, if indirect, plausibility to the point. Graduation trends and the changing geography of donors, with sustained efforts precisely by those same middle-income partners through the creation of their own regional financing facilities (Asian Infrastructure Investment Bank (AIIB), New Development Bank (NDB)), add a key strategic component to the Bank's choices. Enmeshing large EMEs in the web of the Washington-based development institutions is a way to counterbalance their ascendancy, and to ensure their ongoing support to the Bank's capital increases and future lending capacity. While the IBRDs declining equity-to-loans ratio has been justified by its management on grounds of employment of unutilized capacity during the crisis years, qualified inputs have noted that – *ceteris paribus* – income from lending to large middle-income partners, with very little risk of default – most notably China, will help the Bank continue to support low-income fragile borrowers in the future (Birdsall 2007 and 2017). Additionally, it will serve the cause of its capital increases to address future crises, particularly in the face of lackluster economic performance, or outright opposition, by its largest high-income shareholders. Absent changes in its constituent politics however, compensation through privileged lending, may not be enough to contain the drifting of its rising "blend" shareholders.

Finally, the quality of crisis lending by multilateral institutions will remain of paramount importance, in a world where the frequency, intensity and diversity of global shocks have rapidly increased. Relative to the WBG, the debate has mostly verged on the advisability that an institution traditionally dedicated to provide medium- and long-term support to structural development be switched, even if only in part, to crisis prevention and crisis management, a role traditionally covered by the IMF, domestic authorities and, increasingly by regional development banks. While the case has some ground, the question may be off target. As proven by the "crisis complex", the triple challenge posed to developing and developed countries by the food, price and financial crises occurred between 2007 and 2009, confirms the inter-relation of economic, financial and developmental problems across different sectors and time horizons, particularly relative to social and environmental outcomes, and most notably on the poor. The fact that other actors have emerged as potential crisis managers, including new national donors, regional initiatives and private sector actors, has certainly challenged the incumbency of the Bretton Woods Institutions. The future will likely require different sets of expertise, and most plausibly more sustained coordination and convening efforts, as well as increasing resources, if the size of such shocks remains systemic in nature.

The process of economic graduation is destined to continue: low-income countries will improve their conditions and swell the ranks of middle-income countries, while these will progressively move up the ladder reaching high-income status. A major consequence will be the reduced need for development efforts of the kind that have been pursued until recently by the WBG. However, the scale of resources needed to support crises' responses will not decline, as shown by the impact of pandemics, natural disasters, conflict-related and migratory crises.

Versatile mission change is in the WB's own DNA, as proven by the evolutions that it has undergone since its creation in 1944. The WB's ability to continue redefining itself to face these changes will depend on its learning from successes and failures in dealing with the recent crisis complex, and on its Board-cum-Management's capacity to satisfactorily balance internal and external equilibria. At the Board, shareholders will have to put particular care in balancing the evolving development priorities with IBRD governance reforms in the context of the growing role of EMEs, China in particular, and of the ongoing preeminence of the US-cum-European member states. Externally, the Bank will need to enhance the development impact of its cooperation with the IMF and the traditional regional banks, while also working towards development-effective interaction with the new BRICS-controlled MDBs (most notably the AIIB and NDB). Finally, and perhaps less marginally that one might think, the ability of its top management to successfully navigate these challenges through effective adaptation, without disheartening the organization's first-rate staff, will be key to the endeavour.

Notes

1 The term normally refers to the two main lending bodies of the World Bank Group, IBRD and IDA (thus excluding MIGA, IFC and ICSID). In this study, it is used interchangeably to refer to either the World Bank Group (post-2013 reform) or IBRD-cum-IDA before then. Otherwise, mention of the specific lending body that applies is provided in the text.

2 The quality of supported actions and the targeting of the most vulnerable people inside countries, for instance, did not appear consistently satisfactory (IEG World Bank Group 2013). The main culprits have been found in scarce per-country allocations (due to a particularly low grant component in the Program, and to the absence of allocable IDA resources at the time), low administrative budgets, and quick policy designs, which have at times resulted in rush analytical diagnostics and poorly staffed projects.

3 The aim is to end extreme poverty by reducing the percentage of people living on less than USD 1.25 a day to 3% by 2030 and to boost prosperity among the poorest 40% in all countries. The World Bank Group has also targeted 2020 to cut extreme poverty to 9% of the world's population.

4 The comparison excludes the IMF – crisis-lender par excellence, the EIB – due to its lending at market – as opposed to below-market, rates and the EU.

5 The amount refers to gross commitments of IBRD, IDA and IFC, including "Recipient-Executed Trust Fund (RETF) commitments, and MIGA gross issuance. RETF commitments include all recipient-executed grants, and therefore total WBG commitments differ from the amount reported in the Bank Group Corporate Scorecard, which includes only a subset of trust-funded activities." World Bank Group Finances (2017).

6 In 2009–2010 the Bank (IBRD and IDA) increased its lending by 125%, compared to the additional combined percentage increase in lending by other regional banks (ADB, AfDB, EBRD and IDB), that amounted to 83%. Overall, the Bank was able to raise its lending commitments by USD 29 billion, vis-à-vis USD 19 billion of increased commitments by the other regional banks (IEG 2012 – II: 27). Over the same period, the Bank also increased its lending by a higher percent compared to a wider sub-sample of other donors (127% vis-à-vis 75%, ibid). Data, however, exclude the EU, the IMF and the EIB from the comparison, arguing about their relative dissimiliarity with respect to the WB vocation as a multilateral development bank.

7 Cote d'Ivoire, India, Nigeria, Pakistan, Papua New Guinea, Sao Tome, Senegal, Uzbekistan, Vietnam and Yemen.

8 The 2008–2011 contraction in its equity-to-loans ratio was justified by the WB's management as a conscious choice, endorsed by the Board, to tap existing unutilized lending capacity precisely to support international crisis response. A detailed comparison of IFIs lending positions and instruments during the crisis is provided in IEG (2012 – II).

9 Over FY 09–10 the Bank's development policy financing (IBRD and IDA, DPF/DPO) in total lending reached a share of nearly 40% (up from 25% in FY07) (World Bank OPCS 2015). In absolute values, over the 2005–2011 period, pre-crisis DPL IBRD and IDA commitments (FY 05–07) averaged USD 6.7 billion. Post-crisis (FY 09–10) the Bank (IBRD and IDA) more than trebled its DPL, averaging at USD 20.7 billion (IEG 2012 – II).

10 On the problems related to proper evaluation of long-term Bank-sponsored projects see Ravallion (2015).

11 The relation between these dynamics and the IDA contributions by large donors is in turn a major bone of contention, see Vestergaard and Wade (2013).

12 Net gains have been reaped by fast growing EMEs (among top winners: China up by 1.64%, South Korea by 0.58%, Turkey by 0.55%, and Mexico by 0.50%), while losses have been initially incurred by mature industrialized large shareholders (with deepest reductions experienced by Japan, down by 1.01%, the US down by 0.51%, France and the UK down by 0.55%, and Germany, down by 0.48%). Apparently, and different from the adaptation of the Group's lending and programs to external stimuli, the attempt at redistributing IBRD shares occurred according to relative gains maximization and rational bargaining by large shareholders (Baroncelli 2018). In spite of early good intentions, the EU MS could not coordinate effectively at the Board (with evidence of collective principality failures, as some EU MS focused on "not losing more than other EU MS"). The US veto power was left intact. The gains that were expected by "developing and transitioning countries" (DTCs) at group level have not materialized: their shifting from pre-reform 42.60% voting rights to 47.19% post-reform, and the simultaneous decrease from 57.40% to 52.81% for the group of developed shareholders has occurred along multiple graduations of former low- and middle-income partners from their status to the next income categories, respectively. However, their being lumped together as "DTCs" for the purpose of assessing the voice reform gains, has overestimated the gains of low- and middle-income shareholders, while underestimating the losses of high income ones.

13 Tension has further grown in 2017, after the attempts by President Jim Yong Kim to enroll the US Administration in an initiative to promote Gender Equality, sponsored by one of President Donald Trump's aid, his daughter Ivanka. To fully appreciate the importance the WB's President diplomatic efforts towards Washington it should not be forgotten, however, that the post has been traditionally appointed under the auspices of the US Presidency. Both President Jim Yong Kim and its predecessors owe their position to the preeminent role that the US exert on the institution, both via its top position in subscriptions and shares, and by virtue of its privilege in having the last say in appointing the top managerial role of the organization.

14 In the future, however, the Group will have to do more to address unmet legitimacy and representation concerns of low-income partners. Demographic surges, in conjunction with political, social, health and environmental instability make poverty needs particularly acute in Africa, the region whose shareholders have the lowest voting powers at the Board (5.58% combined voting powers of the three African constituencies, as of March 2017).

15 'Not only are we helping them along the development path, but the lessons we learn in China … are very helpful to other middle income countries', President Jim Yong Kim, quoted in Edwards and Igoe (2017).

16 In 2016 China obtained almost USD 2 billion in IBRD loan approvals, which placed it behind Peru, India, and Kazakhstan (Birdsall 2017).

17 These are devised to 'address development challenges that require integration across five areas of specialization' (*ibidem*), namely Climate Change; Fragility, Conflict and Violence; Gender; Jobs; Public–Private Partnerships. Both the

Global Practices and the Cross-Cutting Solution Areas have been devised to foster knowledge-sharing across the different institutions and units of the Bank Group. The move has responded to calls for sharpened early warnings, improved diagnostics and better responses to country-based and system-level development demands.

18 SCDs should assess development constraints and priorities based on the Bank's work, done in consultation with national authorities: while cooperation plays well for inclusion, it has been noted, it may reduce the role of independent assessment conducted by the Bank's staff (Ravallion 2015).

19 In the aftermath of the crisis, the BRICs countries helped to stabilize trade and investment and provided a cushion to the system-wide setback induced by the financial crises (IMF 2011: 8). In 2010, emerging donors supported the UN World Food Programme with USD 87.1 million and the UN Emergency Response Funds with USD 90.6 million (the US, in turn, the largest donor of humanitarian aid in 2010 at about USD 4.9 billion, limited its channeling through the UN Central Emergency Response Fund to USD 10 million). In 2012, emerging donors' contribution to total aid was estimated between 7% and 10%. In 2013 China provided USD 7.1 billion in development aid, to 121 countries – mostly concentrated in Sub-Saharan Africa, while in the same year the United Arab Emirates had more than quadrupled the volume of its total development assistance, reaching a staggering 1.2 ODA/GNI ratio in 2015, which placed it second after Sweden in the OECD ranking. Between 2010 and 2014, Turkey's ODA rose more than threefold reaching a total USD 3.4 billion. Recent projections place the full contributions of non-DAC donors at 20% of total aid by 2020. The main non-DAC donors are currently: Brazil, Bulgaria, China, Cuba, Cyprus, Czech Republic, Estonia, Hungary, Iceland, India, Israel, Kuwait, Latvia, Lithuania, Malta, Mexico, Poland, Romania, Russia, Saudi Arabia, Slovak Republic, Slovenia, South Africa, Taiwan, Thailand, Turkey, United Arab Emirates and Venezuela.

20 Non-ODA flows – including loans from the WB – have gained increased relevance for developing countries. As an example, FDI from OECD sources have more than doubled across the first decade of the new millennium, becoming 1.7 times as large as total ODA in 2011 (Gleave and Morris 2015). Recent developments have however impacted on that trend: refugee-related ODA has increased, while FDI into developing countries, while on balance stable, have witnessed changes in direction (South–South increasingly adding to North–South) and dynamics (rise in cross-border mergers-acquisitions over greenfield investments) (UN 2017).

21 Jin-Yong Cai, quit the IFC in 2015, a year before his post as President expired; IBRD Managing Director Caroline Anstey and Senior VP Pamela Cox, the two apexes President Jim Yong Kim had put in charge of restructuring had left by the end of 2013; Bertrand Badré (Managing Director and Chief Financial Officer for the Group) left in 2016. While Cai and Badré's departures were linked to voices of privileged lending to Chinese banks (*Financial Times*, 6 November 2015), Anstey and Cox cases appeared connected with their performance in the reform process pursued by President Jim Yong Kim (Bretton Woods Project 2013a).

22 Author's Interview with WB's officer (March 2017).

23 A detailed analysis of the Bank's weaknesses (and potential) in taking up the role of development knowledge leader is provided in Ravallion (2015).

References

Atkinson, A. (2015), *Inequality: What Can Be Done?*, Cambridge, MA and London: Harvard University Press.

Baroncelli, E. (2011), 'The EU at the World Bank: Institutional and Policy Performance', *Journal of European Integration*, 33 (6): 637–650.

Baroncelli, E. (2013), 'Eclecticism and the Study of Delegation between Global Governors: The EU, the World Bank, and Trust-Funded Development in Sub-Saharan Africa', *Rivista Italiana di Politiche Pubbliche*, 1: 131–158.

Baroncelli, E. (2018), *The European Union, the World Bank and the Policymaking of Aid: Cooperation among Developers*, London: Routledge.

Birdsall, N. (2007), 'The World Bank: Towards a Global Club', Center for Global Development Essay, May 2007, also in Bradford, C. Jr. and Linn, J. (eds) (2006) *Global Governance Reform: Breaking the Stalemate*, Washington, DC: Brookings Institution.

Birdsall, N. (2017), 'Getting to Yes on a World Bank Recapitalization', Center for Global Development, Views from the Center Blog, 11 August 2017.

Bretton Woods Project (2013a), 'World Bank's New Strategy: Deliverology for the Private Sector?', The Bretton Woods Update, 86, 26 June.

Bretton Woods Project (2013b), 'World Bank Group Strategy: Who Benefits?', The Bretton Woods Update, 3 October.

Chelsky, J., Morel, C. and Kabir, M. (2013), 'Investment Financing in the Wake of the Crisis: The Role of Multilateral Development Banks', *Economic Premise*, 121, June, PREM The World Bank, Washington.

Chen, S. M. R. and Ravallion, M. (2009), 'Are There Lasting Impacts of Aid to Poor Areas?', *Journal of Public Economics*, 93 (3–4): 512–528.

Deaton, A. (2013), *The Great Escape*, Princeton, NJ and Oxford: Princeton University Press.

Edwards, S. and Igoe, M. (2017), 'What's at stake in the World Bank's quest for a capital increase?', Inside Development/World Bank Annual Meetings, Devex, 13 October.

Gilbert, C., Powell, A. and Vines, D. (1999), 'Positioning the World Bank', *Economic Journal*, 109: 598–633.

Gleave, M. and Morris, S. (2015), 'The World Bank at 75', Center for Global Development, CGD Policy Paper 058, March.

IEG (2012 – I), 'The World Bank Group's Response to the Global Economic Crisis – Phase I', The Independent Evaluation Group, Washington, DC: The World Bank Group.

IEG (2012 – II), 'The World Bank Group's Response to the Global Economic Crisis – Phase II', The Independent Evaluation Group, Washington, DC: The World Bank Group.

IEG World Bank Group (2013), *The World Bank Group and the Global Food Crisis. An Evaluation of the World Bank Group Response*, Washington, DC: IBRD.

IEG World Bank Group (2014), *Learning and Results in World Bank Operations: How the Bank Learns*, Independent Evaluation Group, Washington, DC: World Bank.

IEG World Bank Group (2016), *Knowledge-Based Country Programs, An evaluation of World Bank Group Experience*, Washington, DC: IBRD.

IMF (2011), *New Growth Drivers for Low-Income Countries: The Role of BRICs*, Washington DC: The International Monetary Fund.

Kapur, D. (2015), 'Escape from the World Bank', *Project Syndicate*, 16 October.

Milanovic, B. (2011), *The Haves and the Have-Nots*, New York: Basic Books.

Piketty, T. (2014), *Capital in the Twenty-First Century*, Harvard and New York, Cambridge, MA and London: The Belknap Press of Harvard University Press.

Ravallion, M. (2015), 'The World Bank: Why It Is Still Needed and Why It Still Disappoints', Center for Global Development Working Paper 400, April.

Sandefur, J. and Patel, D. (2016), 'World Bank Presidents, Ranked: From McNamara to Kim', Views from the Center for Global Economic Development, CGDEV Blog, 9 September.

UN (2017), 'Global context for achieving the 2030 Agenda for Sustainable Development International financial flows and external debt', Development Issues No. 10, Development Strategy and Policy Analysis Unit, Development Policy and Analysis Division, Department of Economic and Social Affairs, The United Nations. Available at: https://www.un.org/development/desa/dpad/wpcontent/uploads/sites/45/publication/dsp_policy_10.pdf (accessed: 15 March 2018).

Vestergaard, J. and Wade, R. (2013), 'Protecting Power: How Western States Retain Their Dominant Voice in the World Bank's governance reform', *World Development*, 46: 153–164.

Vestergaard, J. and Wade, R. (2015), 'Still in the Woods: Gridlock in the IMF and the World Bank Puts Multilateralism at Risk', *Global Policy*, 6 (1): 1–12.

Winters, M. (2011), 'The World Bank and the Global Financial Crisis: The Re-emergence of Lending to Middle Income Countries', *The Whitehead Journal of Diplomacy and International Relations*, 12 (2): 57–72.

Woods, N. (2010), 'Global Governance after the Financial Crisis: A New Multilateralism or the Last Gasp of the Great Powers?', *Global Policy*, 1 (1): 51–63.

World Bank (2014), World Bank Annual Report 2014, Washington, DC: World Bank.

World Bank (2015), World Bank Annual Report 2015, Washington, DC: World Bank.

World Bank Group Finances (2017), *Annual Report*, Washington, DC: The World Bank.

World Bank OPCS (2015), 'Development Policy Financing Retrospective – Results and Sustainability', Operation Policy and Country Services (OPCS), Washington, DC: The World Bank Group.

4 Competing visions of the Western international economic order and the Chinese Belt and Road Initiative

Uzma Ashraf

Introduction

The US-led Western political-economic order is becoming increasingly fragmented while losing its vigor; it is suffering through internal rifts and a loss of confidence in multilateralism and international institutions. The fragmentation is the result of internal fault lines and threat perceptions emanating from non-traditional security elements, including terrorism and migratory crises, as well as rising military and economic competition from non-Western powers such as China and India. The recent US withdrawal from the Paris Climate deal and abandoning of the Trans-Pacific Partnership (TPP) reflects the rift between the US and its traditional allies. The EU is passing through challenging times: the Brexit, the migration and refugees crises, and security issues, to just name a few amongst the many problematic issues (John 2017). The sovereign debt crises have subsided, yet conflicting national (political and economic) interests continue to dominate the power relationships within the Union as well as between the EU and the international institutions (Barton 2017:169–174; *Financial Times* 2017b).

Disillusionment arising from the deep economic recession of the Global Financial Crisis (GFC), and a US political leadership seemingly uninterested in nurturing the Western order – along with its tenets of human rights, democracy and economic freedom – are paving the way for populism, nationalist sentiments and heightened insecurity. The once overly optimistic conception of the Western liberal value system is suffering from a loss of confidence. Fukuyama's "end of history" – the end point of mankind's ideological evolution and the universalization of Western democracy as the final form of human government – is meeting its most formidable challenge ever.

However, this is not the first time that the Western order comes under pressure. Famously, Joseph S. Nye, suggested that the Western order is

> largely limited to a group of like-minded states centered on the Atlantic littoral [and] did not include many large countries such as China, India,

and the Soviet bloc states, and ... did not always have benign effects on non-members.

Nye 2017

As a consequence, since its creation in 1945, the Western political-economic order has always been challenged by those countries that felt to be excluded from global policy making. Historically, Asia did not play a significant role in either designing the post-War institutional architecture, that is the Western political-economic order, or in setting the Global Economic Governance (GEG) agenda. In more recent decades, the center of gravity of the global economy has shifted towards Asia, increasing pressures for global governance reforms, including requests for a fairer representation of emerging economies within Bretton Woods institutions. Today, Asia is home to 4.5 billion people (out of a total 7.2 billion world population) and contains the fastest growing economies of the world; by all projections, it is bound to overtake all other continents economically and militarily by 2040. Yet, Asia does not have the clout, independence and legitimacy it feels it deserves in international affairs and institutions.

This includes the specific sub-sector of international affairs covering development cooperation and development financing. Since the 2002 Monterrey Conference on Financing for Development (and the subsequent meeting in Doha), new entrants on the global development scene from the ranks of emerging economies, private funds and newly-established South–South cooperation institutions, have redefined global development cooperation parameters. Asia has now taken the lead in promoting global infrastructure-based development, which has become less popular for most of the Western Development Finance Institutions (DFIs).

In guarding strategic global interests, the Association of South East Asian Nations (ASEAN) has been particularly active in this field through the ASEAN-led Regional Comprehensive Economic Partnership (RCEP).[1] At a country level, China, which neither approved nor adopted the Western political-economic order established at the end of the Second World War, has been quietly challenging such an order. Since the 2000s, from Africa to Latin America, Beijing has been carrying out an enormous effort to re-write the rules of foreign economic engagement. Since the 2010s, China also seems to be reimagining the rules of the geostrategic "great game" in Central and Southern Asia through its *sui generis* economic, legal and political cooperation.[2] Both successes are attached to the so-called Beijing Consensus cooperation model, which is presented as apolitical and non-interfering into the domestic affairs of other countries and is characterized by a strong focus on infrastructure development.

This chapter argues that the Chinese Belt and Road Initiative (BRI) may represent the move that could eventually shift the world's equilibrium eastwards. However, unlike the prevalent perception in many Western policy circles, I argue that the BRI, the Renminbi internationalization and the strategic construction of the Asian Development Finance Institutions (ADFIs) do not necessarily mark the beginning of the end for the Western order. This chapter shows that the Chinese-led ADFIs have so far, to a certain extent, emulated the structure and development objectives of the Western order, albeit without many of its defects. While it remains too early to comment on the sustainability of the Chinese-led ADFIs, the BRI, if implemented prudently, could contribute to bridging the trillion dollars a year infrastructure gap in Asia. I also argue that the main players of the Western order, as manifested under the Bretton Woods institutional philosophy, instead of remaining *spectators* of the tectonic shift in Asia, have an opportunity to engage constructively in redesigning the economic and financial architecture of this region, and beyond.

This chapter is organized as follows: section 2 looks at the origin of the Western order. Section 3 discusses the relation between Asia and the Western order. Section 4 discusses the rise of China; its sub-sections discuss Chinese-led domestic and regional DFIs and Chinese efforts at creating a competing global monetary order through the Renminbi internationalization. Section 5 discusses the BRI and analyzes the China–Pakistan Economic Corridor, the test-case and one of the most ambitious projects in the BRI. Section 6 discusses the lessons learnt from China's foray into GEG. The final section evaluates the prospects for a complementary, rather than adversarial, relation between the Western and the Asian orders.

Origins of the Western GEG order

Since 1944, the US steered the establishment of the Bretton Woods institutions – the World Bank (WB), the International Monetary Fund (IMF) and the International Trade Organization (ITO) – with an original mandate to *rebuild* the infrastructures of shattered post-war economies. These institutions have successfully contributed to influencing the domestic political and economic sphere of many developing countries by exporting the Western development model. The portfolios, functions and powers of these institutions have evolved significantly over time – yet, the discourse and mechanisms that allowed a propagation of their interests and value system have largely remained unchanged.

In particular, the Western GEG order was built upon four elements: i) free trade; ii) multilateral economic cooperation through Washington-based institutions; iii) expansion of democracy; and iv) promotion of Western values. Economic historians interpret the establishment of the Bretton Woods institutions as an exceptional result in the history of global financial regimes,[3] given both previous unsuccessful attempts and the large mandate of the newly created institutions (Eichengreen 1992; Mikesell 1994; Cesarano 2006).

Unlike the previous British hegemonic order, the US-led Western order is termed "embedded liberalism",[4] as its purpose was to recast the capitalist system worldwide by providing a *universal* coordination structure (Ruggie 1982). Technically, it was a victory for the US in the garb of *benign multilateralism*: the idea of benevolent economic engagement based on "objective" economic principles, including economic and trade relations centred on comparative advantages, open trade and unrestrained Foreign Direct Investments (FDI) and Foreign Portfolio Investments (FPI).

The IMF was created to coordinate monetary policies and to provide temporary financing arrangements to countries facing BoP problems. Originally based upon a system of fixed exchange rates between the US dollar and gold, and between the US dollar and other currencies (hence also between other currencies and gold), the system was eventually abandoned in favour of a floating exchange system in 1971, a move that gave the US the freedom to "print" as much money as it deemed necessary. The US still enjoys the perks of its currency's global hegemony.

The WB's prime focus was on infrastructure development of the war-torn European economies and to help secure trade interests in the erstwhile colonies with a few independent states in Asia, Africa and Latin America.[5] While there were plans to establish an International Trade Organization (ITO) to coordinate free trade, this was substituted by an agreement (General Agreement on Tariff and Trade) which turned into a permanent institution only in 1995 with the creation of the World Trade Organization (WTO).

The purpose and focus of the Bretton Woods institutions did not remain linear. Soon after creating the WB, the US followed a more bilateral approach and set up the Marshall plan to help reconstruct European economies, thus allowing the WB to focus on infrastructure development in non-European economies. Under Robert McNamara's lead (1968–1980), the WB expanded its services from infrastructure to social services. By the early 1980s, both the IMF and the WB had undergone a major ideological shift that took them to focus on market efficiency and Structural Adjustment Programs (SAPs) in indebted countries. By this time Japan, having recovered from World War II, aggressively sought to increase its influence on global policy matters. On the one hand, this Japanese ambition for influence, and on the other, increased criticism on the SAPs, led to the adoption of the so-called Washington Consensus, which, building on macroeconomic policies already envisioned by SAPs, professed structural growth via macro-stability, low inflation, viable BoP, trade liberalization, deregulation and privatization.[6] This development philosophy was passed on to debtor countries through *conditionality*[7] mechanisms, including by strongly encouraging governments to lift tariff and non-tariff trade barriers to trade and impediments to outside investment and foreign currency transactions. One of the key consequences of Washington Consensus policies is that financial flows to Emerging Markets and Developing Economies (EMDCs) became more short-term and speculative, igniting much of the financial instability of the 1990s.[8]

The Washington Consensus' liberalization philosophy survived well beyond the 1980s and was most notably applied in SAPs administered in Asian, African and Latin American countries. Earlier, under a strategy based on Import Substitution Industrialization (ISI) and export-oriented industrialization, most nations in Latin America (except Chile and Costa Rica) had proved unable to manage their debt crisis, primarily because they were overexposed to external conjunctures, including sharp rises in oil prices.[9] Structural reforms under the Washington Consensus brought in timely IMF support, which alleviated the crises. However, after two decades, the external debt crisis that the consensus was supposed to resolve had only grown deeper and the debts became unsustainable by the late 1990s. In those years only East Asian countries were able to maintain steadfast growth and to significantly reduce poverty – notably, this was precisely the region that refused to follow the consensus policies and rather kept indigenous economic recipes, some of which presented an alternative to the Washington Consensus and later became part of the development model publicized as Beijing Consensus.[10]

By the mid-2000s, the failure of Washington Consensus policies was widely acknowledged even in Western conservative circles. The consensus attracted criticism for its boilerplate approach to development policy and practice of conditionality, which helped diffuse the consensus philosophy around the world but blatantly ignored national peculiarities in its haste to apply universalistic recipes. Later, the augmented Washington Consensus, which incorporated Western practices for corporate governance, anti-corruption, labour markets, WTO agreements, financial codes and standards, open capital accounts, non-intermediate exchange rate regimes, independent central banks/ inflation targeting, social safety nets, and – targeted poverty reduction – received similar criticisms (Rodrik 2006; Fischer 2012).

The Western order and Asia: Japan, the ADB and the ASEAN

Historically, Asia experienced three main international orders. For almost two millennia China was the hegemonic power in Asia. By mid-nineteenth century, the European powers had colonized most of the continent; however, this European order hardly lasted a century, until the end of the Second World War triggered decolonization. In post-colonial Asia, the US brought a partially distinct conception of hegemony, presented in the garb of "containment" of the communist threat to East and South East Asia. American hegemonism leveraged Western democratic values as opposed to communist USSR and China.

During the 1960s, while breeding under US hegemonism and still recovering from the War, Japan steadily stepped up to establish its own regional order based on a mix of Asian and Western values, as well as a hybrid economic model characterized by a developmental state with strong influence over both the real and financial economy. Although Tokyo failed in establishing a Japanese-led order in Asia, its hybrid model proved successful in supporting balanced and inclusive economic growth and development in several East Asian economies. As in Japan, this model employed an Export-Led Growth (ELG) strategy and favored a close relationship between government, businesses and the financial industry.

Tokyo's ambition to elevate its power and international standing was the crucial factor behind the creation of the first Asian financial institutions in the 1960s. In an effort to go outward and to lead an Asian International Organization, the Japanese Prime Minister, Kishi Nobusuke, proposed a number of Japanese-dominated initiatives, including the establishment of an Asian Development Fund (ADF), which was to operate under the slogan "Economic Development for Asia by Asia". Yet, since the US was not willing to cede political control to Tokyo while still financing its economy, and because of the East Asian countries' skepticism of Japanese dominance, the proposal failed.

After making adjustments between its continental ambition and the reality of US regional control, Japan finally led 48 members in the setting-up of the Asian Development Bank (ADB) in August 1966. By opting to remain within the US-led normative and financial framework, Japan was able to secure a matching contribution of USD 300 million from the US[11] and a significant strategic advantage in the initiative (Huang 1975; Krishnamurti 1977; Watanabe 1977). Deep institutional linkages between the ADB and the Japanese Ministry of Finance gave Japan an advantage similar to what the US enjoyed in the WB. On the policy side, the ADB maintained a steady focus on poverty alleviation via infrastructure development, while the WB was already undergoing a dramatic portfolio diversification strategy.

In those same years, the Association of South-East Asian Nations (ASEAN) was being established (1967) as a platform for Asian integration, promoting an "Asian way" to regional unity, prosperity, and sustainable development.[12] Yet, none of its members had the standing to lead regional integration, while Japan was profoundly distrusted by the block. Like many other Asian initiatives, ASEAN also faced major internal challenges as the region remained embroiled in tense rivalries, eventually focusing on a limited free trade agenda.

By the late 1980s, the Japanese economy, which continued to grow by leaps and bounds, seemed to surpass the US economy, making many Japanese believe in a potential overtake. Because of high marginal saving rates, and an over-valued currency, Japanese investors were able to place large investments in the US which, despite turning out to be vastly overpaid, were nonetheless perceived as threatening the US control over its domestic economy. The Japanese economic rise and its ambitious political leadership vying for more international financial influence made the US increasingly wary of Japanese long-term designs and eventually led to a strong opposition to the establishment of an Asian Monetary Fund (AMF).

In the early 1990s, the Japanese economy began sputtering. Its hybrid ELG model, supporting the national aggregate demand and favouring a close relation between government, businesses and finance, faltered on several accounts. Stagflation began, eventually leading to two decades of economic stasis. On the other side, the Japanese model continued proving successful in supporting balanced and inclusive economic growth in other East Asian economies – and most notably in Japan's former colonies, South Korea and Taiwan, on top of Hong Kong and Singapore. All were nonetheless affected by increasing capital liberalization without a backstop of appropriate legal and regulatory institutions, a situation that eventually brought to the 1997 financial crisis, which underscored the limits in the Japanese-inspired state-led model of development and selective liberalization.

Japan's *lost decade* costed the country the opportunity to shape a new Asian order during the late twentieth century.[13] The financial crisis of the 1990s further diminished Japanese ambitions to increase its influence in Asia while also providing the necessary impetus to alternative regional initiatives. The IMF role in the Asian financial crises of the 1990s frustrated many Asian governments, which begun looking for ways to promote the common Asian interests (Arner and Schou-Zibell 2010).[14] Yet, Asia still lacked a clear leader.

The rise of China

Amidst the US–Japanese competing visions for Asia in the 1980s, a third power began to rise, concomitantly becoming interested in joining the multilateral US dominated GEG framework. Under the leadership of Deng Xiaoping, China adopted key economic reforms in 1979 and begun a steady and gradual reform process after experiencing three decades of economic instability. Market liberalization was phased in two stages: i) de-collectivization of agriculture and opening to foreign investments in selected zones beginning from 1979; ii) privatization of most state-owned facilities, lifting of price controls and easing of protectionist policies and state-imposed regulations from the end of the 1980s. Results were remarkable: GDP annual growth rate averaged 9.4% in 1978–2012, compared to 6% in 1953–1978 (Hirst 2015). In contrast with other transition economies, China successfully managed the transition from a planned economy to a mixed economy. While a number of factors make the Chinese case peculiar, its experience in managing the so-called double transition – an abrupt demographic transition and large-scale urbanization – is particularly noteworthy (Yang 2014).[15] In 1980, China joined the WB; three years later, it applied for membership to the ADB and, after another three years of political and diplomatic maneuvering, it eventually became a fully-fledged ADB member in 1986.

Throughout the 1990s, while Japan was caught in internal economic downturn, China maintained a steady economic growth based on labour-intensive sectors, an ELG model and continued economic reforms. China's rise led to an increasing mismatch between its economic clout and its relative influence in the Western order's multilateral DFIs.[16] While there have been relative economic adjustments in the voting weight of EMDCs in the Western DFIs since the 1990s, these were not commensurate to their real weight. By the early 2000s these structural limitations began frustrating China and other emerging economies.[17]

The unwillingness of the Western order to translate increasing EMDCs economic power into relative influence prodded Beijing to establish a new Asian order, which Japan previously proved unable to sustain, by undertaking a number of political and economic multilateral initiatives, including the Shanghai Cooperation Organization (SCO), the New Development Bank

(NDB, also known as the BRICS Bank), the Asian Infrastructure Investment Bank (AIIB), and the Silk Road Fund (SRF).

Beijing claims that these initiatives are primarily aimed at building a network of infrastructures and connectivity hubs to complement the existing Eurasian infrastructures, which mainly serve the Western economic order. Yet, with China increasingly turning into a regional hegemon, fellow Asian countries remain skeptical about these initiatives. Notwithstanding the fact that the mandate and structure of Chinese-promoted IFIs, including the AIIB and the NDB, conform to the prevalent international legal norms, these initiatives have invited much criticism and some counter efforts. The US has opposed the BRI and refused joining the AIIB, while India has also rejected the BRI. In fact, the US has even hinted at a counter-initiative to "contain" Chinese BRI in agreement with India. Similarly, the recent Japanese adoption of a more assertive foreign and security policy, as opposed to post-War pacifism, suggests that Japan's foreign policy will focus more on regional engagements in the next future.

China and the new GEG

The establishment of the NDB in 2014 and AIIB in 2016 illustrates the disillusionment of emerging economies with the Western development agenda. China led the establishment of this multilateral institutional agenda (Jinping 2017). The NDB, created by the BRICS countries (Brazil, Russia, India, China and South Africa) is characterized by an "egalitarian principle", which divides the initial capitalization of USD 50 billion in equal parts among the five founding members while also allocating an equal number of shares among them. Therefore, at the NDB no single member has veto while each enjoys an equal share, a mechanism that avoids the disproportionate influence trap on which the Bretton Woods institutions have discussed for decades. The NDB statute allows other UN member countries to join the Bank, while limiting the total voting weight of non-founding members to a maximum of 45%, while the remaining voting power is reserved to BRICS members (New Development Bank 2018).

The AIIB equally comprises regional and non-regional members, although its governance arrangement gives priority and larger decision-making power to the former: non-regional members cannot be assigned more than 30% of the seats in the non-permanent board of directors (AIIB Articles). The AIIB's initial capital is USD 100 billion, with 20% paid-in and 80% callable. China, which is contributing USD 50 billion, enjoys a 27.5% voting power, which effectively gives it veto power on issues requiring three-fourth majority. Formally established with 57 members in 2015, the Bank has lent about USD 3 billion in the first two years of operation. Three-quarters of its projects are co-financed by the WB or other regional development banks. Although the AIIB's governance structure draws upon other IFIs like the WB and the

ADB, a distinguishing feature of the AIIB is the absence of a resident board of executive directors, usually representing and protecting national interests, thus saving expenses and supporting the "lean" modality of Chinese-led initiatives.

The SCO is an intergovernmental organization set up for political, economic and security cooperation by China, Kazakhstan, Kyrgyzstan, Russia, Tajikistan and Uzbekistan in June 2001. SCO members (with the exception of Uzbekistan) date back to the Shanghai Five group which was founded in 1996. India and Pakistan have joined the SCO as full members in June 2017. The SCO has four observer members (Afghanistan, Belarus, Iran and Mongolia) and six dialogue partners (Azerbaijan, Armenia, Cambodia, Nepal, Turkey and Sri Lanka). While the SCO pre-dates China's activism in GEG and has not engaged in direct financing operations, it is nonetheless instrumental to the promotion of economic and societal cooperation, and could in the future expand its realm to finance BRI related activities.

A comparative look at the objectives of the AIIB, the NDB and the SCO reveals that China is making a deliberate effort to underscore "equality" and "inclusivity" in these multilateral organizations. A distinguishing feature of these organizations is that the "key" values are from typical of EMDCs: while Bretton Woods institutions promoted a Western order founded on the principles of democracy, Chinese-led DFIs present a vision underlining non-interference, non-alignment, and, at least in the NDB case, equality of participating members. Arguably, equality will also be difficult to be maintained in the future of other institutions, considering China's sheer economic size.

Chinese Domestic Financial Institutions

While Chinese-led International DFIs may have been the most visible part of Beijing's "Go Global" strategy, most of the work that led to build that capacity was done via domestic financial institutions in the 1990s. The most significant of these institutions are the China Policy and Commercial Banks, of which the China Development Bank (CDB) and the Export–Import Bank of China (EXIM) are the major banks. China created these financial institutions as part of the "Go Global" and "Go West" strategies to finance national state-invested projects and subsequently used them in overseas investments. Both the CDB and the EXIM Bank have a long experience in funding projects across developing countries and have been engaged in the BRI project.

The CDB was established in 1994 under the direct leadership of the Chinese State Council, which declared it a DFI in 2015. The CDB has become the world's largest DFI with a registered capital of RMB 421 billion (USD 61 billion) and assets grown over RMB 13 trillion (USD 1.89 trillion) by the end of 2016 (China Development Bank 2018). As a Chinese Policy Bank, CDB is tasked with providing sustained support for national economic and social development, foster China's national competitiveness and enhance the interests of its people. The CDB's loan portfolio is extensive: apart from financing infrastructures, it has made solid progress in promoting bilateral financial cooperation with other member countries of the SCO Interbank Association, the China-ASEAN Interbank association and the BRICS Interbank Cooperation Mechanism.[18]

Like the CDB, the EXIM Bank is a state-owned policy bank founded in 1994 under the leadership of the State Council, and dedicated to support China's foreign trade, investments and international economic cooperation in the "Go Global" Chinese strategy. The Bank's mandate is to facilitate national development strategies by developing a clear-cut market position, a well-defined business portfolio, unique functions, sufficient capital, good governance, strict internal controls, safe operations, high quality service and sustainable development capability. The EXIM Bank actively supports China's financial and economic reforms and development projects abroad, including the BRI, with an emphasis on "green finance". The EXIM bank has access to direct credit support from the government and has already financed more than 1000 projects in 49 countries (EXIM 2016).

In 2014 China also set up a Silk Road Fund (SRF) to support BRI projects. The SRF has a total capital of USD 40 billion with capitalization from the State Administration of Foreign Exchange, the China Investment Corporation, the EXIM Bank and the CDB (Silk Road Fund 2017). The SRF was established with a view to finance medium- to long-term primarily equity-based investments to support infrastructure development, resources and energy development, industrial capacity cooperation and financial cooperation projects in BRI countries. Unlike the Bretton Woods institutions, the SRF is a for-profit fund operating on market-based principles and aiming at ensuring reasonable returns on investments.

The Renminbi internationalization

The use and internationalization of the Renminbi (RMB) is a part and parcel of the Chinese strategy to a new GEG order. The NDB and AIIB have used USD for initial capitalization and disbursement, but plan on using alternative currencies, including the RMB, in future dealing. The NDB already issued its first 3 billion RMB-denominated (USD 448 million) bonds for green investment projects in BRICS countries (Dasgupta 2016).

A currency has a key role in setting up a regional or international order. A dominant medium of exchange has always been at the heart of all great empires from the Greeks to the British. More recently, the US dollar relished the unparalleled advantage that no other dominant currency ever benefited, being both a global mean of exchange as well as a global reserve currency – what Valéry Giscard d'Estaing termed as America's "exorbitant privilege". The USD became the global reserve currency after its value was linked to the price of gold in the Bretton Woods system; yet, the USD continued to enjoy its privileged reserve status even after US

President Richard Nixon unilaterally ended the USD convertibility into gold in 1971, effectively giving the Federal Reserve the freedom of deciding money supply levels. The USD global reserve status supported US global dominance both in trade and finance, effectively reinforcing American hegemony.

The RMB internationalization dates back to the late 1990s, when the Chinese government took a series of steps to promote the use of RMB globally. During the last decade, China has been slowly and steadily ramping up transactions in RMB as a strategy to increase its *soft power* and end its dependency on the USD. Beijing has taken many steps in this regard, including mandating the Bank of China with providing liquidity support,[19] signing an increasing number of bilateral currency swap arrangements to avoid liquidity traps (Avgouleas et al. 2014) and promoting the RMB as a regional invoicing currency.[20] The most noticeable achievement was the recent inclusion of the RMB into the IMF's reserve currency basket. In the long term, the internationalization of the RMB as a reserve currency may help China in shielding its domestic economy from the USD volatility.

It is realistic to see, as Brummer contended in 2017, how China, instead of waiting for its currency to evolve organically in existing international markets, has undertaken a mercantilist strategy to create new markets. China is promoting its own national RMB-based infrastructure (Brummer 2017), expecting that the BRI may help finally make gains (Landry and Tang 2017). While most of the BRI projects are being funded in USD, once new trade routes and transportation links will be established, these will provide excellent opportunities for denominating outbound FDI, FPI, loans, trade and payment instruments in RMB, spearheading a true internationalization of the currency. The BRI initiative would thus allow the RMB to become a more freely traded currency on world markets and a more widely acceptable form of settling business deals. To this extent, it is interesting noticing how the Bank of China released the first cross-border RMB index in 2013 and the first Belt and Road RMB exchange rate index in 2015. According to this understanding, it is not the road and the bridges that are at the heart of Beijing's economic and political ambitions under the BRI, but its desire to truly launch the RMB as an internationally traded global reserve currency. This is one of the most important, yet quite frequently ignored, aspects of the BRI, which has especially been overlooked by the Western literature. Another factor often ignored in international analyses is Beijing's leverage to use the RMB's internationalization as a motivating force to drive domestic market reforms which would otherwise be difficult to implement.

Asian countries that mostly relied on the Asian-style ELG model may welcome the "conditionality-free"[21] infrastructure development model under the ADFIs using the RMB as a settlement currency. If the RMB is to become a truly globally traded reserve currency, it would provide a great strategic win for Beijing. However, despite making some progress in the internationalization of the RMB, Beijing's efforts in this regard have not come to full fruition yet. In the future, the availability of Chinese "palatable" financing options for Asian/Eurasian countries – which come without structural and political conditionalities – have the potential to challenge the western order's dominance in Asia, albeit in the long run. Ultimately, this can significantly reduce the relative influence of the western order's financing institutions in Asia, and possibly in Eurasia.

The China–Pakistan Economic Corridor as a BRI study case

The BRI, first announced in 2013, is an ambitious Chinese initiative to reshape the Eurasian continent by building six economic corridors,[22] connecting the underdeveloped regions South and West of China along the lines of the ancient "Silk Road." While the "belt" links Eurasia to China by land, the twenty-first century maritime Silk Road will comprise a string of ports connecting China with South East Asia, South Asia, Africa, the Middle East and Europe through the South China Sea, the Indian Ocean and the Mediterranean Sea. The Chinese-led BRI, unlike projects in the Western international economic order, seems to be an amorphous notion; derived from the China model, constantly evolving and based on a learning-by-doing methodology instead of being rooted in an ideology or expressed through formal legal structures and pre-designed institutional arrangements.

In February 2017, the ADB estimated that developing countries in Asia will need USD 1.7 trillion a year or a total of about USD 26 trillion though 2030 in investments to meet their infrastructure needs. Chinese President Xi Jinping's BRI vision promises Asia over USD 1 trillion in new infrastructure projects (*Financial Times* 2017a),[23] trade agreements and people-to-people ties. To put this into perspective, it is useful recalling that the last occurrence of US spending in major infrastructures abroad was the Marshall Plan, which delivered USD 103 billion in today's currency to help rebuild 16 European countries.

China anticipates that it may not need to export state capital and instead hopes to rely on attracting Chinese and non-Chinese public and private investors to fund projects under the BRI scheme. Such a grand scheme would be completely unimaginable to Western development cooperation modalities without being backed by detailed financing schemes and operational blueprints – as a consequence, the skepticism around the BRI is both justified and understandable. Skepticism is particularly tangible around two major risks: i) the possibility that borrowing countries may not be able to pay back the Chinese loans and; ii) the possibility that many projects will not be financially capable to generate enough revenues to sustain operations in the longer term (Larmer 2017).[24]

In this respect, the BRI's flagship project, the China–Pakistan Economic Corridor (CPEC), presents a test case for China's grand vision of infrastructure-based economic development. The Pakistani case is important for a number of reasons, including the sheer size of the investment (USD 57 billion), the size of the country and the geopolitical context.

Pakistan, throughout the 70 years of its existence, remained part of the Western strategic alliance system while also maintaining a strong partnership with China. CPEC is a promising preposition for Pakistan, a country with 55 million people living below the poverty line, facing extreme energy shortages and remaining a victim as well as a perpetrator of Islamist terrorism. The investment commitments under CPEC promise to have major positive effects upon *Human Development* via: i) energy infrastructure development (over USD 35 billion); ii) development of transportation links – particularly along the impoverished Western route; iii) water security, and; iv) job opportunities for its 207 million population, 60% of which is below 30 years of age. China's financial commitments under CPEC has already contributed to accelerate Pakistan's growth rate from 3.7% in 2013 to about 5.7% in 2017.[25]

CPEC promises Pakistan economic development in three major ways: first, through direct investments – improvement of business environment, enhanced commercial attractiveness of Pakistan's market for investors (which will benefit not only Pakistan but Chinese investors engaged in CPEC), and further industrialization, which will lead to more jobs and further growth. Second, it offers stabilization and improved security situation which will also gear up economic activities and may enable Pakistan to commit more resources to combat terrorism. Third, CPEC strengthens regional integration – infrastructure and transportation routes connectivity between Iran, Pakistan, Afghanistan, China and Central Asia, which involves a market of 2 billion people (if India joins, it will cover more than 3 billion people). It is also hoped that development gains from CPEC would help shrink the recruitment pool for extremists and Islamists. From a strategic perspective, Beijing's almost unconditional support also benefits Pakistan in its relations with the US and India. Such unconditional support from China, however, is unsettling the regional dynamics and Indian aspirations to play an important regional power role. On the domestic political front, interestingly, CPEC projects receive unquestioned support from the civilian and the military leadership owing to the Chinese's principle of "non-interference" in political matters.

On its side, Pakistan is also contributing much to China's Eurasian strategy. Islamabad's potential contribution to the BRI is fundamental, as it can potentially provide: i) a node joining the "Belt" and the "Road"; ii) a strategic alternative to the Strait of Malacca;[26] iii) a plausible Chinese naval base in Gwadar and; iv) a yardstick to calibrate whether China can successfully manage the deep geostrategic regional rivalries and non-traditional security threats to the long-term success of the BRI.

Concurrently, CPEC presents Pakistan with both internal and external challenges. Internally, there is an evident lack of transparency, good governance and appropriate debt-repayment strategies. For CPEC to succeed, good social, political and economic governance institutions are indispensable (Memon 2017).[27] Pakistan's internal political rift on the selection of CPEC routes and distribution of benefits from CPEC projects also amplifies existing interprovincial chasm. The umbrella expectation is that CPEC benefits must equitably reach all parts of Pakistan; however, fair allocation of development benefits is not apolitical in Pakistan. Security and protection of CPEC projects, as well as staff, continues to pose challenges despite more than 10,000 security forces providing protection, yet sustainable security mechanisms are required for the long-term sustainability.

Geopolitical interests can also challenge the stability of the CPEC: India may feel threatened from a stronger Pakistan and tension between India and China can rise as they are both vying for regional influence. India also fears that through CPEC, China would be able to have virtual control of the strategic port of Gwadar, which is touted as China's first military naval outpost. Recently, India has also signaled that CPEC is in violation of international law as it passes through the disputed territory (Northern areas of Pakistan) and the Indian stance was endorsed by the US (Iqbal 2017; Ministry of Defence of Pakistan 2017).[28] In other words, Beijing will have to carefully thread in the 70 year old Indo–Pakistan rivalry, still feeding on Kashmir and, more recently, on Baluchistan and Afghanistan.[29] Cautiousness will be needed: Pakistan remains a nuclear state intricately entangled in regional security affairs in South Asia, and including in places of strategic interest for the US, such as Afghanistan.

CPEC is a part-gambit-part-development calculation for China. If CPEC is successful in delivering the planned and promised development outputs, it will secure China a strategic advantage on multiple fronts: winning regional confidence for its ambitious BRI plan, long-term availability of large markets for trade and manufacturing, an Renminbi market, a secure transit alternative to the strait of Malacca, and an ability to demonstrate to the world that it can secure peace through its economic agenda in the most fragile circumstances. China claims that its path to security passes through economic development. Earlier, it successfully tested this strategy in Xinjiang, and now CPEC represents an enlarged international application of the same policy. Nonetheless, in the next few years, managing security threats in Xinjiang, Baluchistan and at the Pakistan–Afghanistan border to protect its workers and businesses will be a daunting test of Chinese' claims.

The promising aspect for GEG is that CPEC can offer an opportunity for the *convergence* of international agendas in South Asia: complementing Chinese and US security and economic interests in Pakistan and in the region. Curbing domestic terrorism in order to protect the CPEC project has become a priority for both Islamabad and Beijing. Amongst these challenges, therefore, lies the opportunity, in particular for the US, to establish a complementing vision of development, stability and connectivity (Chibber 2017).

Lessons: China's foray into GEG

Asia today requires trillions of dollars in infrastructure development in order to graduate from its "developing" status. If we look at the West's development trajectory, the advanced economies of Europe and the US went through this infrastructure investment phase centuries ago – suggesting that it represents a compulsory development passage. Most efforts in Asia are carried out at the national level while the BRI promises to help bridging part of this infrastructure gap by presenting a regional opportunity to many Asian countries. Beijing's BRI pitch has worked sensationally well: within four years, over 68 countries and organizations have signed up to join an initiative spanning through 60% of the world's population and one-third of the global GDP.

In 1820, China was the world's largest economy – and is the second largest economy today. Starting from a largely dispossessed rural society in 1978, the Government has lifted 500 million people out of poverty, more than any other country in the world, by raising per Capita GDP almost 50-fold, from USD 155 (in today's dollar) to USD 7,590 by 2014. In 1978, three-quarters of the country's industrial production was centrally controlled; by 2010, private firms contributed between two-thirds and three-quarters of China's GDP (Eckart 2016). Beijing promises state-directed investments and market-operated lending in its BRI development model. While in Western development programmes, grants and loans are often bundled with social, economic and public reforms, also entailing international legal obligations, China's programmes do not require structural adjustments programmes.

Undoubtedly, while the Chinese model has lifted half a billion people out of poverty, it also lacked the institutional accountability, rule of law, and soft institutional infrastructures that are indispensable to sustain the gains from economic growth. China is not alone: many Asian countries sit at the bottom of the Corruption Perception Index despite an increase in their economic growth rates.[30] History tells us that sustainable development requires not only infrastructures, but also complementary institutional development.

Indications of challenges are everywhere: protests have taken place in Africa long before they erupted in Vietnam and Myanmar. Nepal and Pakistan (Lo and Zhou 2017; Rana 2017) have just scrapped BRI and CPEC development projects respectively. In Sri Lanka, the Hambantota airport fiasco generated much suspicion regarding Chinese imperialistic design. Some regional countries are turning to Japan as an alternative provider of development financing.

All this suggests that the CPEC can face multiple challenges in the future: from corruption, poor legal and governance structures, political regime fragility and security threats. Most literature from non-BRI countries has debated ad nauseam on the possible negative effects of the BRI design not only on Eurasian countries but also on the Western order. The Asian reception of the BRI (excluding Japan and India), is however, mostly favourable. The leading institutions of the Western order like the WB, the IMF and the ADB, have in most cases not only underwritten the AIIB and other Chinese-led infrastructure projects, but also signed Memorandums of Understanding.

China's foray into GEG presents many challenges to existing global norms. At best the BRI is a work-in-progress conception. It presents a vision so grand (overly speculated in scholarship) that it borders being unrealistic. Arguably, the first test of Chinese's BRI success lies in the successful implementation of CPEC, which in a microcosm presents all the complex challenges the BRI may face on a continental scale.

Conclusion: challenges and opportunities for the Western order

The BRI vision provides unique challenges and opportunities to the US-led Western political-economic order. The preservation of Western security interests and of the Western value system are possibly its two prime concerns in Asia. As China's investments in the BRI region are rising, it will have to attend to security and peace in the region to protect its investments, also by strengthening protection of property rights and rule of law. This shift presents an opportunity to align interests with the West.

Security in South Asia is a major concern for the US. This region remains the world's "decisive geopolitical chessboard" rampant with strategic, security and socio-political conflicts, as well as home to three nuclear states. Embroiled in internal and external terrorist threats, Pakistan especially embodies a wide and complex array of risks that have the potential to destabilize the region, including its meddling in Afghanistan and its reaching-out to Moscow and Ankara.

The US could carve out a balance of power in South Asia by using its leverage right, and offer a trilateral dialogue between Islamabad, Delhi and Beijing, and to make Pakistan commit to serious efforts to combat terrorism. The US still has unique advantages through which it can exert its soft influence (backed by its unmatched military power) to provide for regional security and keep intact the Western order in the region.

Using leverages right is particularly important as Pakistan is becoming economically more stable than it was ten years ago. One of the key reasons of America's failure in Afghanistan is Washington's inability to economically develop Afghanistan. The BRI has the potential to support economic growth in the wider region and an economically stable Afghanistan can provide a respectable exit strategy to Washington. At this juncture, including Afghanistan in CPEC investments (China has recently extended the negotiations) could therefore offer alternatives to the US to pursue peace in South Asia through economic development.

However, the US has a weakening interest to bear the responsibility of preserving the Western order. The "America First" sentiment that swept away the 2016 election campaign in the US was not a sudden populist façade but a manifestation of deeper rifts within the Western camp. The recent US withdrawal from the UNESCO, Paris Agreement, the TPP and Transatlantic Trade and Investment Partnership (TTIP), with the North America Free Trade Agreement (NAFTA) being touted next, illustrates what is becoming to be known as "the withdrawal doctrine", illustrating a weakening US interest in continuing global involvement (Julien 2017). America's economy lacks the ever-increasing capacity of the headiest post-World War II era, its business community shies from losing Chinese markets, and its domestic and overseas commitments have become too costly to afford. In his book, *Civilization*, Niall Ferguson (2012) identified six ideas and institutions, known as the "killer apps" that drove the extraordinary divergence in prosperity between the West and the rest of the world after 1500. These apps include competition, scientific revolution, property rights, modern medicine, consumer society and work ethics. He views that American consumer society has become decadent. The internal fault lines are appearing simultaneously with a rise in external challenges and both are likely to feed on each other.

The rise of China is raising multiple concerns: some valid, some overstated. Some Asian states, in particular, Japan and India, view Beijing weakening regional non-Chinese-led initiatives. Some of the Washington strategists consider the American effort to "integrate" China into the Western order as generating new threats to US primacy in Asia. The top US political leadership has sent many overt messages in reviving the "Indo–Pacific" alliance aimed at *containment*, and has vehemently expressed that "no one nation should put itself into a position of dictating 'one belt, one road'" (Panda 2017). Although appealing to the communist era, the "containment doctrine" could be a dangerous revival; yet, the reality is that hardly any actions has substantiated the announcement made in this regard. On its side, Beijing has not seriously spoken to counter the Indo–Pacific alliance (Louis 2017).

Allison (2013) asserts, "war is not inevitable in the US–China power game of the 21st century." The major power relationship can be managed in many ways: "a positive-sum perspective" (which incentivizes mutual trust, transparency, and economic ties); "a zero-sum perspective" as prevailed during the Cold War (with the potential for Mutually Assured Destruction); and, a relationship that situates somewhere in between the two (Christensen 2006). With respect to the BRI, the US and China would be better off in cooperating on policies that support and complement economic development in the region. For the US, there are various ways to engage, including direct support and leveraging its regulatory experience in creating better business environments for BRI financed projects. The US can also provide an indirect support by channeling resources and efforts through the IFIs in which it holds majority powers.

What is to be expected from Chinese continental ambitions in Eurasia? China lacks the international ideological appeal that the Soviets once held, and its internal rifts are more apparent – yet its economy is stronger and technological capabilities greater, and foreign commitments less burdensome. China has also been slowly and gradually putting into place institutional safeguards advancing its management capacity and branding reputation, such as the ADFI's framework based on the "lean, clean and green" model. Niall Ferguson's view that China may not be able to sustain its great economic gains without instituting *property rights* means that it may be a matter of time before China gets to implement stronger domestic reforms that will allow consolidating the economic and foreign policy progresses it has achieved since the 1980s.

Uniquely, the Western order has much to offer to China's bid in the Eurasian continent and beyond, especially in strengthening the soft institutional infrastructure of good governance and rule of law. By working together they can achieve more, as a system, than they can as the sum of their individual parts.

Notes

1 Includes 10 ASEAN economies and Japan, South Korea, China, India, Australia and New Zealand.
2 The "great game" historically connotes the nineteenth century political and diplomatic rivalry between the British Empire and the Russian Empire to influence and win over Afghanistan and neighbouring Central and South Asia. Both of the Empires, in order to protect their respective trade routes, remained apprehensive of each other's intentions. Finally, this great game of tension ended in September 1895 with the signing of the Pamir Boundary Commission protocol that defined the border between Afghanistan and the Russian Empire. In late 1990s the term "New Great Game" was used to describe the renewed geopolitical interest in the newly created mineral-rich Central Asian States. This New Great Game is distinct from the former nineteenth century Great Game. Membership to the emergent regional platforms, like the SCO, has significantly made it complex for Western powers to continue to play the old great game in Asia.
3 The planning for an international financial and monetary system was under American and British consideration since the Genoa Conference in 1922, which failed to achieve settlement. The chaotic decade of 1920s was a compelling reason to plan for a new international monetary and financial arrangement and the first noteworthy step was the Reciprocal Trade Agreements Act (RTAA) of 1934. Onwards, the US led the course of western value system.
4 Hegemony is the political, economic or military predominance or control of one state over others. The definition was expanded during the nineteenth century to include cultural and social predominance. The British hegemony based on its industrial and cultural supremacy, lasted till 1915. Embedded liberalism, a term coined by John Ruggie in 1982 refers to the global economic system from the end of the Second World War to the 1970s. The system was set up to support a combination of free trade, with the freedom for states to enhance their provision of welfare and to regulate their economies to reduce unemployment.
5 The WBG consists of the IBRD, which lends to governments of middle-income and creditworthy low-income countries; the IDA provides interest-free loans to governments of the poorest countries; the IFC focuses exclusively on the private sector; the MIGA, promotes FDI into developing countries to support economic growth; and, the ICSID provides international facilities for arbitration of investment disputes.

6 The consensus, postulated in 1989 by John Williamson refers to a set of economic policy reforms. The term "Washington" connoted an affirmation of the economic agencies of the US, the IFIs, the FRB and other policy think tanks and can be summarized as: (a) fiscal discipline; (b) deficits reduction; (c) broadened tax regime; (d) market-based real interest rates; and, (e) competitive exchange rates.

7 A borrower government agrees to adjust its economic policies according to the IMF loan conditions, which ensure repayment capacity of the country. Until the early 1980s, the IMF's focus was mostly on macroeconomic policies.

8 Interestingly, just before the Asian financial crises erupted in 1997, the Interim Committee of the IMF was deliberating to modify IMF's Charter to impose upon its members a legal obligation to further open up capital accounts.

9 The Latin America's GDP grew sharply at 5.5% per annum from 1950–1980 under the ISI policies yet it could not lead to a sustained development course.

10 Apart from the four East Asia Tigers, Brazil did almost as well as China until the 1980s; currently, the Indian economy, despite following a different path, is on a rise. See, section 4 for the Export-Led Growth (ELG) model.

11 Originating from Ohashi Kaoru's idea, a feasibility study led by Watanabe Takeshi proposed a regional financing institution to be set up in Asia to complement the WB's with an initial capitalization of USD 1 billion.

12 An informal and personal approach to problem-solving that respects the South East Asian cultural norms, based on quite-diplomacy and consensus.

13 The term, lost decade, originally referred to the Japanese economic situation during the 1990s, is now loosely applied to any ten-year period of economic stagnation.

14 Among the initiatives of those years, the Chiang Mai Initiative (CMI) began as a series of multilateral currency swaps in 2000 following the Asian crisis of 1997 among the ASEAN, the PRC, Japan and South Korea. However, during the GFC, the CMI was multilateralized in 2009 by the ASEAN+3 in order to provide a reserve pooling arrangement. China, Japan and Korea contributed almost 80% of the USD 120 billion, while 20% was contributed by the ASEAN countries.

15 Large-country effect is also likely to produce benefits for China for a longer period of time than is the case for other developing countries owing to the strict family planning.

16 At the time of establishing the Bretton Woods Institutions, relative weight and strength of the founding members delineated their authority and influence. The IMF and the WB did not give equal voting power to their members: the relative voting power of the 188 members is instead based on a combination of capital contribution, size of the economy and financial stability. At the time of establishing the Bretton Woods, the US contributed USD 3.175 billion of the initial USD 10 billion capitalization and received 37.2% voting power. Over the decades, EMDCs have been gradually increasing the size of their economies – yet, bigger economies and larger contributions have not changed voting power proportionately. While the IMF and WB tried multiple times to institute governance reforms to adjust this lag, the US Congress refused approving any reform affecting its veto power and influence. Since the US has always had veto power in these institutions, no reform could eventually be implemented until approved by the US.

17 Within the WB/IMF, China maintains today a voting share of 4.8% despite representing 15% of the world economy, while Japan holds 7.5% of voting power despite representing only 6.5% of the world economy. The ADB imitated the governance system and development philosophy of Bretton Woods Institutions: Japan, as the largest capital contributor, holds the largest voting power (12.84%), followed by the US (12.75%), leaving China, the largest Asian economy, far behind (5.54%). Tellingly, the Chinese voting share was reduced from an original 6.1% in 2006 due to strategic threats, as Japan felt that China was rapidly increasing its military spending and diplomatic capacity. Currently, the EMDCs hold almost 40% of voting power within Western IFIs, while about 60% still lies with OECD countries despite the fact that their contributions have shrunken and their economic size has become comparatively smaller. See the websites of the WB, the IMF and the ADB for voting shares.

18 By end of 2016, the CDB's international loan portfolio exceeded USD 277 billion.

19 The Bank of China is the most internationalized state-owned bank in China and has been leading the cross-border RMB market.

20 In August 2010, the Hong Kong Monetary Authority allowed all authorized institutions to take part in the interbank bond market using Renminbi through a settlement agent and after seeking the People's Bank of China's approval. Hong Kong, Singapore and London all have some international trade settled in Renminbi – with Hong Kong taking the lead.

21 Chinese-sponsored projects often require adherence to the "One-China policy" conditionality. There is, also, an increased emphasis on environmental standards in AIIB projects as its motto is built on "lean, green, clean" development. Other economic conditionalities usually include preferences for Chinese investors/businesses, labour, equipment and machinery, etc. Unlike in Western ODA, in Chinese project financing there are no macroeconomic conditionalities.

22 China–Mongolia–Russia Corridor; New Eurasian Land Bridge; China Central–Asia–West Asia Corridor; China–Indochina Peninsula Corridor; China–Pakistan Corridor; and Bangladesh–China–India–Myanmar Corridor.

23 As of 2016, USD 900 billion worth of projects have been planned or under implementation.

24 The Hambantota airport in Sri Lanka, built for USD 200 million, illustrates both of these risks (apart from strategic and geopolitical undercurrents): the newly constructed airport is called the "world's emptiest airport" and is its unused cargo terminal is being used as a rice storage facility, while the Sri Lankan Government is struggling to service the debt raised to build the airport.

25 Expected growth rate is 5.5% for fiscal year 2018–2019.

26 Over 85% of Chinese oil imports travel through the Strait of Malacca; however, China has another alternative to Malacca through Myanmar, which is underplayed in the literature. Gwadar's strategic significance for China (both as a future naval base and as an alternative to Malacca) seems therefore overly exaggerated.

27 In particular, rule of law is indispensable for the efficient functioning of infrastructure projects.

28 The US issued a string of conflicting statements: initially, endorsing Indian view, that CPEC is in violation of international law, however, subsequent statements endorsed that CPEC will increase development opportunities in South Asia.

29 It is alleged that the separatist elements in Baluchistan are supported by India, which denies providing such support. It is also alleged that Pakistan continues to provide safe havens to some factions of the Taliban, like the Haqqani group,

responsible for attacking US/Afghan forces. Pakistan officially denies this. These mutual "allegations" are only one of the many factors that the rivalry between India and Pakistan (Afghanistan–Pakistan and US–Pakistan) continues to grow.

30 In the 2017 Corruption Perception Index, Afghanistan sat at the bottom 4th position, North Korea at 8th, Cambodia at 19th, Bangladesh at 26th, Russia at 45th, Myanmar at 50th.

References

Allison, G. (2013), *Lee Kuan Yew: The Grand Master's Insights on China, the United States, and the World*, Cambridge: MIT Press.

Arner, D. and Schou-Zibell, L. (2010), *Responding to the Global Financial and Economic Crisis: Meeting the Challenges in Asia*, Working Paper Series on Regional Integration, No. 60, Asian Development Bank.

Avgouleas, E., Arner, D. W. and Ashraf, U. (2014), 'Regional financial arrangements: lessons from the Eurozone crisis for East Asia', in I. Azis and H. S. Shin (Eds.), *Global Shock, Risks, and Asian Financial Reform*, Cheltenham: Edward Elgar Press.

Barton, U. A. (2017), *Rethinking Regulation of International Finance: Law, Policy and Institutions*, Alphen aan den Rijn: Wolters Kluwer.

Brummer, C. (2017), 'The Renminbi and Systemic Risk', *Journal of International Economic Law*, 20(3): 447–507.

Cesarano, F. (2006), *Monetary Theory and Bretton Woods: The Construction of an International Monetary Order*, Cambridge: Cambridge University Press.

Chibber, A. (2017), 'China's Belt and Road Initiative and India's options: Competitive Cooperation', *Journal of Infrastructure Policy and Development*, 1(2) (DOI: 10.24294/jipd.v1i2.83).

China Development Bank (2018), 'About CDB'. Available at: www.cdb.com.cn/English/gykh_512/khjj/ (last accessed: 13 March 2018).

Christensen, T. (2006), 'Fostering Stability or Creating a Monster? The Rise of China and US Policy Toward East-Asia', *International Security*, 31(1): 81–126.

Dasgupta, S. (2016), 'BRICS Bank to kick-off fund raising with Yuan denominated bonds in China', *The Times of India*. Available at: https://timesofindia.indiatimes.com/business/international-business/BRICS-Bank-to-kick-off-fund-raising-with-Yuan-denominated-bonds-in-China/articleshow/51553815.cms (last accessed: 13 March 2018).

Eckart, J. (2016), '8 things you need to know about China's economy', *World Economic Forum*. Available at: https://www.weforum.org/agenda/2016/06/8-facts-about-chinas-economy/ (last accessed: 13 March 2018).

Eichengreen, B. (1992), *Golden Fetters: The Gold Standard and the Great Depression*, Oxford: Oxford University Press.

EXIM Bank (2016), Annual Report. Available at: http://english.eximbank.gov.cn/upload/accessory/20175/2017531315427099615.pdf (last accessed: 13 March 2018).

Ferguson, N. (2012), *Civilization: The West and the Rest*, New York: Penguin Press.

Financial Times (2017a), 'One Belt One Road – and many questions'. Available at: https://www.ft.com/content/d5c54b8e-37d3-11e7-ac89-b01cc67cfeec (last accessed: 13 March 2018).

Financial Times (2017b), 'Conflict over Athens' surplus needles the IMF'. Available at: https://www.ft.com/content/dc636b6a-eed1-11e6-ba01-119a44939bb6 (last accessed: 13 March 2018).

Fischer, S. (2012), 'The Washington Consensus', in F. Bergsten and R. Henning (Eds.), *Global Economics in Extraordinary Times: Essays in Honor of John Williamson*, Washington: Peterson Institute Press (PIIE).

Hirst, T. (2015), 'A brief history of China's economic growth', *World Economic Forum*. Available at: https://www.weforum.org/agenda/2015/07/brief-history-of-china-economic-growth/ (last accessed: 13 March 2018).

Huang, P. (1975), *The Asian Development Bank: Diplomacy and Development in Asia*, New York: Vantage Press.

Iqbal, A. (2017), 'CPEC passes through disputed territory' *DAWN*. Available at: https://www.dawn.com/news/1362283 (last accessed: 13 March 2018).

Jinping, X. (2017), 'Work Together to Build the Silk Road Economic Belt and The 21st Century Maritime Silk Road: Text of President Xi's Speech at Opening of the Belt and Road Forum', *Xinhua News*. Available at: http://news.xinhuanet.com/english/2017-05/14/c_136282982.htm (last accessed: 13 March 2018).

John, P. (2017), 'Creaking at 60: The future of the European Union: Special Report', *The Economist*. Available at: https://www.economist.com/news/special-report/21719188-it-marks-its-60th-birthday-european-union-poor-shape-it-needs-more (last accessed: 13 March 2018).

Julien, C. (2017), 'America First or America Alone? The Withdrawal Agenda', *The Times of Israel*. Available at: https://www.timesofisrael.com/america-first-or-america-alone-trumps-withdrawal-doctrine/ (last accessed: 13 March 2018).

Krishnamurti, R. (1977), 'ADB: The Seeding Days', Manila: Asian Development Bank.

Landry, D. G. and Tang, H. (2017), 'Rise of the Redback: Internationalizing the Chinese Renminbi', *The Diplomat*. Available at: https://thediplomat.com/2017/09/rise-of-the-redback-internationalizing-the-chinese-renminbi/ (last accessed: 13 March 2018).

Larmer, B. (2017), 'What the World's Emptiest International Airport Says About China's Influence', *The New York Times Magazine*. Available at: https://nyti.ms/2eV4xlg (last accessed:13 March 2018).

Liu, Q., Lejot, P. and Arner, D. (2013), *Finance in Asia: Institutions, Regulation and Policy*, London: Routledge.

Lo, K. and Zhou, V. (2017), 'Has scrapped USUSD 2.5 billion Nepal hydro dam deal with Chinese state firm hurt Beijing's Himalayan ambitions?' *The South China Morning Post*. Available at: www.scmp.com/news/china/diplomacy-defence/art-icle/2119725/nepal-cancels-hydro-dam-deal-chinese-state-firm (last accessed: 13 March 2018).

Louis, N. (2017), 'In Asia, Trump keeps talking about Indo-Pacific', *Politico*. Available at: https://www.politico.com/story/2017/11/07/trump-asia-indo-pacific-244657 (last accessed: 13 March 2018).

Memon, A. Q. (2017), 'CPEC debt: Borrowing is not bad if invested in lucrative ventures and assets', *The Express Tribune*. Available at: https://tribune.com.pk/story/1444780/cpec-debt-borrowing-not-bad-invested-lucrative-ventures-assets/ (last accessed: 13 March 2018).

Mikesell, R. F. (1994), *The Bretton Woods Debates: A Memoir*, Princeton: Princeton University Press.

Ministry of Defence of Pakistan (2017), 'US announce support for CPEC': Available at: https://defence.pk/pdf/threads/us-announces-support-for-cpec.524058/ (last accessed: 13 March 2018).

New Development Bank (2018), Organization – Members. Available at: www.int/about-us/organisation/members/ (last accessed: 13 March 2018).

Nye, J. S. (2017), 'Will the Liberal Order Survive? The History of an Idea', *Foreign Affairs*, 96 (1).

Panda, A. (2017), 'Is the Trump Administration About to Take On China's Belt and Road Initiative?' *The Diplomat.* Available at: https://thediplomat.com/2017/10/is-the-trump-administration-about-to-take-on-chinas-belt-and-road-initiative/ (last accessed: 13 March 2018).

Rana, S. (2017), 'Pakistan stops bid to include Diamer-Bhasha Dam in CPEC', *The Express Tribune.* Available at: https://tribune.com.pk/story/1558475/2-pakistan-stops-bid-include-diamer-bhasha-dam-cpec/ (last accessed: 13 March 2018).

Rodrik, D. (2006), 'Goodbye Washington Consensus, Hello Washington Confusion? A Review of the World Bank's Economic Growth in the 1990s: Learning from a Decade of Reform', *Journal of Economic Literature*, 44(4): 973–987.

Ruggie, J. G. (1982), 'International Regimes, Transactions, and Change: Embedded Liberalism in the Post-War Economic Order', *International Organization*, 36(2): 379–415.

Silk Road Fund (2017), 'Overview'. Available at: www.silkroadfund.com.cn/enweb/23775/23767/index.html (last accessed: 13 March 2018).

Watanabe, T. (1977), *Toward a New Asia: Memoirs of the First President of the ADB*, Singapore: Asian Development Bank.

Yang, Y. (2014), 'The Chinese Growth Miracle', in *Handbook of Economic Growth*, 2B. Elsevier Press.

5 Normative trade power Europe?

The case of EU trade agreements with Asian countries

Daniela Sicurelli

Introduction

According to the United Nations Development Program (UNDP 2014), "by increasing GDP and creating new income and employment generation opportunities particularly for vulnerable communities, international trade can promote human development". This pro-poor outcome is especially evident for low- and middle-income countries that mainly export labour-intensive goods and services. The EU is the biggest trader in the world, and accounts for 16.5% of global imports and exports (EU 2017) and a key player in the WTO. It is also the largest world donor of Official Development Assistance (ODA), which makes it a major global economic governance shaper. Consistently with the United Nations Development Programme (UNDP) goals, official documents of European institutions state that, by promoting Preferential Trade Agreements (PTAs), the EU aims at both fostering growth in Europe (European Commission 2006) and contributing to development cooperation (European Commission 2012, 2015). The European Commission (2012) measures the development effects of trade on low- and middle-income countries in terms of "improvement on human development indicators". According to Khorana and Garcia (2013), Lavenex (2014), Feliu and Serra (2015) and Heron (2016), this approach to trade policy confirms the role of the EU as a normative power (Manners 2002), namely a power committed to promoting norms internationally, with the purpose of contributing to "sustainable global economics" and a "more just human development" (Manners 2009a: 23). Others (Heron 2011; Siles Brügge, 2014a, 2014b; Taylor 2016; Hoang and Sicurelli 2017; McKenzie and Meissner 2017), instead, have highlighted a lack of coherence between the self-proclaimed objectives of its trade policy and its actual content.

Negotiations of preferential trade deals with Asian countries offer a test of the domestic incentives and constraints to the emergence of the EU as a normative power through trade. In the 2000s, the interest of European industry and investors in penetrating the dynamic Asian markets has dramatically increased. Due to the highly differentiated income-levels and development models of Asian countries, trade negotiations with those countries are especially challenging for EU trade policy's ambition to take into account the development needs of its negotiating partners. By comparing the texts of the comprehensive trade agreements concluded by the EU with Asian countries in the 2000s, namely South Korea (2009), Singapore (2014) and Vietnam (2015), this chapter supports the literature questioning the ability of the EU to act as a coherent normative power and development promoter through trade. The EU did allow Vietnam (a low–middle-income country, according to World Bank classification) to have greater transition periods than South Korea and Singapore (high-income countries) in promoting liberalization of trade in goods and with greater guarantees against investors in the Investor-State Dispute Settlement (ISDS). Despite these efforts, though, it failed to provide Vietnam with sufficient flexibility clauses that would support the country in its attempts to adjust to the liberalization and regulatory standards proposed by the EU.

Scholars of International Relations provide different interpretations for the lack of coherence in the EU trade policy. Institutionalist and constructivist studies draw a picture of the structural conditions for the lack of coherence in the EU trade policy. Political economy studies integrate those findings and capture the impact of the domestic pressures mobilized around specific negotiations. Building on this latter approach, I investigate the political economy conditions through which EU trade policy can contribute to promoting *Human Development*. I show that different patterns of societal mobilizations emerged in the three negotiations, due to differences in the attractiveness of the EU as a market for its partners, the structure of the economy of those partners and the potential impact of the negotiations upon US competition. These differences affected patterns of political mobilization of domestic organized groups, and ultimately undermined the efforts of the EU to pursue its declared normative goal of consistently promoting *Human Development* through trade in the region.

This chapter is structured as follows: the first part traces the evolution of the trade policy strategies of the European Commission since 2006. The second part reviews the International Relations literature explaining the motivations behind EU preferences in trade negotiations and the lack of coherence in pursuing its strategic goals. The third part compares the content of EU trade agreements with Korea, Singapore and Vietnam, focusing on relevant issues from a normative and development perspective. The fourth part traces the impact of European domestic pressures on the EU negotiating positions with these three Asian partners. Finally, the conclusions comment on the challenges the EU faces when it comes to playing a coherent role in pursuing growth, development and normative goals through trade, and discusses the implications of these findings for future trade negotiations.

The EU trade policy strategies in the 2000s

As a response to the stalemate of the multilateral negotiations within the WTO – the so-called Doha round – the European Commission issued three communications aimed at clarifying the objectives and guiding principles for the negotiation of future preferential trade agreements. The Communication "Global Europe. Competing in the World" (European Commission 2006) focuses on economic interests, and states

> we should … factor other issues and the wider role of trade policy in EU external relations into bilateral trade developments. But in order for trade policy to help create jobs and drive growth, economic factors must play a primary role in the choice of future FTAs.

For this purpose, the document identifies Asia as a priority region for EU trade policy. In this context, in 2007, the EU started trade negotiations with ASEAN and South Korea. Negotiations with ASEAN, though, stalled in 2009. Since then the EU opted for negotiating bilateral trade agreements with single ASEAN members as stepping stones for a future inter-regional deal. As part of the same Asian package, it negotiated the first comprehensive trade agreement with an Asian country, namely South Korea, eventually signing the agreement in 2009.

The 2006 Communication's focus on the economic interests of the EU raised harsh reactions among NGOs and governments of lower-income countries, which expressed concerns about the development implications of the European trade policy. These reactions compelled the European Commission (2012) to reformulate its trade policy goals and to take into account the need of "Tailoring trade and investment policy for those countries most in need". The Communication explained that in order to support low- and middle-economies in their attempt to adjust to international standards, the EU should pursue a flexible approach to the promotion of liberalization commitments and of tariff and non-tariff barriers. By providing low- and middle-income countries with greater flexibility clauses than high income countries, the EU thus promoted a differentiated approach to liberalization according to the development level of its trade partners.

A third European Communication entitled "Trade for All. Towards a more responsible trade and investment policy" (2015) went further in expressing concerns for the needs of developing countries by stating that "The new approach also involves using trade agreements and trade preference programs as levers to promote, around the world, values like sustainable development, human rights, fair and ethical trade and the fight against corruption". In doing so, the document states, "the EU needs to keep a flexible approach to FTA negotiations to take account of the economic realities of its partners".

In 2014 and 2015 the EU concluded respectively its second and third preferential trade deals with Asian states, namely Singapore and Vietnam. Given the different development levels of these two countries, a comparison between the trade agreements they have concluded with the EU represents a test of the ability of the EU to effectively respond in a differentiated way to the development needs of its trade partners.

Explaining the negotiating positions of the EU

The EU-stated ambition to play a normative role through trade has raised broad attention among scholars of International Relations active both in empirical and theoretical research on the determinants of EU trade policy.

A first group of scholars considers EU trade policy as a manifestation of its normative power. From this perspective, Van den Hoven (2006), Manners (2009b), Khorana and Garcia (2013), Lavenex (2014), Feliu and Serra (2015) and Garcia and Masselot (2015) claim that a distinctive feature of the EU as a trade actor is a commitment to export its constitutive norms. According to these studies, the EU is bound by its own values and principles when promoting and negotiating trade agreements, including democracy, the rule of law, sustainable development and human rights.

A second group of scholars, adopting a critical theory approach, argues that hegemonic ambitions are the main drivers of EU trade negotiations. From this perspective, empirical research on the negotiations of Economic Partnership Agreements (EPAs) with the African Caribbean and Pacific (ACP) countries suggests that the EU self-representation as an ethical actor is instrumental to legitimizing power relations over developing countries in an attempt to foster the interests of major European industries (Bailey and Bossuyt 2013; Langan 2014, 2016; Price and Nunn 2016).

In between these opposite representations of the EU trade policy, other empirical studies depict a more nuanced image of the EU as a trade and normative actor. Institutionalist and constructivist research focuses on the structural context that affects EU trade policy-making. Institutionalists demonstrate that the multiple veto players (Young and Peterson 2014), the heterogeneous organizational preferences of European institutions (McKenzie and Meissner 2017) and the compartmentalization of the EU policy process concerning trade and human rights negotiations (Sicurelli 2015a) challenge policy coherence in the way the EU pursues economic, development and normative goals through trade. Constructivist studies, instead, point at the impact of conflicting narratives in the EU policy-making, which affect the negotiation of preferential trade agreements. They argue that the liberalization imperative and the strategic reference to the WTO as an external constrain has dominated the EU position during the negotiations with Korea. This imperative has empowered exporters and importers and marginalized protectionist positions within the EU (Siles Brügge 2011). On the contrary, in the negotiations with the ACP group, the position of civil society organizations and ACP governments successfully challenged the free trade institutional narrative. In particular, they identified a contradiction between the rhetoric of the external constrain and the actual commitment of the EU to promote regulatory standards that fall beyond the WTO jurisdiction. In order to respond to that criticism and downplay the coercive element of the Economic Partnership Agreements, EU negotiators had to provide negotiating partners with relevant flexibility measures such as long transition periods, a broad list of sensitive products and rendezvous clauses on trade in services and investments, to support them in the process of liberalization and in their attempt to fulfil the EU regulatory standards (Heron 2014, 2016).

Mainstream political economy studies complement institutionalist and constructivist analyses of the determinants of EU trade policy. They claim that, within the opportunities and constrains represented by the institutional and normative structure of the EU, pressures exerted by domestic interest groups and NGOs have a strong impact over the negotiating position of the European Commission. The configuration of those pressures varies according to the EU negotiating partner and may be dominated by protectionist groups (Falkner 2007; De Bièvre and Eckhardt 2011), exporters (Elsig and Dupont 2012), import dependent groups (Eckhardt and Poletti 2016) or coalitions between industries and NGOs (Kelemen and Vogel 2010; Trommer 2014; Poletti and Sicurelli 2016). The variables contributing to the shaping of those mobilization patterns include the attractiveness of the market of the negotiating partners, the structure of their economies and the competition with other trade powers. The mobilization of different configurations of interest groups around single trade deals, in turn, accounts for the lack of consistency in the way the EU integrates liberalization and development imperatives in the practice of bilateral trade negotiations. These competing views will be assessed in the next sections.

The trade agreements with South Korea, Singapore and Vietnam

According to the Commission's communications (2012, 2015), the EU should propose deep liberalization commitments and hard enforcement measures to the most advanced economies, namely Korea and Singapore, and greater flexibility clauses to Vietnam in order to support the process of liberalization and adjustment to EU-sponsored regulatory standards. A comparison of the EU agreements with these three Asian countries, however, only partially confirms these expectations. As Table 5.1 shows, this comparison will focus on selected issues with implications for development cooperation included in each of the trade agreements negotiated by the EU with Asian countries, namely market access, services liberalization, government procurement, investment, sustainable development and human rights.

In terms of access of EU products into Vietnam's market, the EU provides the latter with a larger transition period (ten years after the entry into force of the Free Trade Agreements (FTA) as opposed to five years agreed with Korea and Singapore). In turn, in the agreements with Korea and Singapore, the EU agreed to eliminate its tariffs within five years after the entry into force of the FTA, while in the case of Vietnam the EU has obtained a longer

Table 5.1 Selected provisions in the trade agreements between the EU and Asian countries

	EU–Korea	EU–Singapore	EU–Vietnam
Market access	Both parties have agreed to eliminate virtually all tariffs at the latest five years after the entry into force of the FTA.	Both parties have agreed to eliminate virtually all tariffs at the latest five years after the entry into force of the FTA.	Vietnam and the EU respectively agreed to eliminate virtually all tariffs line at the latest ten and seven years after the entry into force of the FTA.
Services	Reciprocal commitment to services liberalization, with the exception of EU postal services.	Reciprocal commitment to services liberalization, including EU postal services.	Reciprocal commitment to services liberalization, including EU postal services.
Government procurement	Confirming and extending GPA commitments for both parties.	Confirming and extending GPA commitments for both parties.	Confirming EU GPA commitments and asking Vietnam to comply to standards fully in line with the GPA.
Investment	No ISDS (agreement negotiated before the enforcement of the Lisbon Treaty).	ISDS, with no emphasis on state right to regulate. No appeal mechanism.	ISDS, with emphasis on state right to regulate. Appeal mechanism.
Sustainable development	Calling for ratification and enforcement of all the core ILO conventions and to effectively implement all multilateral environment agreements to which they are party. "Allowing the parties the freedom to regulate according to their own collective preferences. Co-operation activities also have a role to play e.g. through policy-dialogue, on trade related global environmental issues, employment and social policies, human resources development, labour relations and social	Calling for ratification and enforcement of all the core UN environmental and labour conventions compatibly with "domestic circumstances". Monitoring mechanism: government consultations, advisory groups (civil society), Panel of experts.	Calling for ratification and enforcement of all the core UN environmental and labour conventions compatibly with "domestic circumstances". Government consultations, advisory groups (civil society), Panel of experts with detailed procedures and conditions.

dialogue. The Commission services do not aim at harmonisation of social and environmental provisions with parties to trade agreements, but rather at progressing through dialogue and cooperation to make economic and trade-related endeavours sustainable in the long term" (EC, 2010: 6).

In contrast to the strict unilateral rules of the GSP Plus provisions (see above), to which the GSP eligible ASEAN countries in the past were reluctant to abide to, the second paragraph of this quotation seems to give a lot of flexibility and room of manoeuvre to the EU negotiators of a sustainability clause in an EU–ASEAN FTA. This is evidently a sound and safe approach, taking into account the social and environmental "development gaps" between the individual ASEAN countries. However, it also fully explains the phrasing in the EU-Korea FTA of October 2010:

"The Parties recognise that it is not their intention in this Chapter to harmonise the labour or environment standards of the Parties, but to strengthen their trade relations and cooperation in ways that promote sustainable development …" (Art. 13.1, 3).

Civil society dialogue mechanism, government consultations, panel of experts.

| Human rights | Vague linkage clause with the Framework Agreement. Dialogue as an enforcement mechanism. | Clear institutional linkage with the PCA. Dialogue as an enforcement mechanism. | Clear institutional linkage with the PCA. Dialogue as an enforcement mechanism. |

transition period, seven years, to open up its market. Service liberalization involves a higher number of sectors in the cases of the EU FTAs with
Singapore and Vietnam in contrast to the agreement with Korea.

Both agreements with Singapore and Vietnam include an ISDS, differently from the agreement with Korea.[1] The trade agreement with Vietnam
includes more safeguard clauses for the state regulatory autonomy against
disputes with investors, namely an appeal mechanism and the explicit protection of the state's right to regulate. On government procurement, the trade
agreement imposes on Vietnam a relatively harder commitment than those
with Korea and Singapore, considering that Vietnam is not a member of the
WTO Government Procurement Agreement (GPA). While trade agreements
with Korea and Singapore confirm and extend GPA commitments, Vietnam
is asked to adjust its government procurement sector to comply with GPA
standards. According to Vietnamese governmental and non-governmental
sources, this undermines the distinctive features of Vietnam's national socialist
market economy, which requires heavy state intervention (Sicurelli 2015b). As
the EU admits "The government procurement chapter of the 'EU-Vietnam
FTA' achieves a degree of transparency and procedural fairness comparable
to other FTAs that the EU has signed with developed and more advanced
developing countries" (EU Delegation to Vietnam 2016). These reforms are
especially costly for Vietnam, due to the structure of its economy based on an
intrusive role of the state over the economy. Despite the official definition of
Vietnam's economy as a "socialist-oriented market economy", the EU and the
US, among others, have not yet recognized Vietnam as a country with "market
economy" status.

In respect to the chapter on sustainable development, the EU provides
both Singapore and Vietnam with flexibility clauses, agreeing to take into
account possible domestic obstacles to ratification and enforcement of core
labour and environmental conventions, on the basis that the parties to the
agreements should ratify international labour and environmental law compatibly with their respective "domestic circumstances". Nevertheless, it imposes
more detailed enforcement procedures on Vietnam than on the other two
countries. While the EU–Korea agreements explicitly refer to "civil society"
as an actor that should be involved in the monitoring stage of the implementation of the agreement, trade agreements with Singapore and Vietnam do
not use that term.[2] Still, those agreements require a balanced representation
of economic, social and environmental stakeholders, including employers and
workers' organizations in the overseeing process. Compared to the agreements
with the other two Asian countries, the FTA with Vietnam is more detailed in
the procedures and conditions for the activation of government consultations,
advisory groups and panel of experts. Given the lack of recognition in Vietnam
of independent trade unions and pluralist interest group representation, those
conditions appear especially hard for the country.

Finally, the three agreements refer to human rights as essential elements of
cooperation between the parties. Each of them is included within a broader

partnership (the EU–Korea Framework Agreement, 2010; the EU–Singapore Partnership and Cooperation Agreement, PCA, 2013; and the EU–Vietnam PCA, 2012) that calls the parties to cooperate on multiple sectors, including international human right standards. While the EU–Korea FTA provides a vague linkage clause between the trade agreement and the framework agreement, the EU–Singapore and EU–Vietnam deals establish a clear institutional linkage with the Political Cooperation Agreement (PCA). The EU–Korea agreement states "The present Agreement shall be an integral part of the ... overall bilateral relations as governed by the Framework Agreement. It constitutes a specific Agreement giving effect to the trade provisions within the meaning of the Framework Agreement". By contrast, the agreements with Singapore and Vietnam specify that the PCA and the PTA "shall form part of a common institutional framework". These differences are especially remarkable if one considers that negotiations on sustainable development and human rights did not raise any particular friction in the case of the EU–Korea agreement, while they triggered heavy resistances from Singapore and Vietnam (Sicurelli 2015a; McKenzie and Meissner 2017).

Preference formation in the EU trade policy

EU–Korea negotiations

In 2007, when the US signed a trade agreement with Korea (KORUS), the Asian country emerged as a priority for European trade policy. By that time, Korea represented a growing interest for European exporters, especially in the services sector (Copenhagen Economics and Francois 2007). In 2009, the EU was the second largest market for Korean exports, and the third source of Korean imports. In turn, Korea ranked 12th as an export destination and 9th as a source of imports for the EU (Cooper et al. 2011). By that time, imports from Korea to the EU amounted to EUR 32.5 million, while EU exports amounted to EUR 21.6 million. European exporters were especially interested in increasing their market share in Asia as a reaction to the conclusion of KORUS and pushed the European Commission to conclude an agreement that would provide them with at least comparable conditions than their US counterparts. In order to address these demands, the EU was able to obtain KORUS-plus provisions in the liberalization of financial and legal services and in other sectors (Woolcock 2014). In addition to exporter interest groups, import-dependent interests, especially retailers represented by Eurocommerce, actively lobbied the Commission, which agreed with Korea on deep reciprocal liberalization commitments (Eckhardt and Poletti 2016).

In this context, the protectionist positions of the European car industry, concerned by the implications of a trade agreement that would open the European market to imports of Korean cars, found little support in the European Commission. In particular, the Commission did not accept the European Automobile Manufacturers' Association's (ACEA) request to include high non-trade barriers concerning unstandardized emission testing in the agreement and only reached a compromise with ACEA on rules of origin and duty drawback (Siles Brügge 2014c).

European companies aiming to expand their investment opportunities in Asia also lobbied the European Commission. Since Korea was a member of the GPA, negotiations on government procurement focused on the possibility to include GPA plus commitments. Under the KORUS agreement, Korea and the US had agreed to liberalize the government procurements of a higher number of public agencies than required by the GPA (Cooper et al. 2011). Against this background, European investors were interested in obtaining an agreement that would provide them with at least the same opportunities their American counterparts had.

Since the Doha negotiations, environmental, development and human rights NGOs, as well as the European Trade Union Confederation (ETUC) had lobbied the European Commission to promote the integration of sustainable development norms into WTO law (Young 2007; Poletti and Sicurelli 2012; Hilary 2014). After the stalemate of the Doha negotiations, those NGOs lobbied for the inclusion of a chapter on sustainable development in the preferential trade negotiations (Sicurelli 2015a; Poletti and Sicurelli 2016). Nevertheless, negotiations with Korea did not mobilize strong pressures for fully binding commitments on sustainable development. On the labor front, ETUC merely asked the Commission to be included in civil society dialogue in the monitoring stage of the implementation of the trade agreement. In general, ETUC supported the European strategy of pushing for a free trade deal aiming primarily at creating growth and jobs in both the negotiating sides (Healy 2015). Even though it had expressed criticism against the provisions included in the sustainability chapter of EU trade agreements with Central America, Peru and Colombia, calling, in vain, for the trade agreements not to be signed (Hilary 2014), it finally welcomed the final text of the agreement with Korea. General Secretary John Monks considered it "on balance a good deal" and stressed, "It's important that all Europe's industrial sectors do profit from this agreement and that it creates new jobs" (ETUC 2010).

In the end, Korea and the EU decided not to subject labour and environmental issues to the agreement's dispute settlement mechanism, which means they agreed on a trade deal that includes less binding sustainable development provision than the KORUS. Similarly, the low salience of the agreement with Korea for human rights activists accounts for position of the European Commission in favour of a minimalist linkage between the trade agreement and the PCA between the two members.

EU–Singapore negotiations

Since 2006, the EU has had a positive trade balance with Singapore, both in goods and services. At the same time, Singapore is the second Asian investor in the EU. In 2010, imports from Singapore to the EU amounted to EUR

19 billion, and exports to EUR 24.5 billion. In the same year, in preparation of the negotiations with Singapore, the European Commission opened an online industry consultation, which mobilized multiple industry organizations. As shown by the synthesis of the contributions to the survey published in the Commission's website (European Commission 2010), exporters in the automotive and energy sectors, and investors in the service sector, were mostly active in the context of negotiations with Singapore. For those European industries, Singapore represented a major destination of exports and investments and an important regional hub for the ASEAN region. Thus, even industries that were not directly interested in increasing their trade and investment relations with Singapore participated to the survey, reckoning that the EU–Singapore FTA could become a template for future trade agreements with other ASEAN members (European Commission 2010). For these reasons and due to the absence of import-competing groups with a stake in the negotiations, the surveyed industries effectively pushed for the inclusion of high reciprocal commitments in terms of market access and services liberalization.

Since Singapore is a member of the GPA, proposing GPA standards of government procurement liberalization was not a conflictual matter. Yet, European investors responding to the Commission's survey expressed a clear interest in the promotion of transparent rules allowing European Companies to compete with Singapore's Government-Linked-Corporations (*ibidem*). Similarly, the inclusion of an ISDS in the agreement with Singapore was not a controversial issue, since the country had already concluded trade and investment agreements, which included this mechanism.

As for negotiations with Korea, both labour rights and the environment did emerge as highly salient issues also in the negotiations with Singapore (McKenzie and Meissner 2017). The European Commission proposed Singapore to agree on a chapter on sustainable development built on the model of the EU–Korea agreement, and accepted Singapore's request to include a clause allowing the parties to invoke domestic constraints for ratification and enforcement of International Labour Organization (ILO) and environmental conventions. In contrast to negotiations with Korea, trade unions and human rights activists (International Federation on Human Rights), mobilized during the EU–Singapore negotiations (FIDH 2007). Even though the European Parliament did not take an explicit position in support of human right NGOs, it appears that such pressures led to a more explicit link between the EU–Singapore FTA and PCA than in the EU–Korea agreement.

EU–Vietnam negotiations

As in the case of Korea, negotiations with Vietnam especially mobilized exporter and import-dependent associations. The EU is the largest destination of Vietnamese goods and, at the same time, the second largest two-way partner (after China). In 2013, when negotiations started, Vietnam's exports to the EU amounted to EUR 21 billion, exports from the South East Asian country to the EU only amounted to EUR 6 billion. Furthermore, as the structure of the Vietnamese industry is based on low-tech manufacturing and cheap labour, this has contributed to the mobilization of European import-dependent associations interested in steering the deal. Indeed, these organizations that profit from importing low-cost intermediate products for their production process are interested in lowering European barriers to imported goods. These groups actively mobilized during the preparation of the European Commission's position and obtained relatively high commitments to liberalization from Vietnam (Eckhardt and Poletti 2016). Import-competing interests in the agriculture sector, under the umbrella of COPA-COGECA, and textile sector (represented by Euratex) also mobilized in order to promote higher sustainability standards in the production processes of their competitor industries in Vietnam (Sicurelli 2015a). Despite the strong resistance initially expressed by Vietnamese government institutions against the protectionist undertones of the European positions on sustainable development (Hoang 2016),[3] European interest groups were eventually able to promote high anti-dumping standards and provisions protecting rice and sugar, among other agriculture products, as well as a special treatment for textiles in the chapter on Rules of Origin. The European Commission likely used the attractiveness of the European market as a bargaining chip to obtain those concessions.

The EU was the sixth largest foreign investor in Vietnam in 2013. The growing interest of European investors in ASEAN markets, the heavy role of the state in the Vietnamese economy and the high corruption in Vietnamese public procurements have raised pressures within the EU for adopting GPA liberalization standards comparable to those included in the trade agreement with Korea and Singapore. Competition of European investors with their US counterparts also affected pressures for high levels of liberalization in the investment sector. As a reaction to these pressures, the EU obtained Trans-Pacific Partnership-plus (TPP-plus) norms on liberalization of public procurement (Hoang and Sicurelli 2017).

During the negotiations of the EU–Vietnam agreement, the ISDS became a strongly contested issue in Europe in the context of the Transatlantic Trade and Investment Partnership (TTIP). European NGOs were especially vocal against the risk that an ISDS would threaten the policy space of Vietnam state institutions associated to this instrument. Those NGOs were especially influential in Germany, Austria and France (Bauer 2016). In reaction to those pressures, in 2015 the European Commission proposed a revised version of the ISDS, the Investment Court System, in the negotiation of future bilateral agreements, which allows the host state to appeal against a ruling of a standing tribunal and which includes an explicit reference to the state's right to regulate. The agreement with Vietnam was the first to be concluded after that revision and was therefore considered by the European Commission as a model for future agreements.

Differently from the cases of Korea and Singapore, negotiations with Vietnam were influenced by a coalition of import-competing firms, mainly represented by Euratex, and NGOs (such as Action Aid, FIDH, Vietnam Committee on Human Rights and ETUC), interested in promoting a chapter on sustainable development which would impose high standards of labour protection and clear enforcement procedures. The European Parliament also supported those pressures (Sicurelli 2015a). In order to address those pressures, the EU was firmly committed to obtain a more ambitious chapter than that included in the agreement with Singapore. As a result, as far as commitments to sustainable development are concerned, the agreement with Vietnam reiterates the clause that calls on the parties to ratify international labour and environmental treaties compatibly with "domestic circumstances", but imposes more rigid enforcement rules, as compared to that with Singapore.

Finally, the NGO community mobilized for the inclusion of binding human rights clauses in the negotiations. As a reaction, the Commission confirmed the linkage clause to the PCA it had already promoted in the negotiations with Singapore. Nevertheless, it did not accept to carry out a preliminary human rights impact assessment of the trade agreement. In contrast to the issue of labour rights, as a matter of fact, negotiations with Singapore on the human rights clause did not mobilize industry associations in support of NGO pressures.

Conclusions

The comparison of the trade agreements concluded by the EU with Korea, Singapore and Vietnam shows that the EU has been only partially coherent in its declared attempt to create the opportunities to stimulate investments and trade, as well as promote sustainable development in lower-income partners by tailoring its trade policy to the development needs of its partners. The EU did provide Vietnam with more flexibility clauses than Singapore and Korea, but it also put relatively stronger pressures upon Vietnam to adjust to regulatory standards.

By tracing the decision-making process in the EU, this chapter suggests that the mobilization of domestic interest groups and NGOs in the context of the specific negotiations has contributed to this contradictory outcome. A common feature of negotiations with the three Asian countries is that they mainly mobilized exporter and investment interests aiming at increasing their opportunity for market access in the growing Asian market. Import-dependent associations also effectively lobbied the European Commission, especially in the negotiations with Korea and Vietnam. The dominant role of exporters, investors and importers in the shaping of a European negotiating position explains the highly reciprocal liberalization commitments in each of the three agreements. Competition with the US for access to the East Asian markets seems to have increased pressures for trade and investment liberalization, especially in the cases of Korea and Vietnam. At the same time, European protectionist interests were able to obtain preferential conditions, especially in the negotiations with Vietnam. The ranking of Vietnam's economy at the lowest end of global value chains has triggered strong defensive positions among European import-competing groups that proved able to shape the negotiating position of the Commission by promoting regulatory barriers to Vietnam's products.

According to the EU discourse, the EU is a normative shaper of global economic governance, and its trade policy is meant to foster *Human Development*. Yet, based on the analysis of the political economy dynamics triggered by negotiations with Korea, Singapore and Vietnam, it is fair to conclude that domestic contradictory pressures affected the attempt of the EU to pursue its declared development goals. Existing tensions between EU domestic commercial interests to expand European inexpensive imports, high value-added exports and investment opportunities while protecting European sensitive industries, on the one hand, and pressures to support lower-income countries in their adjusting to international regulatory and human rights standards, on the other hand, represents a challenge to the ability of the EU to tailor its trade deals to the development needs of its partners. The effects of this tension are especially evident in the negotiations with labour-intensive countries with which the EU is highly integrated in global value chains. In these negotiations, the mobilization of import-dependent firms in the EU makes it less likely to engage in the promotion of costly social standards.

Notes

1 The Lisbon Treaty (enforced in 2009) establishes exclusive competences of the EU concerning investment liberalization. Negotiations for the EU–Korea agreement started before the enforcement of the treaty. Thus, the European Commission did not have the mandate to negotiate provisions concerning an ISDS.
2 Both in Singapore and Vietnam NGOs have started proliferating the 1990s. In 1991 the Minister of Information and the Art in Singapore formally promulgated the concept of civil society (Lee 2002). Yet, the People's Action Party, which won each election since 1959, maintained strict restrictions on NGOs, especially those involved in human right promotion (Ortman 2015). In Vietnam, instead, the Communist Party does not officially recognize the use of the concept of civil society, and consider it a Western concept (interview, Research Institution, Hanoi, January 2015).
3 Addo (2015) effectively synthetizes the terms of the debate about the sustainable development versus protectionist implications of the inclusion of labour standards in trade agreements.

References

Addo, K. (2015). *Core Labour Standards and International Trade: Lessons from the Regional Context*. New York: Springer.
Bailey, D. and Bossuyt, F. (2013). 'The European Union as a conveniently-conflicted counter-hegemon through trade', *Journal of Contemporary Political Research*, 9(4): 561–577.

Bauer, M. (2016). 'The political power of evoking fear: the shining example of Germany's anti-TTIP campaign movement', *European View*, 15(2): 193–212.

Cooper, W. H., Jurenas, R. and Platzer, M. D. (2011). 'EU–South Korea Free Trade Agreement and Its Implications for the United States', Report, Congressional Research Service, 7-5700.

Copenhagen Economics and Joe Francois (2007). 'A quantitative analysis of a potential Free Trade Agreement between the EU and South Korea', study prepared for the European Commission, DG Trade, Brussels.

De Bièvre, D. and Eckhardt, J. (2011). 'Interest groups and EU anti-dumping policy', *Journal of European Public Policy*, 18(3), 339–360.

Eckhardt, J. and Poletti, A. (2016). 'The politics of global value chains: import-dependent firms and EU–Asia trade agreements', *Journal of European Public Policy*, 23(10), 1543–1562.

Elsig, M. and Dupont, C. (2012). 'European Union meets South Korea: bureaucratic interests, exporter discrimination and the negotiations of trade agreements', *Journal of Common Market Studies*, 50(3): 492–507.

ETUC (2010). 'EU Trade Commissioner and ETUC's General Secretary discuss labour standards and trade policy', Press release, Brussels, 13/04/2010.

EU (2017). *European Union by Topics*. Trade. https://europa.eu/european-union/topics/trade_en.

EU Delegation to Vietnam (2016). *Guide to the EU-Vietnam Free Trade Agreement*, June, http://trade.ec.europa.eu/doclib/docs/2016/june/tradoc_154622.pdf.

European Commission (2006). *Global Europe: Competing in the World*, COM (2006) 567 final, 4 October.

European Commission (2010). *Results of the industry consultation from 2010 on a possible EU Singapore trade Agreement*, http://trade.ec.europa.eu.

European Commission (2012). *Trade, growth and development Tailoring trade and investment policy for those countries most in need*, Final Communication to the Parliament, the Council and the European Economic and Social Committee, SEC(2012) 87 final.

European Commission (2015). Trade for all. Towards a more responsible trade and investment policy, 14 October, http://trade.ec.europa.eu/doclib/docs/2015/october/tradoc_153846.pdf.

Falkner, R. (2007). 'The political economy of "normative power" Europe: EU environmental leadership in international biotechnology regulation', *Journal of European Public Policy*, 14(4): 507–526.

Feliu, L. and Serra, F. (2015). 'The European Union as a "normative power" and the normative voice of the European Parliament', in S. Stavridis and D. Irrera (Eds.), *The European Parliament and Its International Relations* (pp. 17–34), London: Routledge.

FIDH (2007). Position Paper on Economic Partnership Agreements (EPA) and Human Rights, June, https://www.fidh.org/IMG/pdf/APE_final_eng.pdf.

Garcia, M. and Masselot, A. (2015). 'EU-Asia Free Trade Agreements as tools for social norm/legislation transfer', *Asia Europe Journal*, 13(3): 241–252.

Healy, T. (2015). 'Canadian and European Unions and the Canada-EU CETA negotiations', in A. Bieler, B. Ciccaglione, J. Hilary and I. Lindberg (Eds.), *Free Trade and Transnational Labour* (pp. 59–70), London and New York: Routledge.

Heron, T. (2011). 'Asymmetric bargaining and development trade-offs in the CARIFORUM-European Union Economic Partnership Agreement', *Review of International Political Economy*, 18(3): 328–357.

Heron, T. (2014). 'Trading in development: norms and institutions in the making/unmaking of European Union–African, Caribbean and Pacific trade and development cooperation', *Contemporary Politics*, 20(1): 10–22.

Heron, T. (2016). 'Trading in development: norms and institutions in the making/unmaking of European Union-African, Caribbean and Pacific trade and development cooperation', in M. Carbone and J. Orbie (Eds.), *The Trade–Development Nexus in the European Union: Differentiation, Coherence and Norms* (pp. 10–12), London and New York: Routledge.

Hilary, J. (2014). 'European trade unions and free trade: between international solidarity and perceived self-interest', *Globalizations*, 11(1): 47–57.

Hoang, H. H. (2016). 'Normative power Europe through trade: Vietnamese perceptions', *International Relations*, 30(2): 176–205.

Hoang, H. H. and Sicurelli, D. (2017). 'The EU's preferential trade agreements with Singapore and Vietnam. Market vs. normative imperatives', *Contemporary Politics*, 1(19): 369–387.

Kelemen, D. and Vogel, D. (2010). 'Trading places: the role of the United States and the European Union in international environmental politics', *Comparative Political Studies*, 43(4): 427–456.

Khorana, S. and Garcia, M. (2013). 'European Union–India trade negotiations: one step forward, one back?', *Journal of Common Market Studies*, 51(4): 684–700.

Langan, M. (2014). 'Decent work and indecent trade agendas: the European Union and ACP countries', *Contemporary Politics*, 20(1): 23–35.

Langan, M. (2016). *The Moral Economy of EU Association with Africa*, London and New York: Routledge.

Lavenex, S. (2014). 'The power of functionalist extension: how EU rules travel', *Journal of European Public Policy*, 21(6): 885–903.

Lee, T. (2002). 'The politics of civil society in Singapore', *Asian Studies Review*, 26: 97–117.

Manners, I. (2002). 'Normative power Europe? A contradiction in terms?', *Journal of Common Market Studies*, 40(2): 235–258.

Manners, I. (2009a). 'The EU's normative power in changing world politics', in A. Gerrits (Ed.), *Normative Power Europe in a Changing World: A Discussion* (pp. 9–24). The Hague: Netherlands Institute of International Relations.

Manners, I. (2009b). 'The social dimension of EU trade policies: reflections from a normative power perspective', *European Foreign Affairs Review*, 14(5): 785–803.

McKenzie, L. and Meissner, K. L. (2017). 'Human rights conditionality in European Union trade negotiations: the case of the EU–Singapore FTA', *Journal of Common Market Studies*, 55(4): 832–849.

Ortman, S. (2015). 'Political change and civil society coalitions in Singapore', *Government and Opposition*, 50(1): 119–139.

Poletti, A. and Sicurelli, D. (2012). 'The EU as a promoter of environmental norms in the Doha round', *West European Politics*, 35(4): 911–932.

Poletti, A. and Sicurelli, D. (2016). 'The European Union, preferential trade agreements, and the international regulation of sustainable biofuels', *Journal of Common Market Studies*, 54(2): 249–266.

Price, S. and Nunn, A. (2016). 'Managing neo-liberalisation through the sustainable development agenda: the EU-ACP trade relationship and world market expansion', *Third World Thematics: A TWQ Journal*, 1(4): 454–469.

Sicurelli, D. (2015a). 'The EU as a promoter of human rights in bilateral trade agreements: the case of the negotiations with Vietnam', *Journal of Contemporary European Research*, 11 (2): 230–245.

Sicurelli, D. (2015b). 'The EU as a norm promoter through trade. The perceptions of Vietnamese elites', *Asia Europe Journal*, 13(1): 23–39.

Siles-Brügge, G. (2011). 'Resisting protectionism after the crisis: strategic economic discourse and the EU–Korea free trade agreement', *New Political Economy*, 6(5): 627–653.

Siles-Brügge, G. (2014a). *Constructing European Union Trade Policy: A Global Idea of Europe*, Basingstoke: Palgrave Macmillan.

Siles-Brügge, G. (2014b). 'EU trade and development policy beyond the ACP: subordinating developmental to commercial imperatives in the reform of GSP', *Contemporary Politics*, 20(1): 49–62.

Siles-Brügge, G. (2014c). 'Resisting "Protectionism": The EU–Korea Free Trade Agreement', in G. Siles-Brügge (Ed), *Constructing European Union Trade Policy: A Global Idea of Europe* (pp. 97–124), Basingstoke: Palgrave Macmillan.

Taylor, I. (2016). 'Bait and switch: the European Union's incoherency towards Africa', *Insight on Africa*, 8(2): 1–16.

Trommer, S. (2014). 'Legal opportunity in trade negotiations: international law, opportunity structures and the political economy of trade agreements', *New Political Economy*, 19(1): 1–20.

UNDP (2014). Human and Trade Development. Central Asia Human Development Series. Report, available at http://hdr.undp.org/sites/default/files/ca_trade_and_hd_paper_eng_web_2.pdf.pdf.

Van den Hoven, A. (2006). 'European Union regulatory capitalism and multilateral trade negotiations', in S. Lucarelli and I. Manners (Eds.), *Values and Principles in European Foreign Policy* (pp. 185–200). London and New York: Routledge.

Woolcock, S. (2014). 'Differentiation within reciprocity: the European Union approach to preferential trade agreements', *Contemporary Politics*, 20(1): 36–48.

Young, A. R. (2007). 'Trade Politics ain't what it used to be: the European Union in the Doha Round', *Journal of Common Market Studies*, 45(4): 789–811.

Young, A. and Peterson, J. (2014). *Parochial Global Europe: 21st Century Trade Politics*, Oxford: Oxford University Press.

6 Is China colonizing Africa?

Africa–China relations in a shifting Global Economic Governance system

Adams Bodomo

Introduction

China's twenty-first century foray into Africa is marked and defined to the international world not so much by the two parties but by more than one decade of Western responses, even criticisms of China's activities in Africa (Berger and Wissenbach 2007; Wissenbach 2008, 2009; Bodomo 2009, 2010). Africa–China relations are thus defined and determined not just by Africa and China but also by Western reactions to the relation between them. To Westerners and some Africans, China's Africa foreign policy often appears as a new form of economic imperialism (e.g. Games 2005), as a pure capitalist investment (e.g. Hilsum 2006) or as a neo-colonial venture (e.g. Jack Straw's speech in 2006 and Sanusi 2013).[1]

This chapter argues that framing China's Africa foreign policy by using dichotomous and oppositional categories – such as those of generous/self-interested; genuine/covetous; cooperative/exploitative; or inclusive/unilateral – is ill-suited to describe not only one of the most complex and successful country-to-region cooperation experiences in contemporary international relations, but also one of the most significant manifestations of the paradigmatic shift that China is bringing to the Global Economic Governance (GEG) system.

The colonialism/neocolonialism charge

Is China colonizing Africa? After more than two decades of intense Africa–China relations, what was initially seen as a non-issue has become one of the most recurrent research questions in contemporary International Relations and Development Studies. Even a cursory search on the internet and a cursory look at both academic and non-academic literature could produce a list of articles openly alluding to Chinese colonialism, neo-colonialism or new colonialism (see, for instance, Junbo 2007; Esposito et al. 2014; Esposito and Tse 2015).

An obvious starting point to answer the question would be defining what people mean when they talk of *colonialism* and *neo-colonialism*, especially in regards to Africa–China relations. Jian Junbo from Fudan University in Shanghai aptly summarizes a common understanding of classical colonialism as beginning from the 15th century [and] commonly consisting of foreigners *occupying* distant lands, controlling their economic and political affairs and exploiting their material resources through unfair or one-sided trade practices or simply by force. By that definition European states acted as colonizing powers in Africa and Asia, but they went far beyond colonialism through the slave trade, proxy wars, and imposing cultural norms.

Junbo, 2007

This reading of colonialism is in line with standard definitions of the term: "a political-economic phenomenon whereby various European nations explored, *conquered, settled,* and *exploited* large areas of the world";[2] a

practice of domination, which involves the subjugation of one people to another ... [Since] the term colony comes from the Latin word *colonus*, meaning farmer, the root reminds us that the practice of colonialism usually involved the *transfer of population* to a new territory, where the arrivals lived as *permanent settlers* while maintaining political allegiance to their country of origin.[3]

Colonialism was tackled by independence movements in the 1940s and 1950s in both Asia and Africa. Indigenous independent movements, often helped by the competition among superpowers in the early stages of the Cold War, managed to gain in representation, international visibility and legitimacy throughout the 1950s, at times transitioning towards peaceful and orderly national self-determination processes and at other times culminating in national revolutions and independence wars. The decolonization process in Africa and Asia resulted in national independence in most cases: between the end of the 1940s and the end of the 1970s, more than 100 new states joined the UN, most of which as a result of the decolonization process. However, the attempts to develop economically independent nation states were soon to face difficulties. Many of these countries had limited state structures left by the colonial administration, scant infrastructures, poorly qualified human resources and weak ethnic or linguistic bonds. New and mostly inexperienced government administrations often went from a period of exuberance and defiance towards the former colonial masters, through political experimentation and consolidation, only to eventually find themselves running adrift on budget, security and national cohesion problems. When many of these administrations began looking again at European countries for political and financial support, power relations between former colonizers and newly-created administrations took new, and yet not necessarily less compelling forms of exploitation – which were to become later known as *neocolonialism*. Junbo (2007) describes these new forms of power relation as

a new colonialism paradigm ... as some Western nations became new colonizing powers through capital investments and high-tech production.

This neo-colonialism embraces all aspects of classical colonialism *except* for occupying foreign lands, since all states in Africa remain technically independent. In this neo-colonialism, the exploiting power controls weaker states' economic resources and political systems and exploits their wealth under the name of liberal capitalism.

Other definitions of neocolonialism include the

subtle propagation of socio-economic and political activity by former colonial rulers aimed at reinforcing capitalism, neo-liberal globalization, and cultural subjugation of their former colonies. In a neo-colonial state, the former colonial masters ensure that the newly independent colonies remain dependent on them for economic and political direction,[4]

with some operationalizations of the concept spelling out activities such as the

retention of military bases, exploitation of resources, preferential trade treaties, imposed unification of colonies, conditional aid, and defense treaties. It also includes artificially created countries or combining countries into a group or federation.[5]

So, if we were to adopt standard definitions of *"colonialism"* and *"neocolonialism"*, where would today's China's Africa policy lie in all this? Is China a colonizing power when it engages Africa? Has China skipped the colonial stage, honing its skills at exerting economic and political influence without having to engage in any military occupation? Or has China inaugurated a new cooperation model, which eschews all the defining features of previous Africa–West international relations?

Views vary widely: academics, politicians, diplomats, journalists and self-proclaimed experts often put themselves into one of two oppositional camps – in favour or against China – hoisting their foundational flags. Many understand the Chinese venture as indeed colonialist in nature, and yet a type of benign colonialism.[6] Others are deeply suspicious of the general tendency to instrumentally use the charge of colonialism as a way of giving classical colonialism a more human reading while handing the Chinese a harsher judgement of what they would both deserve.[7]

One point that can be firmly established is that, if we compare standardly accepted definitions of *Colonialism* to the records of government officials from Jack Straw to Sanusi Lamido Sanusi (2013), one would legitimately conclude that there is a tendency to whitewash or downplay the real nature of colonialism which involved *forcible occupation of land* followed by an often *violent occupation* accompanied by *political and military subjugation*. As obvious as it might be, it is useful recalling that, contrary to Europe, China never engaged in unilateral military activities in Africa and never set-up civilian administrations dependent from the government in Beijing.

On the other side, charges of *neocolonialism* are more difficult to assess, as China's relations with Africa do indeed fit many of neocolonialism's characterizing features. For example, Chinese nationals have come to Africa in unprecedented numbers; as Sanou Mbaye, a former senior official at the African Development Bank put it in the early 2010s

> more Chinese have come to Africa in the past ten years than Europeans in the past 400. First came Chinese from state-owned companies, but more and more arrive solo or stay behind after finishing contract work.
>
> Economist 2011

On the economic exploitation charge, it is a fact that several African countries have seen a number of civilian riots against Chinese businesses and workers, denouncing both the loss of businesses opportunities to what they perceive as unfair competition and barren entries to job opportunities reserved to Chinese nationals. On the political dependency charge, it should be noted that African diplomats often refer to a number of Chinese practices betraying how the Chinese government perceives and treats African government representatives as junior partners (Raudino 2016).

How shall we deal with the *neo-colonial* charge then? I argue that an objective and balanced way to approach the topic is to take a closer look at the historical and factual features of China's political, economic and cultural engagement in Africa. This would provide an opportunity to separate myths from facts and to concentrate on an objective evaluation of China's activities in the continent.

The roots of Africa–China relations

The Chinese presence in Africa stretches back to the fifteenth century when Admiral Zheng He sailed to the East African coast on a trading mission, opening the continent to trade exchanges with the Far East. In contemporary history, significant cooperation between Africa and China was established in the larger context of Africa–Asia relations during the 1955 Bandung Conference, which brought together for the first time most independent African and Asian countries resisting the pressure to be drawn into the Cold War. Many of these countries subsequently joined the "Nonaligned Movement", an alliance against colonialism, neo-colonialism and imperialism, which refused falling in any of the two military blocks and focused instead on economic development cooperation.

China, in the meantime, became a secondary and yet active Cold War player, in an era characterized by superpower skirmishes for ideological and economic influence in the developing world. In the 1960s, Maoist China became particularly active in Africa through foreign assistance programmes supporting socialist leaders, which paid for flagship programmes such as the prominent Tazara railway, linking the port of Dar es Salam in Tanzania to inland Zambia (Monson 2009). Because of its Cold War era economic cooperation activities in Africa, China accumulated large amounts of political capital and personal trust from many African leaders, which subsequently resulted in crucial support to

Beijing, particularly within the aegis of the UN, including during China's 1971 bid to a permanent representation within the UN Security Council (UNSC).

China's Cold War era presence in Africa was nonetheless very limited when compared to the intensified cooperation of the 1990s, which further increased since the turn of the Millennium. In 2000, China created the Forum on China–Africa Cooperation (FOCAC), a most significant event in the development of country-to-region political and economic relations.[8] This model of regional cooperation has overshadowed political and economic fora that had long existed before between Africa and its former colonial masters, such as the Franco–African summits and the Commonwealth group meetings with the UK, and has subsequently been emulated by new investment competitors from the global South, including India (Broadman 2008; Chand 2011) and Turkey (Amra, 2001; Vicky 2011).

The launch of FOCAC inaugurated a new cooperation strategy and was symptomatic of a major overhaul of Africa–China relations in the making. In those same years, China's intensified quest for oil and raw materials brought Beijing to multiply its embassies in Africa, to open dozens of Confucius Institutes and to increase the number of government-sponsored programmes, including vocational trainings and scholarships offered to African nationals.[9] While this campaign has often been portrayed by the West as a continuation of the same old European quest for raw materials, I argue that there are fundamental differences in this reinvigorated Africa–China relation. I develop this argument by outlining some of the features that allow distinguishing Chinese social and economic engagements in Africa from European and other competitors' engagements, before giving a brief exposure of what lessons these competitors can learn from China's success and what we should conclude on the colonialist/neocolonialist charge.

The nature of today's Chinese engagement in Africa

Historically, there is much truth to the claim that China's twenty-first century foray into Africa was mainly driven by its need for commodities, which were, and continue being, essential to its large manufacturing economy. Trade between Africa and China began growing exponentially in the early 2000s, when China's import of African commodities accounted for over 90% of total imports from Africa (data between 2004 and 2011), with oil and fuel accounting for the lion's share (64% of the total China–Africa trade in 2009), followed by iron ore and metals (24%) and other bulk commodities, food and other agricultural products (5%) (Raudino 2016).

In the early 2000s, Africa also provided China with profitable market access opportunities for its manufactured goods: a WB publication suggests that in 2004 as much as 87% of all Chinese exports to Africa were machinery and equipment, textile, apparel and other manufactured products (Raudino 2016). Chinese exports to Africa have also traditionally been more diversified than Chinese imports from Africa: using the Herfindahl-Hirschman index, Broadman (Broadman et al. 2007) found that Africa's exports to China are highly concentrated in a few oil- and mineral-producing states, while the same index suggested a considerably greater diversity among the main African importers of Chinese manufactured goods.

Notwithstanding the above, there are a number of reasons why the relation between Africa and China cannot simply be defined in purely commercial terms. From an historical perspective, China engaged Africa long before its economic boom of the 1990s, having promoted anti-colonial solidarity since the 1950s and having subsequently sustained many newly independent African countries in their quest for international legitimacy and recognition. China has traditionally been a staunch supporter of non-interference and avoided any direct meddling in African elections, civilian conflicts or regional wars, while nonetheless remaining an active contributor towards UN peacekeeping operations in the continent – to the point that it has today become the largest contributor of blue helmets among UNSC P5 members. Since 1949, China and Africa have reciprocally sustained their value systems in international fora, consistently advancing a developmental model that privileges "universal" economic rights over "Western-centered" human and political rights. Because of this, it would be reductive, simplistic and unfair to categorize China's engagement in Africa as purely driven by its need for resources.

What is most important, Chinese economic involvement in Africa has also evolved considerably in these last twenty years, to the point that what already represented a relative novelty in the early 2000s, can today be seen as a truly revolutionary cooperation model. This is particularly noticeable with respect to: i) focus on economic relations rather than development assistance; ii) nature of investments and efficacy of implementation; iii) conditions of engagement; and iv) discourse on equality of partnership. These features put Chinese investments partially in contrast with Western development programmes in Africa, so there necessarily has to be a comparison.

Focus on economic relations rather than development assistance

A key feature of Chinese engagement in Africa is a relatively high ratio of Foreign Direct Investments (FDI) to Official Development Assistance (ODA) and trade to ODA when compared to the West. While western ODA volumes to Africa have continued surging since decolonization, in the early 2000s China took a different path by channeling increasing resources to FDI and trade creation.

The centrality of: i) a positive Trade Balance (particularly via integration in global value chains and exports to hard currency markets); and ii) inwards FDIs (particularly via technology transfer in sectors with high value-adding potential) as key drivers of growth has been discussed for a long time in international development circles.[10] Yet, this key point has fell on deaf ears for an equally long time, and this despite the fact that a growing number of African and international economists had consistently been pointing at it.[11] As a result, while the West remained focused on traditional (grants and technical assistance) and innovative (blending financing instruments) ODA paradigms of development despite a self-professed focus on the importance of the "trade not aid" cooperation model, China was truly capitalizing on it, both in its policies and rhetoric.

This clearly emerges from investment statistics. African FDI inward flows fluctuate widely from year to year and data from different sources are often discrepant – yet, there is emerging evidence that China is turning into the single most important provider of Greenfield and Brownfield investments to Africa. In 2016, China was the largest investor in Africa by FDI flow value and the third largest by number of new FDI projects.[12] Looking at FDI stock, all metrics suggest that China is quickly approaching the US and other European leading investors; according to UNCTAD, in 2016, China had the fourth largest stock of investments (USD 35 billion) after the US (USD 64 billion), UK (USD 58 billion) and France (USD 54 billion), and before South Africa and Italy (USD 22 billion each) and India (USD 17 billion). What remains most impressive is the pace at which Chinese FDI stock in Africa is growing: +170% between 2010 and 2015, while for traditional investment partners this figure either remained in the low two-digits (US 16% and UK 23%) or moved altogether into negative territory (France –3.8%) due to the consequences of the 2008 financial crisis (UNCTAD 2017).

Trade-wise, there is no doubt that China has become the most important bilateral trading partner for the African continent – bilateral trade accounted for USD 120 billion in 2016 against USD 33 billion for the US and USD 166 billion for the whole of Europe and Central Asia.[13] While both the West and China have a heavily skewed trade balance structure with Africa – with overly positive current accounts in all African countries with the exception of few commodity exporters – as Chinese investments diversify, so does its trade structure with Africa.

Nature of investments and efficacy of implementation

Contrary to much of the Western rhetoric on Chinese investments in Africa, these have gone beyond resource extraction for a long time now: Sautman and Yan (2007) already noticed in the mid-2000s that, while roughly 75% of American FDI to Africa was concentrated in oil, 64% of Chinese FDI to Africa between 1979 and 2000 while natural resources accounted for 28% only. Today, in an average year, China invests in African constructions as much as it invests in mining, with manufacturing coming third. In absolute terms this translates into China having become the largest foreign investor in African infrastructures. Increasing investment and trade diversification in the last few years also show from China's new African partners: recently, Chinese investments have increasingly concentrated both in resource-scarce countries – such as Ethiopia, which has few resources to offer but a 100 million people-strong market – and in mature and diversified economies, including Egypt and South Africa.[14] These recent patterns are soothing criticisms from those who saw a skewed distribution of investments during the early Chinese moves in Africa, as these were mostly focused in resource-rich and industry-poor countries

Being a centralized and authoritarian polity, China enjoys an indisputable advantage in the implementation of its projects. Because of its own lack of Western-style electoral democracy and civil society participation to political life, Chinese authorities have been able to steer an incredibly ambitious administrative and economic reform agenda with an unprecedented level of effectiveness. As much human rights-based criticism as this might have attracted in the West, China managed the most stunning feat in the history of public development policies: lifting some 500 million people – roughly half of its population – out of poverty in the space of three decades: 1981–2012.[15] This could only be achieved because of Beijing's interventionist and centralized governance model: none of the most successful Western-style electoral democracies could come close to the breakneck growth rates achieved by China.

Beijing has succeeded in translating this governance, and management modality in its relation with Africa, setting up investment programmes more speedily and efficiently than most of its Western competitors.

Conditions of engagement

There has been much myth-making around the contention that Chinese investments in Africa are unconditional and without asking questions. The reality, however, is that China negotiates conditions of engagement, which are both economic and diplomatic. Most overseas Chinese investments are carried out via State-Owned Enterprises, which come with a heavy set of economic ties, including on the sourcing of all production factors: capital, machineries and labour used in Chinese investments are mostly sourced from China. Equally, there are a number of political conditions asked to African Governments, the most important being allegiance within International Organizations with respect to voting behaviour, and the "One China policy" condition, e.g. the request to oppose the recognition of Taiwan as the sovereign and independent Republic of China. The impact of Beijing's sustained diplomatic campaign in Africa has become obvious in the 1990s and 2000s: Taiwan has lost official recognition from a number of African countries and today maintains official diplomatic relations with only one country – Swaziland, renamed eSwatini in 2018; any such countries in Africa and elsewhere are under constant pressure from Beijing, which tries to woo them by offering investments and development assistance programmes.

While the sum of Western FDI stocks remains very large in Africa, and while many African countries are continuing to accept fresh, heavily conditioned Western investments, these facts do not gainsay the fact that Western conditionalities have often fired back, and that the Chinese no-political-questions-asked engagement modality has proved more successful altogether. When given an opportunity in the early 2000s, most African governments have been delighted to drop Western contractors and to embrace Chinese loans and investment offers. To this extent, it is difficult to understate the importance that decades of accumulated African resentment at externally-imposed and often arbitrary conditionalities played upon African leaders' decision on taking a new business course. Notorious cases include Angolan oil fields in the early 2000s. The recent departure of the long-time Zimbabwean leader, Robert Mugabe, will prove a testing case in verifying the future market position of China in Zimbabwe: arguably, after almost 15 years of sour relations, the UK and other Western countries are now ill-positioned to gain back their influence and economic leverage in the country.

Discourse on the equality of partnership

Beijing brings to Africa a particularly attractive and rather refreshing approach with regards to the discourse around its political and economic relations – called here a *new language of engagement*. China comes to Africa with words and phrases in its lexicon bag like "brother", "comrades in arms against neo-colonialism", "people of the developing world comparing notes", "win-win partnerships" and similar, all centering around the theme of South–South cooperation.

African leaders are not naïve. Yet, given decades of neo-colonial discourse involving former European colonial masters handing down conditionalities on its former African subjects, this approach from the Chinese government has proved rather refreshing to post-anti-imperialist movements in Africa, being indeed music in the ears of many African leaders tired of being dictated to by Western Ministries, development agencies and International Financial Institutions.

At least in its public statements, China refrains from being judgemental about the internal political machinations of African countries, as opposed to the West's socio-political conditionalities vented on proudly open information platforms. These requests often include regime change and formal democratization before large humanitarian and development programmes can be mobilized in countries with anti-West leaderships and desperate economic and humanitarian conditions, including Zimbabwe and Sudan in the recent past.

Such conditionalities create "two weights and two measures" differences with the many cases in which Western countries have done business and extended development assistance to pro-West African dictators – from Hosni Mubarak of Egypt and Omar Bongo of Gabon in the very recent past, to Paul Biya of Cameroon, Teodoro Obiang of Equatorial Guinea and Denis Sassou of the Republic of the Congo in the present. The use of such double standards has not gone unnoticed in the African civil society, which appreciates the Chinese ability to separate politics from investments and ideology from the moral imperative of meeting African people's basic needs.

China's success in Africa: lessons for other investors

Arguably, the most important lesson international investors can learn from Chinese ventures in Africa is risk taking. Prior to the era of globalization of investments, Africa was faced with what many referred to as the marginalization of Africa. The end of the Cold War in the 1990s was read by some to mean that Africa would no longer be a geopolitically-relevant region, and much less economically so. However, China read otherwise and while others appeared to be relaxing, it entered Africa in full force, also venturing into war-torn and rather unstable political economies. The result of this strategy paid off handsomely. Cases in point are Angola, Sudan and Zimbabwe, which all were embroiled in civil wars or political instability when China engaged with them and which have today become among the most important sources of Chinese imports of primary commodities as well as Beijing's key diplomatic partners in Sub-Saharan Africa.

From a moral perspective, both Africa and China have long argued that economics must supersede politics, as it could be seen as morally wrong to deny much needed investments and its attendant benefits, including employment and better standards of living, to struggling populations. Being ruled by leaders falling short of Western democratic standards should not be upheld as a formal justification to deny investments to economies in need of external stimuli. This is also in the West's own interest: as others are arguing in this volume, China's Africa investment strategy is only one leg of the multi-faceted diplomatic, economic, financial and cultural strategy that Beijing has been putting in place in the developing world with a view to advance an alternative GEG system.

While Western and Chinese international institutions – two powerful GEG shapers – may eventually come closer and work complementarily, the former group has an interest in undergoing a strong stock-taking and self-introspective exercise informed by China's extraordinarily successful expansion into Africa.

Conclusion

One of the most recurrent questions in development and international studies when looking at Africa–China relations – whether or not China is *colonizing* Africa – cannot be answered with a straight "yes" or "no" answer. Using dichotomous and oppositional categories is ill-suited to describe an intricate relation characterized by centuries of commercial and cultural exchanges and, more recently, by decades of intense political, economic and cultural engagement. This said, most scholars would agree that there is wide ground to dismiss the contention that China is *colonizing* Africa, at least in the historical meaning of the term *colonialism*. On the other hand, a discussion around Chinese *neocolonialism* certainly needs more balance.

China is strongly invested into Africa. Its fast growing economy means that China's present world share of mineral fuels import (46.5% in 2014), metal ores imports (19.8%) and metal products imports (14.1%) will continue rising for the foreseeable future, and that Beijing will continue outsourcing large portions of these from Africa (Roberts et al. 2016).[16] Remarkably, notwithstanding its attention to Africa, only about 4% of Chinese FDI outflows go to Africa, meaning that there is large room for scaling what has been done so far.[17] To this extent, there is little doubt that China will continue reshaping the African economy and rewriting the rules on profitable investments in the continent. The issue of investment is important not only in itself, but also in bringing to the fore many of the current concepts often involved in rethinking Africa–Asian relations, including soft power (Hartig 2015; van Staden 2015; Waserman 2015; Bodomo 2016), symmetry (Bodomo 2009, 2015), agency (Mohan and Lampert 2012) and exploitation (Sanusi 2013).

The original features of Chinese investments (focus on economic relations; nature of investments and efficacy of implementation; conditions of engagement, and; discourse on the equality of partnership) have shaped the African economic environment in a rather profound way, to the extent that we can talk of a paradigm shift. China is not just following in the footsteps of the West but charting a different path to investment and economic cooperation.

Undoubtedly, not all is positive in this new approach: China needs to rein in its own private companies and private individual investors and traders in Africa by coordinating and working with African governments, business associations and human right organizations to identify poor and abusive business practices and engage them. There is also a lot of room for improvement as far as the relative weight of industry engagement is concerned: China has to continue going beyond "palaces and petroleum" (Kiggundu 2011) and must do more than just speedily building infrastructures to facilitate its oil and natural resource extraction, continuing diversification into the higher echelons of agricultural processing and manufacturing, and becoming more brave in technology transfer (Li 2016). Beyond the realm of ontological reality, China also does not seem to have done a good enough job in explaining itself and justifying what it does in Africa and how it does it (Bodomo 2015, 2016, 2017).

If China can improve on these elements, it could come to play an even more effective role in the globalization of foreign investments in the decades to come, not just in Africa, but throughout the world. We might then start asking ourselves the next question: Is China (neo)colonizing the world?

Notes

1 Former British Foreign Secretary Jack Straw's address in Nigeria in February 2006 suggested that what China was doing in Africa then was much the same as Britain had done 150 years before. Former Nigerian central bank Governor Sanusi Lamido Sanusi also alluded to the same thing in 2013.
2 Enclopedia Britannica Online, available at: https://www.britannica.com/topic/colonialism (last accessed: 21 March 2018).
3 Stanford Encyclopedia of Philosophy Online, available at: https://plato.stanford.edu/entries/colonialism/ (last accessed: 21 March 2018).
4 Internet Encyclopedia of Philosophy Online, available at: www.iep.utm.edu/neocolon/ (last accessed: 21 March 2018).
5 Encyclopedia of the New American Nation Online, available at: www.americanforeignrelations.com/A-D/Colonialism-and-Neocolonialism-Neocolonialism.html (last accessed: 21 March 2018).
6 As suggested, many (in fact most) of the publicized views do not come from Africans or Chinese, but from Westerners. Many opinions emerge from anecdotal evidence; for instance, Karl Muth from Northwestern University, who witnessed

Chinese activities in Uganda in 2013 suggests that the "Chinese were seen as friendly colonizers and often compared favourably to the British … Africa, tired of begging Europe and the Americans for money, happily accepted investment from the Chinese … In essence, the difference is that, today, Africa is asking to be colonized and China has accepted the invitation". Eagle Headline Online Discussion, available at: www.eagleheadline.com/archives/566 (last accessed: 21 March 2018).

7 "Calling it colonizing kind (of) whitewashes colonization, or demonizes China's investment of Africa. Usually when we're talking about the specific colonization, we're actually talking about genocide towards natives, slave trade, forcibly converting people to Christianity … the literal colonization sounds much more peaceful and not as harmful as the historic colonization … it's a very subtle trick to call it colonizing, [because it] leaves room for the imagination that past brutal colonization is just happening in Africa, which is not true". Quora Online Discussion, available at: https://www.quora.com/Is-China-colonizing-Africa (last accessed: 21 March 2018).

8 FOCAC is a triennial gathering of African and Chinese leaders alternating between African capitals and Beijing, where China – Africa development cooperation agendas are outlined and assessed. So far there have been seven meetings: FOCAC 2000 in Beijing (Ministerial); FOCAC 2003 in Addis Ababa (Ministerial); FOCAC 2006 in Beijing (Summit); FOCAC 2009 in Sharm El Sheik (Ministerial); FOCAC 2012 in Beijing (Ministerial); FOCAC 2015 in Johannesburg (Summit); FOCAC 2018 in Beijing (Summit).

9 China has today the largest diplomatic network in Africa.

10 At Government level, former South African President Thabo Mbeki was among the first to raise the issue of FDIs during the Tokyo International Conference on African Development (TICAD) in 1998.

11 See in particular the work of Moyo (2009, 2010).

12 According to UNCTAD 2017 World Investment Reports, in 2016 China invested USD 36 billion in Greenfield projects in Africa, followed by United Arab Emirates (USD 11 billion); Morocco (USD 4.7 billion); Saudi Arabia and Italy (USD 4 billion each). In that year China also had one of the strongest Brownfield portfolio of activities (cross-border M&A) in the continent.

13 Data retrieved from WB's Database "World Integrated Trade Solutions". Available at: https://wits.worldbank.org/ (last accessed: 15 March 2018).

14 A review of total Chinese FDI flows stretching back to 2003 reveals that by 2017 Egypt had become the first recipient country; South Africa the 4th; Ethiopia the 6th and Morocco the 10th. Source: fDi market.

15 Data from the World Bank in China.

16 Concerning oil, China is getting roughly one-third of its oil needs from Africa. It is estimated that China will peak energy needs in 2040; while it is greening its economy and it is continuing purchases in West Asia (Middle East), where it is exposed to political and security volatility and a much higher competition from the US, it is foreseen that China's interest for African known reserves – the world's largest – will continue to be on the rise.

17 Indeed, in one interview to the media, the author has drawn attention to the fact that if China is said to be colonizing Africa because it is investing so much in Africa, it might also mean that China is actually colonizing the rest of the world more than it is colonizing Africa, since Chinese investments in Africa are actually less than 10% of its total global investment, the vulnerability argument notwithstanding.

References

Amra, R. (2001), 'Suleimaniye Minarets on the Midrand: Turkey's Economic Incipience in Africa', in *Perspectives on Emerging Powers in Africa*, 9. Available at: (www.pambazuka.org/images/Emerging%20Powers%20newsletter%20May%20 2011/Issue%209%20May%202011.pdf) (last accessed: 2 July 2011).

Berger, B. and Wissenbach, U. (2007), 'EU–China–Africa trilateral development cooperation: common challenges and new directions', *German Development Institute*, Discussion Paper. Available at: www.diegdi.de/CMSHomepage/openwebcms3. nsf/(ynDK_contentByKey)/ADMR7BRFHU/USD FILE/BergerWissenbachEU-China-Africa.pdf (last accessed: 6 July 2011).

Bodomo, A. (2009), 'Africa–China relations: symmetry, soft power and South Africa', *China Review*, 9(2): 169–178.

Bodomo, A. (2010), 'The African trading community in Guangzhou: an emerging bridge for Africa–China relations', *China Quarterly*, 203: 693–707.

Bodomo, A. (2011), *La Globalizacion de las Inversiones en Africa*, Madrid: Los Libros de la Catarata.

Bodomo, A. (2013), 'African diaspora remittances are better than foreign aid funds: diaspora-driven development in the 21st century', *World Economics*, 14(4): 21–28.

Bodomo, A. (2015), 'African soft power in China', *African East-Asian Affairs*, 2: 76–97.

Bodomo, A. (2016), 'The rise of Chinese soft power in Africa', China Policy Institute Blog, the University of Nottingham. Available at: http://blogs.nottingham.ac.uk/ chinapolicyinstitute/2016/03/24/the-rising-of-chinese-soft-power-in-africa/ (last accessed: 15 March 2018).

Bodomo, A. (2017), *The Globalization of Foreign Investment in Africa: The Role of Europe, China and India*, Bingley: Emerald Publishing.

Broadman, G., Isik, G., Plaza, S., Ye, X. and Yoshino, Y. (2007), *Africa Silk Road*, Washington, DC: World Bank.

Broadman, H. (2008), 'China and India go into Africa: new deals in the developing world', *Foreign Affairs*, 87(2): 95–109.

Chand, M. (2011), 'A two-way street: India brands its Africa diplomacy. Perspectives on emerging powers in Africa'. Available at: www.pambazuka.org/images/ Emerging%20Powers%20newsletter%20May%202011/Issue%209%20May%20 2011.pdf (last accessed: 2 July 2011).

Economist (2011), 'The Chinese in Africa – Trying to pull together'.

Esposito, M. and Tse, T. (2015), 'China in Africa: a modern story of colonization?', *EconoMonitor*. Available at: www.economonitor.com/blog/2015/10/is-africa-becoming-chinas-new-derivatives-a-modern-story-of-colonization/ (last accessed: 18 April 2018).

Esposito, M., Tse, T. and Al-Sayed M. (2014), 'Recolonizing Africa: a modern Chinese story?' *CNBC news*. Available at: www.cnbc.com/2014/12/30/recolonizing-africa-a-modern-chinese-story.html (last accessed: 18 April 2016).

Fang, X. (2008), 'Sino-European cooperation: opportunities and challenges', Shanghai Institute of International Studies.

Games, D. (2005), 'Chinese the new economic imperialists in Africa', *Business Day,* February.

Hartig, F. (2015), 'Confucius institutes in Africa – a new soft power instrument in the making?', Paper read at the Afraso Conference on Africa – Asia Encounters, Cape Town, March 24–26.

Hilsum, L. (2006), 'China's offer to Africa: pure capitalism', *New Statesman*. Available at: https://www.newstatesman.com/node/164688 (last accessed: 15 March 2018).

Junbo, J. (2007), 'From capitalism to colonialism', *Asia Times Online*. Available at: www.atimes.com/atimes/China/IA05Ad01.html (last accessed: 15 March 2018).

Kiggundu, M. N. (2011), 'China's economic relations with Africa: beyond palaces and petroleum', Paper presented at the Oxfam HKU Workshop on Africa – China Relations, May.

Li, A. (2016), 'Technical assistance and technology transfer between China and Africa from TAZARA to Huawei', Manuscript, Peking University.

Mohan, G. and Lampert, B. (2012), 'Negotiating China: Reinserting African agency into China–Africa relations', *African Affairs*, 112(446): 92–110.

Monson, J. (2009), *Africa's Freedom Railway: How a Chinese Development Project Changed Lives and Livelihoods in Tanzania*, Bloomington: Indiana University Press.

Moyo, D. (2009), *Dead Aid: Why Aid Is Not Working and How There is Another Way for Africa*, New York: Farrar, Straus and Giroux.

Moyo, D. (2010), *How the West Was Lost: Fifty Years of Economic Folly – And the Stark Choices that Lie Ahead*, New York: Farrar, Straus and Giroux.

Mwesigwa, B. (2008), 'Africa–China–EU relations: a view from Africa', Shanghai Institute of International Studies.

Raudino, S. (2016), *Development Aid and Sustainable Economic Growth in Africa: The Limits of Western and Chinese Engagements*, London: Palgrave MacMillan.

Roberts, C. I., Saunders T., Spence, G. and Cassidy, N. (2016), 'China's evolving demand for commodities', in *Structural Change in China: Implications for Australia and the World*, Conference Proceeding, Sydney: Reserve Bank of Australia.

Sanusi, L. (2013), 'Africa must get real about Chinese ties', *Financial Times*. Available at: www.ft.com/cms/s/0/562692b0-898c-11e2-ad3f-00144feabdc0.html#axzz476hHV2XM (last accessed: 11 March 2013).

Sautman, B. and Yan, H. (2007), 'Wind from the East: China and Africa's Development', in NGOs Conference on China in Africa, Shanghai.

UNCTAD (2017), *World Investment Report 2017: Investment and the Digital Economy, United Nations Publication*. Available at: http://unctad.org/en/PublicationsLibrary/wir2015_en.pdf (last accessed: 15 March 2018).

Van Staden, C. (2015), 'Hostile imaginaries: internet activism, the poaching controversy and Chinese soft power in Africa', Paper read at the Afraso Conference on Africa–Asia Encounters, Cape Town, March 24–26.

Vicky, A. (2011), 'Turkey moves into Africa', *Le Monde Diplomatique*. Available at: http://mondediplo.com/2011/05/08turkey (last accessed: 4 July 2011).

Wassermann, H. (2015), 'China–Africa media contestations and collaborations', Paper read at the Afraso Conference on Africa–Asia Encounters, Cape Town, March 24–26.

Wissenbach, U. (2008), *The Renaissance or the End of Geopolitics? Towards Trilateral Cooperation in Africa*, Shanghai: Institute of International Studies. Available at: www.siis.org.cn/Sh_Yj_Cms/Mgz/200802/2008928113740SY6K.PDF (last accessed: 15 March 2018).

Wissenbach, U. (2009), 'The EU's response to China's Africa safari: can triangulation match needs?', *European Journal of Development Research,* 21(4): 662–674.

7 Economic crises and political downturns in South America

Are MERCOSUR's neoliberal roots a constraint on Human Development?

Roberto Lampa

Introduction

This chapter investigates the political and economic dynamics that contributed to trigger fast changes in MERCOSUR's recent past (2013–2016): on the one hand, GDP contraction or stagnation, fiscal adjustments, increasing unemployment, capital flight, external constraints on the BoP and, therefore, sharp devaluations among member states' currencies (CEPAL 2016). On the other hand, the end of the "second wave of incorporation" by left governments in Argentina and Brazil[1] and the regressive changes in Uruguay's economic policy,[2] highlighting sudden developments in the political economy of the sub-regional alliance (IMF 2015a; INE 2017; World Bank 2017). The chapter suggests that, in the period 2003–2012, the inherent tensions between the redistributive national policies of Argentina, Brazil and Uruguay on the one side, and MERCOSUR's hyper-liberal trade, fiscal and monetary policies on the other, produced contradictory and yet positive outcomes. This was mostly possible thanks to the positive external juncture that lasted till 2012.

Beginning in the early 2000s, domestic economic policies inspired by neo-developmentalist (particularly in Brazil) and structuralist (particularly in Argentina) recipes sustained the national aggregate demand of most MERCOSUR countries by means of either fiscal expansionary policies or subsidized consumption, including via concessionary utility tariffs and free access to healthcare and education. During this period, most MERCOSUR governments implemented cash transfer programmes such as the *Asignación Universal por Hijo* in Argentina, the *Bolsa Familia* in Brazil and the *Astori Tributary Reform* in Uruguay, often matched with a robust fiscal stimulus. In the Argentinian case, these measures were complemented with a new attempt to implement import substitution, whereas in Uruguay an ambitious tax reform served as a key redistributive tool. These policies generally resulted in sustained and prolonged growth and a dramatic reduction of poverty; yet, the expansion of consumption and investments also caused an increased need for hard currency reserves to pay for imports.

Since the mid 1990s, MERCOSUR had however been following the theoretical recipe known as "open-regionalism" or *regionalismo abierto* (CEPAL 1994), heavily inspired by orthodox economic theory, whereby "competitiveness" and "internal and external equilibria" were portrayed as the most important goals. Open regionalism assumed that regional integration and South–South cooperation might have been useful only provided that they did not affect the openness of South American economies to non-regional economies, in order to benefit from so-called open-market globalization policies. In turn, such a relatively high degree of openness implied both the financialization[3] – particularly in Brazil (Bin 2016; Lavinas 2016) – and trans-nationalization[4] of member state economies. These phenomena ignited at their own turn a steady outflow of capitals, which quickly depleted the foreign national reserves of MERCOSUR central banks (Gaggero 2011; Gaggero et al. 2013; IMF 2015a).

Such contradictory forces had not generated major drawbacks in the period 2003–2012 because: i) the terms of trade were favourable to MERCOSUR countries; ii) the out-regional demand – mainly Chinese – for MERCOSUR products remained robust and; iii) the Latin American balance of capital remained in positive territory as a consequence of strong international commodity prices balancing an increasing outflow of foreign reserves due to increased domestic consumption. However, as soon as the external scenario worsened in 2012, increasing legal capital outflows and illegal capital flight on the one side, and a sharp decrease in Foreign Direct Investment (FDI) and Foreign Portfolio Investments (FPI) inflows on the other, led to a severe external constraint on the BoP of the main sub-regional economies, including Argentina.

In 2013–2016, such a deteriorating economic outlook inescapably affected the popularity of the progressive national governments that had been in charge for a decade, including *Frente para la Victoria* in Argentina; *Partido dos Trabalhadores* in Brazil and; *Frente Amplio* in Uruguay. At this stage, the December 2015 electoral success of the right wing government of Mauricio Macri in Argentina and the 2016 soft *coup d'état* carried out in Brazil by a conservative coalition led by Michel Temer, paved the way for severe fiscal adjustments; devaluations and; fiscal austerity policies aimed at undoing many of the inclusionary social policies of the previous fifteen years.

One of the questions surfacing among Latin American researchers is how the successful socio-economic results achieved during those fifteen years could be reversed so quickly. Notoriously, the trade structure of MERCOSUR economies is heavily dependent upon commodity exports, suffering from periodic cycles of volatility. As bull-bear cycles in international commodity markets are notorious problems marring the BoP of economies relying on the primary sector,[5] one would have expected MERCOSUR regional coordination and institutional reforms to complement the redistributive and demand-oriented policies of MERCOSUR member countries with the exporting needs of the block. Instead, a lack of regional initiative left the important social achievements of the progressive governments of Brazil (Lula and Rousseff, 2003–2016), Argentina (Nestor and Cristina Kirchner, 2003–2015) and Uruguay (Tabaré Vazquez and José Mujica, 2004–2015), extremely vulnerable to a worsening external scenario. A different institutional framework, including an effective implementation of the *Banco del Sur*, a monetary fund established in 2009 with the aim of lending hard currency to member states to prevent recurrent BoP crises, could have avoided some of the most damaging consequences of the external shocks that hit the region since the 2008 financial crisis, while also constraining the implementation of unilateral and uncoordinated national austerity policies.

The chapter is structured as follows: section II recalls the most important social achievements of MERCOSUR countries in the period 2003–2012 (while showing the political changes that made possible such achievements) together with the sudden stop of 2013–2016, which eventually turned into a change in the political cycle in Argentina and Brazil. Section III explores the hypothesis that the crises of several MERCOSUR countries after 2013 might be a product of the inconsistences between the aims of the national policies of these member states and the lack of regional institutions able to guarantee the compatibility between these national policies and the external economic scenario. From this perspective, we recognize two different stages: a first period (2003–2012) in which a positive external conjuncture allowed almost all MERCOSUR governments to pay for redistributive and demand-led policies and; a second period (2013–2016) characterized by a sharp deterioration of the international outlook, which, along with the lack of a regional framework protecting and coordinating national policies, entailed a rapid deterioration of the economic fundamentals of MERCOSUR national economies. Finally, section IV draws some conclusions about the limits of the progressive policies and expansionary business cycles that characterized MERCOSUR in the past decade, suggesting some possible lines of institutional reform.

Economic growth and Human Development in 2003–2016: mixed progress and new crises

Broadly speaking, all MERCOSUR countries experienced similar economic trends during the so-called progressive cycle that began in 2003. During a first phase until 2011–2012, good economic performances guaranteed robust growth and meaningful advances in terms of *Human Development*. In a second phase, the deterioration of the external scenario determined a reversal of such an expansionary tendency, which eventually turned into a severe crisis in 2015, bringing to an end the progressive cycle.

In the 2003–2014 period, Brazilian GDP per capita grew at an annual rate of 2.5%; poverty decreased from 35.8% of the population to 15.9% in 2012; extreme poverty from 15.2% to 5.3%. Accordingly, 31.5 million Brazilians (of which 16 million were in extreme poverty) exited poverty during the first decade of the *Partido dos Trabalhadores'* administrations (Weisbrot et al. 2014). In particular, the *Bolsa Família*[6] represented 60% of the income for the population in extreme poverty and 17.6% for the people in poverty. In addition, the share of GDP dedicated to education spending[7] increased from 4.6% of GDP in 2003 to 6.1% in 2011. Accordingly, the Gini index fell from 0.59 to 0.53 and unemployment (which reached 13.0% in 2003) decreased to 5.4% in 2013. Nevertheless, after growing at a rate of 7.6% in 2010, the subsequent year the Brazilian economy entered a recessionary period. Economic growth slowed down to 3.9% in 2011, 1.8% in 2012 and 2.7% in 2013. In 2014, Brazil grew only at a rate of 0.1%, entering into recession for two consecutive quarters (Serrano and Summa 2015).

While these trends were mostly due to the worsening international economic conditions – as witnessed by the sharp decline in the average annual growth of exports in the 2011–2014 and 2004–2010 periods, respectively 1.6% and 5.2% – the macro prudential measures, implemented by the Rousseff government in response to this external scenario, further fuelled them. In particular, the rate of growth of real disposable income fell from 5.3% in 2004–2010 to 1.2% in 2011–2014 (Serrano and Summa 2015). As a result, for the first time in over a decade, the Gini index increased from 0.559 to 0.567 in 2011–2012, whereas extreme poverty also went up from 5.4% to 5.9% in 2012–2013 (Economic Commission for Latin America and the Caribbean (ECLAC) stat). From this perspective, the institutional crisis begun in 2015 and culminated with the parliamentary coup of 2016 determined both a change in the political cycle and a further worsening of the economic outlook. GDP decreased by –3.5% in both 2015 and 2016; unemployment peaked to 13.4% in 2017 (from 6.8% in 2014). The WB recently estimated that – from the beginning of 2016 to the end of 2017 – 2.5 to 3.6 million Brazilians have fallen back into poverty (World Bank 2017).

Coming from the catastrophic crisis of 2001, the Argentinian economy also experienced a dramatic growth of 63% during the years 2004–2014.[8] More importantly, poverty decreased from almost half of the population in 2001 (45.5%) to approximately one-seventh of the population in 2010 (14.3%). Extreme poverty also experienced a sharp decline, from almost one-third of the population in 2001 (29.2%) to approximately one in fifteen in 2010 (6.6%). The Gini index showed a similar trend, decreasing from 0.54 (in 2002) to 0.44 (in 2011). In the same years, unemployment fell from 18.4% to 8%. (Weisbrot et al. 2011). In those same years, the "Universal Allocation per Child" (*Asignación Universal por Hijo*), a social programme aimed at reducing poverty vastly reduced child mortality (Weisbrot et al. 2011). However, in 2012–2015, the unfavourable change in the external scenario severely affected the Argentinian economy, determining a (almost) zero economic growth, as a result of the alternation between two years of recession (2012, –1.9%; 2014, –2.6%) and two years of recovery (2.3% in 2014; 2.1% in 2015). This alternation was determined essentially by the trend of public expenditures (which decreased in 2012 and 2014 and, vice versa, increased in 2013 and 2015), since both investments (–1%) and exports (–8.7%) contracted in this period.[9] The predictable consequences were an increase in poverty and extreme poverty between 2013 and 2014, from 18% to 20.6% and from 4.3% to 5% respectively, and a lack of progress in the distribution of income (0.423%) between 2012 and 2014, notwithstanding the capital controls introduced in 2012 and the increase in social expenditures.[10] The change in the political cycle of December 2015 (Macri's presidency) determined a further worsening of such economic outlook: in 2016 GDP contracted by 2.3% and inflation peaked to 40.3% (the highest in the past fourteen years), determining a remarkable increase in poverty rates (+3.9%) (UCA 2017).

Finally, Uruguay also displayed similar dynamics. The country's social indicators were seriously affected by the economic recession of 1999–2002 (Ibáñez presidency; neoliberal "Colorado" administration), as shown by *Human Development* analyses (UNDP 2013): in 2004 the education poverty rate[11] got to its highest level (65.8%), the housing crowding rate peaked to 23.4%, and the durable goods index[12] reflected the severe consequences of the crisis by getting to a rate of 0.54[13] in 2006. However, since the political change of 2005 (Tabaré Vazquez presidency; centre-leftist "*Frente Amplio*" administration) Uruguay dramatically improved both social conditions and social inclusion, as shown by a drop in the poverty rate (12.4%) and extreme poverty being almost eradicated (0.5%) by 2012 (IMF 2015b). Accordingly, the number of children below the poverty line shrank to 25% in 2011 (OECD 2014). The Gini index showed a similar trend, decreasing to 0.379 in 2012, whereas unemployment and vulnerable employment rates dropped to 5.5% (the minimum historical value) and 22% respectively. Finally, the education poverty rate fell to 59.8%; the housing crowding rate dropped to 13.73% and the durable goods index shrank to 0.18. Nevertheless, such promising trends significantly slowed down in the following years. Extreme poverty remained unvaried in 2013, decreasing to 0.3% in 2014 and 2015 and, eventually, to 0.2% in 2016. Poverty initially contracted in 2013 (11.5%) and 2014 (9.7%) but stagnated in the following two years. At the same time, the job market was characterized by a meaningful increase in both unemployment and vulnerable employment rates: in 2016, they reached 7.8% and 25.3% respectively. Furthermore, the Gini index showed an increase in the country's inequality, getting to 0.386 in 2015 and rebounding to 0.383 in 2016 (INE 2017). Nevertheless, it is important to stress that Uruguay never entered a recession: differently from Brazil and Argentina, its worst performance was an extremely moderate GDP growth in 2015 (+0.37%).[14]

By way of conclusion, it can be said that, with the partial exception of Uruguay, after 2012 there was a sharp change in the economic policies of the region, which had a strong impact on economic performances and HDI levels. Because this change was also inspired by a changing external scenario, the following paragraphs investigate how both national and regional institutions in the MERCOSUR region were dealing with such external scenario.

Open regionalism as a constraint on Latin America's growth sustainability

CEPAL (1994: 8–12) defines "open regionalism" or *regionalismo abierto* as

> a process of increasing economic interdependence on a regional scale, promoted by means of either preferential agreements or specific policies, carried out in a context of increasing *openness* and *deregulation*, aimed at increasing the competitiveness of regional countries as well as achieving an international economy *more open* and *transparent* ... The *final purpose of* open regionalism is that integration policies *become both compatible and complementary* to the economic policies aimed at *increasing international competitiveness*.

From the mid-1990s until the change in the political cycle in the early 2000s, Latin America has often been portrayed as America's backyard, as well as a sort of laboratory for Washington's foreign and economic policies. This is most emblematically visible in Washington's grip on Latin American economies, with most regional trade initiatives being shaped at the White House, the Department of State and the Department of Commerce and subsequently conveyed to capitals in South America.

The most evident episode in this regard might have been the first Summit of the Americas in Miami, in 1994, which discussed for the first time the creation of a new Regional Trade Agreement (RTA), the Free Trade Area of the Americas (FTAA). The FTAA was understood as an expansion of the North American Free Trade Agreement (NAFTA), whereby it was proposed to eliminate or reduce trade barriers among all countries of the America with the exception of Cuba.

It is important to note how the March 1998 FTAA Ministerial Meeting in San José, Costa Rica, had already emphasized how "the FTAA *can co-exist with bilateral and sub-regional agreements*, to the extent that the rights and obligations under these agreements are not covered by or go beyond the rights and obligations of the FTAA" (Carranza 2003: 1030). The relations between MERCOSUR and the US were formalized by the "four plus one" agreements in 1991, which led to the creation of the *Consejo Consultivo sobre Comercio e Inversión* (Consultative Council on Commerce and Investment) of MERCOSUR. Negotiations between MERCOSUR countries and the US on participation in the FTAA were no longer held by each individual country but organized exclusively through this joint council (Fernández-Jilberto and Hogenboom 1997). In addition, the FTAA was aimed at locking-in a deeper economic integration agenda that, if implemented, would have amounted to a virtual free trade area between the Latin American and US economies. Complementarily, and additionally to WTO regulations, the institutional changes of the new RTA would have reasonably removed all existing barriers to US Foreign Direct Investments (FDI) in the region, thus opening the Latin American markets to a wide range of US service industries (Carranza 2003). These factors suggest that sub-regional agreements played a pivotal role within the broader US economic strategy for Latin America, since the liberalization and openness of South American economies represented a first step towards the introduction of neoliberal rules at the continental level (Escudero 1992; Alvarez 2011).[15]

In this scenario, the birth of MERCOSUR (1991–1995) should not be seen as a stand-alone project of regional integration. It was, firstly and foremostly, a specific "USD 50 billion bet" (Schott 2001) that US companies made on the future of South American economies, since MERCOSUR's destiny was to be absorbed by the FTAA.[16] But it was also, more comprehensively, conceived by the US as part and parcel of its neoliberal-inspired foreign policy agenda among low- and mid-income countries, commonly known as Washington Consensus[17] (Ferrer 1996; Gardini 2007, 2010).

Several domestic factors pushed MERCOSUR governments in accepting the neo-liberal credo in those years. The severe hyperinflation crises that hit Brazil and Argentina between 1989 and 1990 had produced a widespread mistrust towards structuralist economic policies (Sember and Vernengo forthcoming).[18] Vice versa, the effective – at least in the very short-term – monetary stabilization achieved by means of fix exchange rates and commercial openess (since imported goods were cheaper than domestic ones) determined a favourable change of climate towards neoliberal reforms. As a result of these domestic political dynamics, both Brazil and Argentina had already adopted an impressive amount of pro-market reforms before the birth of MERCOSUR. In this context, MERCOSUR was seen as a powerful tool to both deepen and accelerate the ongoing neoliberal transformation of these economies (Manzetti 1993). Therefore, far away from being a mere external imposition on South American governments, MERCOSUR should be interpreted as the result of two convergent agendas, "from within" and "from without" the continent: MERCOSUR was the result of broader changes at the international level *and* of the neo-liberal policies of Presidents Menem of Argentina and Collor of Brazil (Gardini 2007).[19]

By virtue of provisions contained in the MERCOSUR agreement, the degree of openness of member countries rose sharply. The new international trade regulations implied the convergence to a binding common external tariff vis-à-vis the rest of the world's goods and services, as well as the liberalization of intra-member trade, despite the reluctance of both the primary and secondary sectors in Brazil and Argentina, which caused delayed and incomplete implementations (Gardini 2006). At the same time, financial deregulations played a pivotal role: when the mobility of capitals became operative, with no gradualism allowed by the agreements, both the currencies' exchange rates and the net position of the BoP became deeply reliant upon the inflow of short-term capitals, as also evidenced by the severe consequences of the 1994 Mexican *Tequila crisis* on the Argentinian and Uruguayan economies.[20] Increased reliance on short-term flows of foreign capitals limited the room for expansionary fiscal policies, since in peripheral countries financial investors associate a higher fiscal stimulus to a higher expected inflation. In turn, a higher inflation is associated to a forthcoming devaluation (because, otherwise, inflation would imply a lower real exchange rate, reducing the country's competitiveness), which would inescapably affect their capital gains (being the initial investment denominated in local currency).[21] Finally, the new agreement also imposed a quasi-perfect mobility of labour.

The new political scenario determined by the birth of MERCOSUR also had repercussions on the economic debate: across the region, the traditional *structuralist approach* was surpassed by the rise of *neoclassical economics*. The United Nations Economic Commission for Latin America and the Caribbean (*Comisión Económica para América Latina y el Caribe* – CEPAL) was inevitably affected by the new climate: since the new political scenario was highly unfavourable to economic heterodoxy and hostile to classic CEPAL formulations,[22] the new director Gert Rosenthal – an experienced conservative diplomat appointed in 1988 – acknowledged the neoliberal reforms implemented by national governments in the region, although he opposed some specific elements (Ocampo 2000; Bielschowsky 2009).

In Rosenthal's view, the traditional (*structuralist*) Import Substitution Industrialization (ISI) approach developed by CEPAL in the 1960s was biased by an anti-export and anti-rural prejudice. In light of such a prejudice, CEPAL works had become rather repetitive: ISI, for instance, had been maintained for much longer than the circumstances warranted.[23] Instead, in Rosenthal's eyes, the increased degree of openness of the main economies of the region had proved to be effective in moderating both fiscal and monetary policies and, therefore, in contrasting hyperinflation in the late 1980s, notwithstanding a sharp increase in inequality (Rosenthal 1996). Such a view was expressed in detail in a 1994 document – entirely authored by Rosenthal (Bielschowsky 2009) – which can be legitimately considered as the *Manifesto* of CEPAL's new course.

Underpinning this new course was the concept of open regionalism, namely the idea that both a higher degree of global openness and a deeper regional integration were necessary elements to ripe the benefits of "globalization". Hence, the term "regionalism" did not underscore the need to reduce the *openness* of South American economies. Quite the contrary, in CEPAL's view, regional agreements were to be conceived as tools to further integrate (already) *open economies in a more liberalized and transparent economic order* (CEPAL 1994: 23). From this perspective, economic growth was essentially seen as the result of the benign influence from the external sector and inwards FDI.

Accordingly, CEPAL clarified that integration agreements would have been consistent with open regionalism only if they could meet nine requirements: i) an extensive liberalization of markets of goods and services; ii) facilitation of new members' entry; iii) legal certainty and transparent rules; iv) absence of disequilibria in the BoP of the country members; v) moderate levels of protection against third-party competitors; vi) reduction of capital controls and facilitated convertibility of currencies; vii) agreements favourable to the international transfer of technology; viii) fiscal incentives in order to support the relatively less developed countries; and ix) institutional arrangements in order to promote the participation of each country's social sectors (Fuentes 1994: 84).

Based on such premises, CEPAL explicitly praised MERCOSUR as an example of integration, since it represented an ambitious and consistent commitment to extend free market to all the goods produced by its member countries, differently from any other regional agreement (CEPAL 1994: 45). In other words, open regionalism suggested further integration into the world economy by means of regionalization, since the economic interdependency of Latin American countries was inescapably linked to global liberalization and deregulation. Accordingly, open regionalism constituted a clear shift away from the structuralist concept of economic integration through Import-Substitution Industrialization, since it granted a fundamental role to free market mechanisms in allocating resources in the production process (Fernández-Jilberto and Hogenboom 1997).[24] Considering the above, one may legitimately conclude that, around 1994, CEPAL not only acknowledged the neoliberal reforms already implemented in the continent, but also turned into a powerful Global Economic Governance "shaper" actively promoting such reforms across Latin America.

Notwithstanding CEPAL's enthusiastic forecasts, empirical evidence suggests that MERCOSUR economies began running into problems shortly after open regionalism was adopted. The Argentinian bilateral trade deficit with Brazil immediately became a controversial issue that undermined MERCOSUR's integration (Pinto de Andrade et al. 2003). In 1997, Argentinian President Menem proposed a common currency in order to overcome such a persisting problem. In all likelihood, Menem's proposal was merely motivated by Argentinian political contingencies, since there was no economic justification to such a common currency (Licandro 2000): even adopting Mundell's (orthodox) theory of Optimum Currency Areas (OCA) (Mundell 1961), the question of why Brazil should have accepted to join a similar monetary union remained largely unanswered. On the other hand, it is plausible that further integration would have implied an even more open domestic market as well as a more intense cross-border competition, making exchange rate fluctuations even more disruptive of bilateral trade (Eichengreen 1998).

An aprioristic defence of MERCOSUR continued well into the 2000s by governments pertaining to the new political cycle. Broadly speaking, both financial and commercial openness and the fixed exchange rates were situated at the origin of the catastrophic crises of 2001–2002, since they produced, respectively, current account deficits in MERCOSUR's countries and a sharp increase of the external debt denominated in USD in order to defend the fixed exchange rate (O'Connell 2005; Kregel 2014). Analysing the Argentinian default of 2001, the IMF (2003) – which had previously played a pivotal role in determining such a failure – explicitly questioned the role played by

MERCOSUR. In particular, the IMF highlighted that the imbalanced bilateral trade between the two biggest country members (which concentrated Argentina's exports in primary products to Brazil) represented a major vulnerability (IMF 2003: 18). In light of this evidence, IMF concluded that

> MERCOSUR trading arrangement may thus have amplified the effect of the peso's real appreciation by contributing to Argentina's low export share as well as its vulnerability to adverse commodity price developments and, increasingly, to weaker regional demand, particularly from Brazil.
>
> IMF 2003: 24

Despite all this, in December 2002, when the sovereign debt crises had already hit most MERCOSUR member countries, the governments of Argentina and Uruguay[25] still emphasized that, *because of* the creation of MERCOSUR, both countries had moved from semi-autarkic economies, with strong State interventionism, to *liberal market* economies linked to global trade flows and capital mobility. In those governments' eyes, such an important achievement was possible because MERCOSUR's founding countries had recognized the need to be an integral part of economic "globalization". Notwithstanding the catastrophic economic outlook of those days, both administrations insisted that the challenge for MERCOSUR countries *was to continue integrating their economies in the world*; however, they also insisted that the social dimension should not have to be forgotten, for the purposes of social cohesion (ILO 2002). In particular, member states took note of the remarkable increase in income disparities across MERCOSUR countries during the 1990s. Sub-regional governments also emphasized that the existing institutions were already compatible, in theory, with a *different economic policy* (i.e. redistributive and/or expansionary policies), aimed at reducing inequality. By doing so, they implicitly dissented with several analyses recommending a structural institutional reform of MERCOSUR (Arestis et al. 2003; Blyde 2006).

Figure 7.1 shows that the degree of openness of MERCOSUR economies remained almost unvaried throughout the 2002–2012 progressive cycle and the subsequent economic crisis of 2013–2015, with a sharp increase in Uruguay before the 2008 crisis. Under such scenario, the room for expansionary fiscal policies remained highly dependant upon the external conjuncture and the terms of trade.

From this perspective, what is particularly striking is that no capital controls were introduced (or even proposed) despite the severe financial downturn that had already shaken MERCOSUR member states. The Argentinian government likely represents the most outstanding example of relentless capital liberalization. President Menem's 1992 reform of the central bank had aimed at guaranteeing higher capital mobility – meant as a powerful tool to tie the government's hands – thus moderating both fiscal and monetary policies (Sember and Vernengo forthcoming). Because the

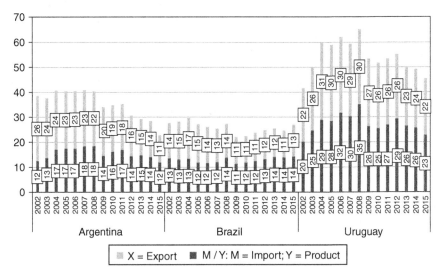

Figure 7.1 Degree of openness (X + M / Y) of MERCOSUR economies

Argentinian and Uruguayan financial sectors were the most open in the region, the 1994 Tequila crisis hit more severely these two countries than any other regional economy. Financialization in Argentina (1990–2003) was so intense that financial investments crowded out real investments, thereby reducing capital accumulation: gross fixed capital formation as a percentage of GDP fell from an average of 20% (1980–1989) to 17% (1990–2005). Only the 2001 sovereign default interrupted such a tendency to financialisation, forcedly closing Argentina's capital account (Demir 2008).

From this perspective, the center-left governments of the region revealed a "revisionist attitude towards multilateralism" according to which the adhesion to regional (i.e. super-national) institutions represented a progressive revival of the unionist (as well as anti-imperialist) projects of Simón Bolívar and Francisco Morazán. However, they deliberately ignored that the increasing trans-nationalization of their economies would have also implied the risk of "middle-income traps",[26] arising from their growing involvement in global dynamics. As a result, Latin America rapidly became more globalized and dependent on transnational dynamics than its political narratives seemed willing to accept (Sanahuja 2017).

At the same time, there is no doubt that the progressive governments that led MERCOSUR member states since the early 2000s imposed a change in the political discourse, which also affected the significance attributed to both MERCOSUR and multilateralism. Nevertheless, the compatibility between an expansionary fiscal policy and the degree of openness (both commercial and financial) of the member states was not even discussed.

The increased dependency on the external scenario inescapably affected the sustainability of the expansionary policies, especially after 2012. Predictably enough, as soon as the external conjuncture worsened, both the current account (particularly in Argentina) and the capital account (particularly in Brazil and Uruguay) reflected the difficult situation of the MERCOSUR economies, imposing fiscal adjustments and social expenditures cuts.

Bilateral trade imbalances and the return of the external constraint on the Argentinian BoP

As anticipated in Section 2, Argentina's economy showed a poor perform-ance starting from 2011–2012. Stated succinctly, two problems affected the economic outlook: first, the bilateral trade with Brazil; second, the extended current account deficit (since 2010 to the present day) which turned into a shortage of reserve currency and, therefore, prompted the introduction of emergency capital controls between October 2011 and December 2015.

Intra-regional trade among MERCOSUR countries has shown struc-tural imbalances since the very foundation of the sub-regional alliance. In short, while MERCOSUR is very important for Argentina's trade patterns (representing more than 30% of its total trade), it is not so relevant for Brazil, accounting for hardly 10% of the Brazilian commercial balance (Noya et al. 2015). Since MERCOSUR countries have a similar international specializa-tion, the sub-regional alliance also operates as an amplifier of global shocks: in the event of an international crisis, not only is Argentina (or Uruguay) dir-ectly affected by the global shock, but also by the recessionary effect that the shock produces on other MERCOSUR's partners members, first and foremost Brazil. From this perspective, Brazil turned into a sort of exogenous variable for Argentina's economy, since any slowdown of the Brazilian economy imme-diately affects Argentina's rate of growth by means of a sharp fall in its exports.

In addition, Argentina also suffers from a structural deficit in the balance of trade with Brazil. In the 2003–2016 period, Argentina ran an uninter-rupted trade deficit with Brazil, which summed USD 36.2 billion. However, almost half of such bilateral imbalance (USD 16.9 billion) was accumulated in the 2010–2015 period. In particular, in 2011 trade deficit with Brazil peaked to 5 billion dollars, which represented approximately one third (32.7%) of the passive items of the balance of trade. This amount is largely superior to both the bilateral deficit with the US (USD 3.5 billion) and Pacific Asia (which includes China, USD 3.1 billion). In other words, Argentina's trade deficit with Brazil was a further structural problem of MERCOSUR, since it was independent from the economic conjuncture: not even during the recessions of Brazil (2009, 2015 and 2016), Argentina was able to re-equilibrate its bilat-eral BoP, as shown in Figure 7.2.

A second problem emerged with the capital account of the Argentinian BoP between 2010 and 2015. For one, it is important to stress that the post-default debt restructuring determined a "forcedly closed" capital account regime in

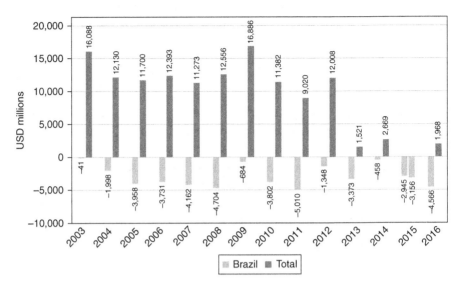

Figure 7.2 Argentina's balance of trade: Brazil versus total (USD millions)
Source: Ministerio de Hacienda (Argentina)

Argentina, a scenario in which capital may not move freely in or out of the country and bond-issuing (denominated in reserve currency) is forbidden. In such a case, any deficit in the current account immediately turns into a stress on the reserve position, since there is no inflow of capital to counterbalance it. From 2010 to the present day, Argentina ran a capital account deficit. On the current account side, no deficit was registered on the balance of trade between 2010 and 2014. Instead, the main determinant of the passive current account was the *investment income* (i.e. the payments to foreign holders of Argentina's debt (via interests) and bonds (via dividends), normally categorized as part of the *Primary Income* or *Factor Income* by the IMF), whose deficit increased of 31.7% between 2009 and 2011 (see Figure 7.3).[27]

This outflow of capital is due to the extraordinary importance that transnational corporations have within the Argentinian industrial sector (Santarcangelo and Perrone 2012). Since the decisions of such firms are highly volatile and independent from any government's economic plan, the deteriorating outlook of 2011–2012 also owes to a change of attitude of such international players, who proved unwilling to leave in Argentina the returns deriving from their investments in Argentina. As no inflow of capital could counterbalance the current account deficit, an impressive outflow of capital severely hit Argentina's monetary reserves in the very same years. Between 2009 and 2011 external assets formation of the non-financial private sector (i.e. the deposits held abroad by Argentinian private and non-financial agents) increased by 67.5%.[28] The combined result was a dramatic reduction

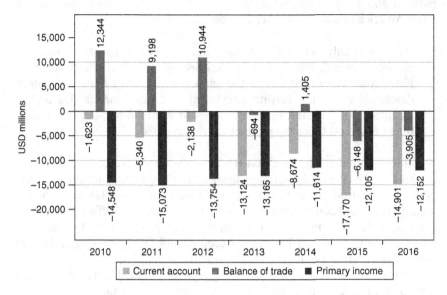

Figure 7.3 Argentina's determinants of current account deficit (USD millions)
Source: INDEC

of international reserve in 2011, corresponding to approximately a quarter of their total amount. The government's response was the introduction of emergency capital controls in October 2011, which however achieved only a stabilization of the economic outlook and not a reversal: in 2015, the investment income deficit was still 16.2% higher than in 2009, while the external assets formation had risen by 32.2%.[29]

What is striking is the lack of a common initiative by MERCOSUR institutions and/or country members. Helping Argentina by means of a credit swap denominated in dollars would have required a minimum effort, particularly for Brazil, whose reserve in dollars amounted to almost USD 400 billion, whereas Argentina's were approximately USD 30 billion, in those days. This notwithstanding, such a rescue plan was not even discussed. At the same time, the Argentinian contingencies of 2011–2015 also highlighted the fragility of MERCOSUR's institutions, particularly in light of the non-implementation of the *Banco del Sur*, MERCOSUR's development bank, whose original mandate was rescuing member countries in the event of a BoP crisis.

Capital volatility and financialization in Brazil and Uruguay

In his inaugural address to the extraordinary 1969 ECLAC session, the Chilean Chancellor, Gabriel Valdés (1969), exemplified a most extraordinary paradox about capital flows between the mid- and low-income countries of Latin America and their Northern hegemon:

> It is commonly believed that our continet receives a *factual* financial-aid from abroad. The data show the opposite. It is possible to state that Latin America contributes to the financing of United States and other developed countries. Private investment in Latin America has always meant, and still means, that the amount of capital flown-out of the continent is several times bigger than the one invested.

Valdés pointed to the fact that the *Primary Income* voice in the current accounts of the US and Western European countries counted on large amounts of profit repatriation and debt servicing deriving from US investments (equity and loans) across Latin America. These flows easily offset, and largely surpassed, the US and Western European net investments (FDI and FPI voices in the Capital and Financial Account) and ODA (*Secondary Income* voice of the current account) in Latin America. Capital flight, whereby Latin American nationals had long exported capitals to the US via illegal and unrecorded means, contributed in the net outflow of capital from the Latin American region to the US and Europe.

The disruptive role played by an open capital account had been debated in Latin American economic circles for a long time, particularly during the so-called "Developmentalist stage", approximately covering the period between the late 1940s and the early 1980s (Prebisch 1946; Sunkel and Paz 1970). In the 1990s the question of the impact of *short-term* capital movements on the real economy re-ignited the debate: as new financial products and technological developments on capital market infrastructures begun allowing for much swifter, substantial and speculative uses of international liquidity, many saw a qualitative difference between the impact of short-term and long-term capital movements. The Tequila crisis of 1994 provided a most fitting scenario for such revival of the debate (Musacchio 2012).

More recently, even the IMF, which in the 1990s and 2000s was among the staunchest supporters of radical capital liberalization, begun questioning its theoretical premises. In their analysis of the decade going from 2002 to 2012, Kose and Prasad (2012) show how the causal effect of capital account liberalization on growth had been irrelevant in emerging markets. Furthermore, they show how the increases in capital flows from industrialized to developing countries represented a pro-cyclical element, since foreign investors proved willing to lend in good times, but pulled back as soon as the macroeconomic outlook worsened, thus amplifying swings in the peripheral business cycle. Accordingly, abrupt capital outflows acted as triggers of several financial crises in emerging markets.

Ostry et al. (2016) have calculated about 150 episodes of surges in capital inflows in more than 50 emerging market economies since 1980, concluding that capital account openness consistently figured as a risk-factor in those cycles. In addition, Siddiqui (2014) shows that the overall increase in foreign capital inflows during the last decade had a relevant appreciation-effect on domestic currencies. In turn, such an appreciation induced a restrictive monetary policy, with higher rates of interest. The overall effect was that domestic investors were negatively affected both by the loss of competiveness and by the credit crunch. Therefore, by allowing the unrestricted inflow of foreign capital, emerging countries have often undermined their own domestic market and increased their dependency on foreign investors to sustain higher economic growth rates.

Table 7.1 shows a similar trend in Brazil. The rate of interest remained high, independently from output levels, even during the years of GDP contraction, acting as a pro-cyclical factor of recession. The explanation lays in the necessity to attract a robust inflow of short-term capital, in order to achieve a surplus in the financial account capable of compensating the current account deficit. The importance of this inflow of capital was such that total reserves in USD got to 373 billion in 2012.

Along these lines, Azis and Shin (2015) emphasize that, in the post-2008 scenario, the "easy money" policy (Quantitative Easing and Tapering among others) in advanced economies has negatively affected emerging markets, creating widespread financial instability. In simplified terms, such outcome depended on the negative interest rate policy of the central bank of the northern hemisphere, which displaced speculative capitals towards emerging markets. The relationship between arbitrage/speculative opportunities and "easy money" has been explored in depth by Kaltenbrunner and Painceira (2016). For one, the notorious *carry trade*[30] in the emerging markets should

Table 7.1 Brazil's economic indicators

Year	GDP variation (%)	Annual nominal interest rate (%)	Current account (USD million)	Financial account (USD million)	Total reserves (USD billion)
2003	1.1	16.3	4,177	−157	49.3
2004	5.8	17.7	11,679	−3,532	52.9
2005	3.2	18.0	13,985	13,144	53.8
2006	4.0	13.2	13,643	16,152	85.8
2007	6.1	11.2	1,551	88,330	180.3
2008	5.1	13.7	−28,192	28,302	193.8
2009	−0.1	8.7	−24,302	70,172	238.5
2010	7.5	10.7	−75,824	125,112	287.6
2011	4.0	10.9	−77,032	137,879	352.0
2012	1.9	7.1	−74,218	92,853	373.2
2013	3.0	9.9	−74,839	67,877	358.8
2014	0.5	11.7	−104,181	111,431	363.6
2015	−3.8	14.2	−59,434	56,714	356.5

Source: WB/CEPAL/Banco Central do Brasil

not be considered an aberration of otherwise perfectly working markets, but a structural feature of the international monetary system, namely financialization.[31] In addition, Kaltenbrunner and Painceira (2016) apply such an interpretative hypothesis to Brazil, highlighting how capital flows have been characterized by extreme volatility over recent years, irrespective of Brazil's sound fundamentals and its position as net currency creditor. Instead, it has been largely shaped by conditions on international financial markets. In Brazil, cumulative 12-months short-term capital flows surged from an outflow of USD 8 billion at the beginning of 2000 to more than USD 60 billion and USD 50 billion at the end of 2007 and 2010 respectively. Brazil's total stock of outstanding short-term external liabilities reached 46.1% of GDP in June 2008 and 39.7% of GDP in March 2011, compared to only 28% of GDP before the crisis in 1999. Foreign investors' participation in the Brazilian stock market increased from below 25% to more than 50% at the end of 2014.

A similar policy also characterized Uruguay and, after change in the political cycle in 2015, Argentina. On September 2016, Argentina, Uruguay and Brazil occupied the three top position in the global ranking of carry trade. The annual expected gain in USD was +5.84%, +5.13% and +4.2% respectively: a exceptional capital gain when compared to the corresponding expected values in the UK (–0.07%) and the Eurozone (–1.88%) (Reuters-El Cronista 2017). The main consequence of these capital movements was a sharp increase in volatility of both capital and exchange rates. Accordingly, rather than letting this excess be "absorbed" in the domestic economy, the Brazilian central bank had accumulated huge foreign exchange reserves as a buffer against sudden stops or capital flight. Foreign exchange reserves in Brazil increased from USD 50 billion in 2004 to USD 364 billion in 2014. Nevertheless, reserve accumulation implied a net resource transfer from Brazil to developed countries: on the one hand, the Brazilian central bank hold low-yielding and safe sovereign bonds; on the other hand, as soon as foreign capital dramatically increased their value, they were repatriated (Painceira 2008). Within this framework, international reserves cannot be used to finance counter-cyclical fiscal policies in times of recession, as illustrated by Table 7.1. Rather, they become the sub-product of financialization and speculative movements of capital. It is noteworthy that Goncalves (2007) reached similar conclusions with regards to Uruguay: notwithstanding the high level of reserves in a country that has a highly dollarized financial sector, further reserve accumulation is constantly needed.

Within this context, regional integration has generally acted as a further element of instability: Azis (2015) stressed that the snowball effect of the Eurozone crisis represented a vivid example of the contagion risk of highly integrated systems. In his view, the market-driven process of regional integration needs to be carefully managed in order to strengthen financial safety and, therefore, to minimize the potential costs in terms of uncertainty and volatility in financial markets.

Many of the aforementioned evidences hold true also with respect to MERCOSUR. Noya et al. (2015) came to conclusions similar to Azis': global shocks tend to affect MERCOSUR countries in similar ways. Furthermore, the second round effects (e.g. the effects produced by the regional linkages as a consequence of an exogenous and extra-regional shock) strengthen the original shock; accordingly, both economic growth and negative global shocks have been amplified by the existence of MERCOSUR. Bresser-Pereira and Holland (2010) noted that MERCOSUR's perfect capital mobility implies that markets avail themselves of arbitrage or speculative opportunities whenever there is some misalignment between active monetary and exchange rate policies. Therefore, contagion and other neighbourhood financial effects could turn regional integration into a controversial issue. Since currencies gradually appreciate until they provoke BoP crises (loss of trade competitiveness often leads to current account deficits, usually sustained by abundant capital flows and, therefore, an excessive "dollarization of liabilities" which increases financial fragility), regional agreements must be modified in order to allow developing countries to neutralize this tendency, or otherwise continue risking that recurring financial crises severely hit member states.

The absence of such regulations, particularly in order to contrast dollarization of liabilities, can be situated at the origin of Uruguay's stress on the BoP in 2015 and 2016. Being a non-industrialized tax haven, Uruguay has always been characterized by both a current account deficit and a Capital and Financial Account surplus. For the very same reasons, capital flight was never an issue: quite the contrary, the country attracted an important amount of flown capitals, particularly from Argentina. However, a sudden tax amnesty announced by president Macri on May 2016 determined an unprecedented outflow of capitals, mostly towards Argentina. In turn, the sudden deterioration of the capital account imposed a fiscal adjustment to the center-left government.

Summarizing, not only did not MERCOSUR implement common controls on capitals, but its member countries did not even coordinate their decisions on this issue. Both the pre-2016 capital flight towards Uruguay and the subsequent capital flight from Uruguay severely question the effectiveness of the MERCOSUR agreements in ensuring effective financial cooperation.

Conclusion

This chapter provides an analysis of three MERCOSUR economies since the early 2000s. Stated succinctly, my argument is that the demand-led and expansionary fiscal policies of 2003–2012 have determined a robust economic growth, which allowed paying for substantial social measures that improved *Human Development* in MERCOSUR countries. Nevertheless, such policies proved to be unsustainable as soon as the external scenario worsened, beginning in 2012. Abrupt changes in the international economic environment determined an external constraint on the Balances of Payments, which affected both the current account in Argentina, whose imbalanced external sector rapidly determined a scarcity of hard currency, and the capital accounts in Brazil and Uruguay. In both cases, the post 2008 downturn of commodity prices broke the camel's back.

A meaningful part of the problem was represented by MERCOSUR's institutions and their inability to defend the social results that had been achieved before. Two aspects deserve special attention: on the one hand, MERCOSUR's imbalanced trade structure, which led to continuous trade deficits of two member countries – Argentina and Uruguay – with Brazil. On the other hand, the absence of common capital controls that led to capital volatility (in Argentina and Uruguay) and financialisation (in Brazil and Uruguay). Furthermore, the non-implementation of the *Banco del Sur* (MERCOSUR's development bank) contributed to the severe lack of hard currency that affected Argentina, determining the introduction of emergency capital controls between October 2011 and December 2015. All these shortcomings can be ascribed to MERCOSUR nature and origins, which are strictly connected to the neoliberal agenda that the US promoted in the 1990s in Latin America.

This critique to MERCOSUR's neoliberal flaws does not imply an aprioristic defence of the previous theoretical background that underpinned several Latin American institutions. Structuralism died out in the 1980s because of its incapacity to adapt to a changing world. Given the new international division of labour and the pivotal role played by transnational corporations, domestic protection worked in some cases but not in others. Several governments implementing ISI policies failed to grasp the complexities attached to market intervention in the neoliberal era, allowing free domestic competition in industries with high fixed costs: for example, in the late 1960s, the annual output of cars and trucks in eight Latin American countries was just 600,000 units shared by 90 firms, giving an average of only 6,700 units per firm (Baer 1972). Ten years later, similar policies became clearly incompatible with the logic of transnational capital.

Nevertheless, some of the social results that were achieved in 2003–2012 could have been preserved by taking a less radical approach to current account liberalization. For instance, the terms upon which FDI was accepted by MERCOSUR countries may have been better negotiated with transnational corporations (following the example of China, which imposed several conditions to FDI) at a sub-regional level, rather than at a national level, while avoiding altogether short-term capital liberalization. A large crowd of mainstream economists (beginning from Stiglitz 2000) convene that, while open current account transactions have become the staple of economic growth worldwide (even if, lately, there is a reversion in trend, led by the Trump administration, due to Asia's increasing strength), hyper-liberal financial account liberalization has been both destabilizing and driven by the interests of a small and closely-knitted community of Western corporate stakeholders.

Notes

1 According to Rossi (2017), "The 'second wave of incorporation' [is] the second major redefinition of the sociopolitical arena in Latin America, caused by the broad and selective inclusion of the popular sectors in the polity after being excluded or disincorporated by military authoritarian regimes and democratic neoliberal reforms". The second wave of incorporation is the turn towards leftist governments happening in the 2000s as a result of the struggle for economic inclusion by the popular sectors, organized in territorialized social movements. It follows the first wave of incorporation, a process that involved a combination of the mobilization of popular claims by labour and/or peasant movements and the policies for channelling those claims into corporatist institutions during the 1930s–1950s.

2 We are not analysing either the case of Paraguay (because of the country's suspension from MERCOSUR in 2012) or of Venezuela (because of the largely disputed membership of the country to MERCOSUR).

3 Financialization is a process whereby financial markets, financial institutions and financial elites gain greater influence over economic policy and economic outcomes. Its principal impacts are to: (1) elevate the significance of the financial sector relative to the real sector; (2) transfer income from the real sector to the financial sector; and (3) increase income inequality and contribute to wage stagnation. Financialization operates through three different conduits: changes in the structure and operation of financial markets; changes in the behavior of non-financial corporations; and changes in economic policy (Palley 2007).

4 In 2009, 65% of the biggest 500 Argentinian firms was owned by non-Argentinian capital (Santarcangelo and Perrone 2012). In the same year, Brazil's top 20 transnational companies had a stock of USD 56 billion in assets abroad, virtually half of the country's total Overseas Foreign Direct Investment stock (USD 114 billion). The top 20 companies produce and sell goods and services worth approximately USD 30 billion and employ 77,000 people abroad: a magnitude comparable to some developed countries (Ramsey et al. 2009).

5 The expansion of exports in primary products is not in itself a guarantee of growth: dozens of countries have known impressive economic expansions under commodity boom periods to subsequently drag into heavy recessions and debt unsustainability once faced with falling commodity prices. On the theory, see: Prebisch (1949), Nurkse (1953) and Furtado (1961).

6 An assistance program where cash payments are made to poor households, on condition that children are both attending school and being vaccinated.

7 In underdeveloped countries, free education reduces poverty expanding household purchasing power, because children are able to receive free meals in school dining halls.

8 Data retrieved from the open access database INDEC of the Argentinian National Institute of Statistics (Instituto Nacional de Estadistica y Censos). Available at: https://www.indec.gob.ar/

9 Ibidem.

10 Data retrieved from the open access data base provided by the CEDLAS-Universidad de La Plata and the World Bank www.cedlas.econo.unlp.edu.ar/wp/en/estadisticas/sedlac/estadisticas/#1496165297107-cedda6d3-6c7d.

11 For example, the percentage of population which did not study at least for nine years.

12 Which measures the unequal distribution of the main durable goods (cars, TVs, computers, washing machines, DVD readers, microwave ovens) among the population, being 0 a perfectly equal and 1 a perfectly unequal distribution

13 Being 0 a "perfectly equal" (and, viceversa, 1 a "perfectly unequal") distribution of durable goods among the population.

14 From this perspective, the (progressive) Astori tax reform of 2008 played a pivotal role, since the decreasing capital inflow started in 2012 did not force the centre-leftist administration to implement any brutal fiscal adjustment. For the very same reasons, Uruguay is also the only MERCOSUR country in which no change in the political cycle took place.

15 From this perspective, in 1991 MERCOSUR shifted away from the original idea contained in the *Foz de Iguazu Statement* of 1985, signed by presidents Raul Alfonsin and José Sarney. In that occasion, the future creation of MERCOSUR was meant as an indigenous initiative to strengthen negotiating capacity against the US and EC, which not only had to represent a commercial agreement, but also a political advancement in order to struggle for the sovereignty of Brazil and Argentina (Figari 2006).

16 One should not forget that both Argentina (*Plan Convertibilidad*) and Brazil (*Plan Real*) implemented, in those days, a fixed exchange rate regime, which reduced enormously the competitiveness of their industries. Furthermore, the Argentinian industrial sector had severely shrunk during the 1980s, because of the neoliberal policies implemented since 1976 and, also, the severe crisis of 1989–1990 (Schorr 2012). An idyllic scenario for the US companies, indeed.

17 See Williamson (1990). Stated succinctly, John Williamson's decalogue consisted of the following recommendations: 1) fiscal conservatism; 2) redirection of public spending from subsidies toward pro-growth measures; 3) tax reform and moderate marginal tax rates; 4) market-determined and moderate (real) interest rates; 5) competitive exchange rates; 6) trade liberalization implying low and uniform tariffs; 7) liberalization of capital market in order to facilitate foreign direct investment; 8) privatization of state enterprises; 9) deregulation of goods market in order to increase competition; and 10) legal security for property rights.

18 One may even say that hyperinflation played the same role that the 1973 Great Inflation had already played in the northern hemisphere against Keynesianism.

19 Fernando Collor de Mello was the President of Brazil from 1990 to 1992, after he had defeated Lula in a controversial second round election in 1989. His economic plan (*Plano Collor*) was characterized by fiscal adjustment, wage deflation, privatizations and free trade. Carlos Saul Menem was the President of Argentina from 1989 to 1999, his *Convertibility Plan* (a fixed exchange regime according to which ARS 1 = USD 1) initially determined a dramatic reduction of inflation and a strong economic growth. However, after 1994's financial contagion the economic outlook rapidly deteriorated, eventually turning into the country's default, in 2001.

20 The so-called Tequila Crisis of 1994 represents the most outstanding example of financial contagion within Latin American countries. A dangerous current-account deficit (7% of GDP) and a sharp decrease in international reserves in Mexico triggered a sharp devaluation of the Mexican peso (around 50% within six months). This in turn caused the local-currency value of the public dollar-linked debt to swell enormously and a crisis of the whole financial sector. The bankruptcy of several banks caused a regional contagion in other Latin American

economies, showing the risks of an "open" capital account, e.g. of an economy characterized by the perfect mobility of capitals.

21 One may also add that fiscal expansionary measures need to rely on a stable income, which by definition cannot be provided by short-term capitals, which are highly volatile and speculative in nature.

22 CEPAL is the UN Economic Commission for Latin America and the Caribbean, founded in 1948. Since the very beginnings, CEPAL was influenced by structuralist economists like Raúl Prebisch, Celso Furtado and Osvaldo Sunkel. The most important formulations of CEPAL dealt with: Import Substitution Industrialization (ISI); capital controls; agrarian reform; taxation on sumptuous consumption.

23 Rosenthal's critique was probably addressed to the unsatisfactory answers that structuralist economists (particularly, those that participated directly in the Argentinian government, such as Juan Vital Sourrouille and Bernardo Grispun) gave to the late 1980s hyperinflation. Broadly speaking, hyperinflation played a crucial role in the neoliberal turn of the early 1990s, since a vast majority of the public opinion associated the monetary stabilization to an increased wealth and purchasing power, thus accepting silently the dramatic fiscal adjustment and the rise in unemployment (Weyland 1996).

24 Juan Alberto Fuentes – the technical coordinator of CEPAL's sub-regional headquarters in Mexico, in those days – acknowledged that at least five of the aforementioned requirements were definitely *orthodox*, from an economist's point of view (Fuentes 1994).

25 Presidency Duhalde (Argentina) and Batlle Ibáñez (Uruguay).

26 The situation in which a country's growth becomes "institutionally constrained" after reaching middle-income levels. For instance, because of the scarcity of reserve currency determined by the increased level of import or the impossibility to implement effective capital controls, etc.

27 Data retrieved from the open access database INDEC of the Argentinian National Institute of Statistics (Instituto Nacional de Estadistica y Censos). Available at: https://www.indec.gob.ar/.

28 Ibidem.

29 Ibidem.

30 *Carry trade* consists of borrowing in a low-interest rate currency (e.g. USD) and converting the borrowed amount into another high-interest rate currency (e.g. BRL), in order to: (a) place such amount on deposit in the second currency offering a higher rate of interest; or (b) invest it into assets (stocks, commodities, bonds, etc.) denominated in the second currency. After such a financial valorisation, the (increased) amount is changed again in the low interest rate currency, netting the speculators an easy capital gain.

31 The authors assume that monetary conditions in the country with the highest liquidity premium will influence monetary conditions all over the world. Therefore, any change in international liquidity preference can lead to large capital (speculative) movements and exchange rate swings, largely independent of economic conditions, since investors continuously seek protection in the currency with the highest liquidity premium. Such a characteristic of the current monetary system has disruptive consequences on emerging economies, since they systematically have to offer higher interest rates in order to maintain capital

inflows. However, high interest rates negatively affect domestic investment, aggregate demand and growth, re-igniting instead capital flows and exchange rate volatility.

References

Alvarez, M. (2011), 'Los 20 años del MERCOSUR: una integración a dos velocidades', *Comercio Exterior*, 108: 7–55.

Arestis, P., Ferrari-Filho, F., Paula, L.F. and Sawyer, M. (2003), 'The Euro and the EMU: lessons for MERCOSUR', in P. Arestis and L.F. Paula (Eds.), *Monetary Union in MERCOSUR: Lessons from EMU*, Aldershot: Edgard Elgar.

Azis, I. (2015), 'Integration, contagion and income distribution', in P. Nijkamp, A. Rose and K. Kourtit (Eds.), *Regional Science Matters. Studies Dedicated to Walter Isard*, New York: Springer-Verlag.

Azis, I. and Shin, H. S. (2015), *Managing Elevated Risk*, Asian Development Bank, New York: Springer-Verlag.

Baer, W. (1972), 'Import substitution and industrialization in Latin America: experiences and interpretations', *Latin American Research Review*, 7 (1): 95–122.

Bin, D. (2016), 'The politics of financialization in Brazil', *World Review of Political Economy*, 7 (1): 106–126.

Bielschowsky, R. (2009), 'Sixty years of ECLAC: structuralism and neo-structuralism', *CEPAL Review*, 97: 171–192.

Blyde, J. S. (2006), 'Convergence dynamics in MERCOSUR', *Journal of Economic Integration*, 21 (4): 784–815.

Bresser-Pereira, L. C. and Holland, M. (2010), 'Common currency and economic integration in MERCOSUL', *Journal of Post Keynesian Economics*, 32 (2): 213–234.

Carranza, M. E. (2003), 'Mercosur, the free trade area of the Americas and the Future of U.S. hegemony in Latin America', *Fordham International Law Journal*, 27 (3): 1029–1065.

CEPAL (1994), *El regionalismo abierto en América Latina y el Caribe. La Integración Económica al Servicio de la Transformación Productiva con Equidad*, Santiago de Chile: United Nations.

CEPAL (2016), *Fiscal Panorama of Latin America and the Caribbean*, Santiago de Chile: United Nations.

Demir, F. (2008), 'Financial liberalization, private investment and portfolio choice: financialization of real sectors in emerging markets', *Journal of Development Economics*, 88: 314–324.

Eichengreen, B. (1998), 'Does MERCOSUR Need a Single Currency?', NBER Working Paper, no. 6821.

Escudero, A. C. (1992), 'MERCOSUR: el nuevo modelo de integración', *Comercio Exterior*, 41 (11): 1041–1048.

Ferrer, A. (1996), 'El MERCOSUR: entre el Consenso de Washington y la integración sustentable', Inter-American Development Bank Conference, 3–5 September, Washington, DC.

Figari, G. M. (2006), 'Democracy and Argentinian foreign policy 1983–2005', *Relaciones Internacionales*, 2 (30): 69–97.

Fuentes, J. A. (1994), 'Open regionalism and economic integration', *CEPAL Review*, 53: 81–89.

Furtado, C. (1961), *Desenvolvimento e Subdesenvolvimento*, Rio de Janeiro: Fundo de Cultura.

Gaggero, J. (2011), 'La fuga de capitales Argentina en el escenario global (2002–2010)', *Documento de Trabajo N° 29*, Buenos Aires: Cefid-Ar.

Gaggero J., Rua, M. and Gaggero, A. (2013), 'Argentina. Fuga de Capitales (2002–2012)', Discussion Workshop: BEPS and the Future of Corporate Taxation, City University of London.

Gardini, G. L. (2006), 'Government-business relations in the construction of MERCOSUR', *Business and Politics*: 8 (1): 1–26.

Gardini, G. L. (2007), 'Who Invented MERCOSUR?', *Diplomacy & Statecraft*, 18 (4): 805–830.

Gardini, G. L. (2010), *The Origins of MERCOSUR. Democracy and Regionalization in South America*, Basingstoke: Palgrave Macmillan.

Goncalves, F. M. (2007), 'The Optimal Level of Foreign Reserves in Financially Dollarized Economies: The Case of Uruguay', IMF Working Paper, No. 07/265.

ILO (2002), *Report on National Dialogue: Argentina and Uruguay*, World Commission on the Social Dimension of Globalization, 2 December 2002.

IMF (2003), *Lessons from the Crisis in Argentina*, 8 October 2003.

IMF (2015a), *Global Financial Stability Report, October 2015: Vulnerabilities, Legacies, and Policy Challenges Risks Rotating to Emerging Markets*, Washington.

IMF (2015b), *IMF Country Report No. 15/82: Uruguay*, Washington.

INE (2017), *Estimación de la pobreza por el método el ingreso*, Montevideo: Uruguay.

Kaltenbrunner, A. and Painceira, J. P. (2016), 'International and Domestic Financialisation in Middle Income Countries: the Brazilian Experience', *Fessud Working Paper Series*, SOAS, No. 146.

Kose, M. A. and Prasad, E. (2012), 'Capital Accounts: Liberalize or Not?, Finance & Development', IMF, Updated: 28 March.

Kregel, J. (2014), 'An alternative view of the Argentine crisis: structural flaws in structural adjustment policy', in *Economic Development and Financial Instability: Selected Essays*, New York: Anthem Press.

Lavinas, L. (2016), *The Takeover of Social Policy by Financialization: the Brazilian Paradox*, Basingstoke: Palgrave Macmillan.

Licandro, F. G. (2000), 'Is MERCOSUR an Optimal Currency Area? A Shock Correlation Perspective', Documentos de Trabajo del Banco Central de Uruguay, 4/2000.

Malamud, A. (2005), 'MERCOSUR turns 15: between rising rhetoric and declining achievement', *Cambridge Review of International Affairs*, 18 (3): 421–436.

Manzetti, L. (1993), 'The political economy of MERCOSUR', *Journal of Interamerican Studies and World Affairs*, 35 (4): 101–141.

Mundell, R. A. (1961), 'A theory of optimum currency areas', *American Economic Review*, 51 (4): 657–665.

Musacchio, A. (2012), 'Mexico's financial crisis of 1994–1995', *Harvard Business School Working Papers*, 12–101.

Noya N., Lanzilotta, B. and Zunino, G. (2015), 'Macroeconomic challenges for MERCOSUR countries in the post-crisis scenario: a Gvar approach', *Revista de Economía*, 22 (2): 63–100.

Nurkse, R. (1953), *Problems of Capital-Formation in Underdeveloped Countries*, Oxford: Oxford University Press.

O'Connell, A. (2005), 'The recent crisis – and recovery – of the Argentine economy: some elements and background', in G.A. Epstein (Ed.), *Financialization and the World Economy*, Cheltenham: Edward Elgar.

Ocampo, J. A. (2000), 'Nuestra agenda', in CEPAL (Ed.), *La CEPAL en sus 50 Años. Notas de un Seminario Conmemorativo*, Santiago de Chile: United Nations.

OECD (2014), *Multi-dimensional Review of Uruguay. Volume 1: Initial Assessment*, Paris: OECD Development Pathways.

Ostry, J. D., Loungani, P. and Furceri, D. (2016), 'Neoliberalism: oversold?', *Finance & Development*, 53 (2): 38–41.

Painceira, J. P. (2008), 'Developing countries in the era of financialisation: from deficit accumulation to reserve accumulation', in C. Lapavitsas (Ed.), *Financialisation in Crisis*, Leiden: Brill.

Palley, T. I. (2007), 'Financialization: what it is and why it matters', *Levy Economics Institute Working Papers*, no. 525, December.

Pinto de Andrade, J., Falcão Silva, M. L. and Trautwein, H. M. (2003), *Prospects of Economic Integration and Incompatible Monetary Policies among MERCOSUR Members*, Institut für Volkswirtschaftslehre, Universität Oldenburg.

Prebisch, R. (1946), 'Panorama general de los problemas de regulación monetaria y crediticia en el continente Americano: América Latina', in Banco de México (Ed.), *Memoria de la Primera Reunión de Técnicos sobre Problemas de Banca Central del Continente Americano*, México, DF.

Prebisch, R. (1949), *El Desarrollo Económico de la América Latina y Algunos de sus Principales Problemas*, Santiago de Chile: CEPAL.

Ramsey, J., Resende, P. and Almeida, A. (2009), 'Trans-nationalization of Brazilian companies: lessons from the top 20', *Latin American Business Review*, 10 (2–3): 117–134.

Reuters-El Cronista (2017), 'Argentina, segunda entre los países más atractivos para el 'carry trade'', 23 March.

Rosenthal, G. (1996), 'Development thinking and policies: the way ahead', *CEPAL Review*, 60: 7–20.

Rossi, F. (2017), *The Poor's Struggle for Political Incorporation. The Piquetero Movement in Argentina*, Cambridge: Cambridge University Press.

Sanahuja, J. A. (2017), 'A "Rashomon" story Latin American views and discourses of global governance and multilateralism', in A. Triandafyllidou (Ed.), *Global Governance From Regional Perspectives: A Critical View*, Oxford: Oxford University Press.

Santarcangelo, J. and Perrone, G. (2012), 'La cúpula empresarial argentina y su rol en el desarrollo económico', *Problemas del Desarrollo*, 168 (43): 37–62.

Schorr, M. (2012), 'Deindustrialization as axis of the re-foundational project of the economy and society in Argentina 1976–1983', *America Latina en la Historia Economica*, 19 (3):31–56.

Schott, J. J. (2001), *Prospects for Free Trade in the Americas*, Washington: Institute for International Economics.

Sember, F. R. and Vernengo, M. (forthcoming), El Banco Central en Tiempos de Convertibilidad (1991–2002), in M. Rougier and F.R. Sember (fothcoming), *El Banco Central de la República Argentina en la Promoción del Desarrollo (1935–2015)*, Buenos Aires: Lenguaje Claro Ed.

Serrano, F. and Summa, R. (2015), 'Aggregate Demand and the Slowdown of Brazilian Economic Growth from 2011–2014', CEPR Working Papers, August.

Siddiqui, K. (2014), 'Flows of foreign capital into developing countries: a critical review', *Journal of International Business and Economics*, 2 (1): 29–46.

Stiglitz, J. (2000), 'Capital Market Liberalization, Economic Growth, and Instability', *World Development*, 28 (6): 1075–1086.

Sunkel, O. and Paz, P. (1970), *El Subdesarrollo Latinoamericano y la Teoría del Desarrollo*, Ciudad de México: Siglo Veintiuno Editores.

UCA (2017), 'Pobreza Extrema e Inseguridad Alimentaria en la Argentina Urbana (2010–2016)', Buenos Aires: Universidad Católica Argentina.

UNDP (2013), 'Desigualdad Multidimensional y Dinámica de la Pobreza en Uruguay en los años Recientes', Uruguay: El Futuro en Foco. Cuadernos sobre Desarrollo Humano, 2: 11–65.

Weisbrot, M., Ray, R., Montecino, J. A. and Kozameh, S. (2011), 'The Argentine Success Story and its Implications', CEPR Working Papers, October.

Weisbrot, M., Johnston, J. and Lefebvre, S. (2014), 'The Brazilian Economy in Transition: Macroeconomic Policy, Labor and Inequality', CEPR Working Papers, September.

Weyland, K. (1996), 'Neopopulism and neoliberalism in Latin America: unexpected affinities', *Studies in Comparative International Development*, 31 (3): 3–31.

Williamson, J. (1990), 'What Washington means by policy reform', in J. Williamson (Ed.), *Latin American Adjustment: How Much Has Happened?*, Washington: Institute for International Economics.

World Bank (2017), 'Country Poverty Brief: Brazil', October 2017.

8 Commodity economies and international assistance

Lessons drawn from Ukraine's experience

Sergey Korablin

Introduction

While the political reasons for Official Development Assistance (ODA) can vary on a country-by-country and case-by-case basis, the economic determinants seem to be fairly standard. Usually, they relate to low national income; high public and private debt; imbalances in the BoP; forex deficits; domestic currency depreciations and; inflationary pressures. The economic treatment prescribed by international creditors is also fairly standard: it usually includes budgetary austerity; tight monetary policy; privatization and; deregulation associated with trade liberalization. The conventional wisdom behind this approach goes under the name of "Washington Consensus".

The term was introduced and described by Williamson in 1989–1990 as a set of economic policy instruments recommended to Latin America economies to cope with their then economic and financial problems (Williamson 1990). Williamson explicitly pointed out that the recommendations were based on a common view of the US government, the US top bureaucracy, the International Financial Institutions (IFIs) and the right-wing economic think tanks based in Washington, DC. Despite Williamson's disagreement and his numerous subsequent explanations (2004), the "Washington Consensus" was almost immediately perceived as a practical manifesto of the neo-liberal doctrine and received various prominent critiques (Marangos 2008).

A partial incorporation of these critical views led to the emergence of so-called "second-generation reforms" that enriched the initial set of Williamson's ten instruments with another ten tools reflecting the crucial role of social institutions in the successful growth of any developing economy. While the "original" Washington Consensus was largely based on macroeconomic orthodoxy (Naim 1999), its "augmented" version was strengthened by such elements as anti-corruption, corporate governance, prudent opening of the capital account, independent central banks, inflation targeting, social safety nets and targeted poverty reduction (Rodrik 2006). Many noticed how the updated list of those recommendations was clearly incomplete. In particular, it did not include a proposal by Birdsall et al. (2001), which envisaged the opening of rich countries' domestic markets to products originating from the poorest economies.

After the experience of the Great Recession (2007–2012) and the IMF Managing Director's acknowledgement that the "Washington Consensus is now behind us" (Strauss-Kahn 2011), the Fund's officials have become reluctant to even mention the term, let alone to use it as an explicit paradigm. Nevertheless, the "augmented Washington Consensus" is still used in current programmes of the Fund, characterized by its traditional macroeconomic emphasis on minimum budget deficits and inflation, while however remaining oblivious of any consideration regarding the needs for technical development and technical modernization among its client countries.

This, at least, is evident in the case of the Extended Fund Facility (EFF) programme under which Ukraine has been cooperating with the IMF since 2015.[1] Despite the obvious advantages of the programme, the EFF continues to reflect one of the most controversial features of all IMF instruments – the reluctance to consider the technological limitations of developing countries and their dependency on global business and commodity cycles. This is especially evident after the surge of interest on this topic in the aftermath of the Great Recession, along with the recognition of the limited capacity of flexible exchange rates to ease adverse external shocks in a weak financial system (Ebeke and Fouejieu Azangue 2015).

The IMF's unwillingness to recognize (or deal with) the direct economic and financial dependency of the developing world on global commodity cycles is especially striking after the 2008–2009 fall of commodity market prices, which shed fresh light on the financial fragility and vulnerability of commodity-dependent economies (Kinda, Mlachila and Ouedraogo 2016). Since many ODA recipient countries are commodity-dependent developing economies, their ability to cope with their structural and contingent problems is severely dependent upon external commodity conjunctures. If these are favourable, commodity-dependent developing countries normally get a chance to balance their trade, attract additional foreign loans and investments – including FDI –, improve their BoP and reduce their financial and public deficits together with debt burdens. However, in case of negative commodity shocks, these countries enter a vicious economic cycle fueled by their small size, commodity dependency and – normally – undeveloped financial markets.

Considering the above, one would assume that ODA should intervene counter-cyclically in commodity-dependent economies, and focus on technology development, and encourage the production of higher value-added goods. This should be a direct and primary goal; without economic diversification away from the primary sector, a recipient country will never be prepared to shoulder adverse commodity shocks.

This idea is not new: it was already stressed by Stiglitz (1998, 2004) and Rodrik (2006) during the most heated phases of the Washington Consensus debate. The same topic has also been extensively covered by Reinert (2004,

2007) and Studwell (2013). Nevertheless, these arguments have mostly fallen on deaf ears, as mainstream models of economic development continue to be focused on the "invisible hand", much to the contentment of donor countries, who are happy to receive raw materials and market access in exchange for their financial support.

While the Governments of LDCs, LICs and MICs have the ultimate responsibility to acquire know-how and production capacity, ODA could do much more to multiply their opportunities. This would also help ODA donors to achieve two additional goals: avoid accusations of exploiting beneficiary countries and, secondly, minimize the risk of turning ODA into an endless exercise finalized at providing limited amounts of free fish, rather than fishing rods and skills.

The case of Ukraine is rather indicative: its economic cycles from 1996 to 2015 demonstrate a deep dependence on the commodity conjuncture: flourishing under high commodity prices but unable to balance basic financial needs during commodity recessions. Tellingly, since 1995, Ukraine has requested IMF assistance only during low commodity price cycles, while easily foregoing international macroeconomic support as soon as commodity prices recovered.

Ukraine's difficult beginning: the 1990s

In August 2018, Ukraine celebrated its 27th independence day. These were difficult years because of the changes occurred in Ukraine's society, state institutions and national economy. On the one hand, one must recognize the systemic reforms through which Ukraine has embraced private property, introduced a functioning national market, created its own currency and financial system, developed the SME sector, achieved the recognition of market status by the international community, strengthened its business presence in global markets and accessed and actively contributed to the work of International Financial Institutions (IFIs), particularly with reference to their efforts in stabilizing Ukraine's economy and overcome the impact of the 2008–2009 recession.

At the same time, it should be noted that Ukraine's economic progression lags far behind both the initial expectations and the country's potential. In the period 1991–2013,[2] Ukraine's real GDP fell by 30%.[3] According to the WB's data,[4] this was the worst result in the world during those 23 years. Out of 157 countries recording and sharing their GDP statistics since 1990, only three countries experienced a decline: Ukraine held the unenviable record, followed by Georgia (–18.9%) and Central African Republic (–1.9%). In all other countries the GDP increased, with performances spanning from minimal growth in Tajikistan (3.6%) and Zimbabwe (8.4%), to the exceptional performances of China (+836%) and Equatorial Guinea (+8216%).

It should be noted that the most dramatic decline in Ukraine's economy took place in the 1990s, that is, during the first nine years of its independence, when Ukraine lost almost 60% of its GDP.[5] In percentage terms, this collapse is twice the size of the fall of the US economy during the Great Depression (1929–1939). In fact, Ukraine's economy has not yet recovered from that shock, either in terms of quantity or quality. Therefore, when discussing the current financial problems of Ukraine, one should do so by considering the broader context of the national production model and the place Ukraine occupies in the global economic structure.

The "lagging growth" model

The reasons of Ukraine's depression in the 1990s are manifold. The "divorce" from the former Soviet Union together with a quick opening of its domestic market immediately put several Ukrainian industries under strain, due to the severe external competition that eventually jeopardized the country's ability to gradually adapt to the new economic environment. The USSR economy had developed and existed as a single economic monolith during more than 70 years; that economic–financial–industrial complex was in its own way unique, and in many cases lacked protective capacity or reserve markets.

Ukraine also lacked mature government institutions, experience of tough domestic and foreign competition and real-world cooperation practices, particularly with its previous ideological opponents. Instead, the country had a chaotic mixture of goals and was following different models of economic development, implementing rather confused measures widely labeled as "radical structural reforms". These were mostly associated with the Washington Consensus concepts.[6] Given these conditions, the fall of the Ukrainian economy in the 1990s should be seen more as a natural consequence of serious mistakes rather than the unexpected result of well-planned market reforms.

Yet, its subsequent economic shocks, cannot, and should not, be explained by simply making reference to the peculiarities of the post-Soviet recession, traumas of the 1993–1994 hyperinflation,[7] weaknesses of the Hryvnia (UAH) exchange rate[8] or chronic problems in the public financial sector.

The economic shocks are instead to be explained by the dependency of the Ukrainian economy on its primary sector and, therefore, on international commodity cycles. This is proved by the fact that, since the 2000s, Ukraine's economy showed not only declines, but also sudden and powerful rallies: for example, in 2000–2007 the GDP grew at an yearly average of 7.5% and the Hryvnia experienced a sharp strengthening, which could not simply be attributed to the active accumulation of foreign exchange in the international reserves of the central bank – the National Bank of Ukraine (NBU).

The Ukrainian GDP grew for the first time in 2000 (+5.9%). However, the dynamics that followed were rather erratic. Even in prosperous years, Ukraine's economic growth remained unstable and GDP rate fluctuated from 12.1% (2004) to 2.7% (2005). Since the beginning of the Great Recession

(2007), Ukraine was again amid the weakest performers: in 2009 the GDP fell by a whopping 14.8%, reaching again the podium of the world's worse performing economies, along with Northern Mariana Islands (–17.5%) and Lithuania (–14.8%). Between late 2008 and 2017, Ukraine's GDP declined during 18 of the 34 quarters.

High default risks, foreign exchange fever and depreciation of the national currency define the "lagging growth" model, which best describes Ukraine's development pattern (Korablin 2016). The main feature of this model is long-term underperformance not only when compared to dynamic competitors but even when compared to average performers. As Ukraine is unable to ignite a virtuous cycles of growth and continues stagnating at the bottom of all key economic indicators – including productivity, value adding capacity and diversification – the different negative elements of the economy become mutually reinforcing, while contributing in reiterating a vicious cycle of stagnation and underperformance, whose intensity can increase over time. Economic underperformance is self-nurturing: poverty alone is a sufficient condition for its reproduction.

Ukraine provides a fitting example of such dynamics, as its heavy reliance on the primary sector has severely constrained its growth opportunities, and left the economy at the mercy of the external conjuncture. Even without considering the war period of 2014–2017, from 2000 to 2013 Ukraine's GDP increased by only 70.3%. That is one of the lowest results among all the republics of the former Soviet Union. Ukraine was even outperformed by the mostly rural Kyrgyz Republic (85.2%), while other resource-rich central Asian republics were growing by leaps and bounds: Tajikistan (GDP increased by 2.9 times), Turkmenistan (3.1 times) and Azerbaijan (4.8 times). Ukraine was also lagging behind the group of developing countries – both those with low (92.7%) and middle (122.4%) per capita income.

Because of these structural limits, and the inordinate privatization that followed the "divorce" from the Soviet Union, the Ukrainian economy missed out on the many opportunities it could have made out of its previous status. However hard it is to believe, in 1987 Ukraine was, after Russia, the most developed and industrialized of the USSR Republics. In that year, the Chinese GDP was only 4.2 times the Ukrainian GDP, despite having a 25-fold larger labour force than Ukraine. By 2013, China's GDP had become 52 times larger than Ukraine's GDP at market exchange rates, and by 2016, 120 times larger.[9]

Ukraine: a small commodity economy

Because of its fundamentals, Ukraine's economy can be described as small, open, commodity dependent and financially undeveloped. More specifically: i) Ukraine's share in global GDP is about 0.12% (2015); ii) Ukraine's ratios of exports/GDP and imports/GDP have both been constantly fluctuating around 50%; iii) Ukraine competes successfully on global markets only in a limited number of commodity segments and low value-added manufactures, mainly in the niches of agricultural products, ferrous metals and basic chemical categories; and iv) international rating agencies assess Ukraine's sovereign debt as either highly speculative ("B-", according to Standard and Poor's and Fitch) or extremely speculative ("Caa2", according to Moody's).

Because of the structure of the Ukrainian economy, the dynamics of growth are significantly dependent upon price fluctuations of raw materials, which Ukraine successfully produces and exports. In particular, Ukraine exports large quantities of steel, wheat, sunflower oil and nitrogen fertilizers; as most other commodities, these are all low value-added goods. Further, because Ukrainian production is too small to influence world prices, Ukraine's role is reduced to a price-taker. The lack of domestic capacity to replace technology and capital-intensive imports and the absence of long-term investments and consistent financial inflows from abroad, make Ukraine highly dependent upon international boom-and-bust cycles in primary commodities.

Figure 8.1 shows the dynamics of world price indices for a number of key Ukrainian export commodities: steel, wheat, sunflower oil and urea (quarterly breakdown, 1995–2016).[10]

Despite the different amplitude of price fluctuations in Ukrainian export commodities, they all approximately have the same profile: i) "failure" in the late 1990s; ii) recovery and rapid rise in 2000–2007; iii) deep decline during 2008–2009; iv) growth in 2010–2011; and v) protracted decline in 2012–2016. A weighting and subsequent aggregation of price indices in Figure 8.1 provides a rough estimate of the dynamics of a composite price index for Ukraine's exports in the period 1995–2016 (Figure 8.2).

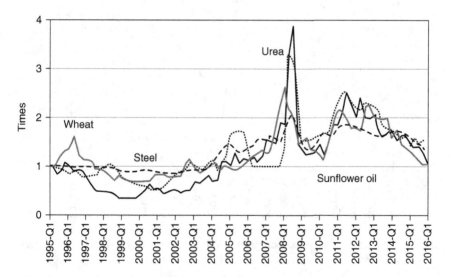

Figure 8.1 Global price indices for some key commodities of Ukraine's exports: wheat, steel, urea and sunflower oil (1995 Q1 = 1), 1995–2016

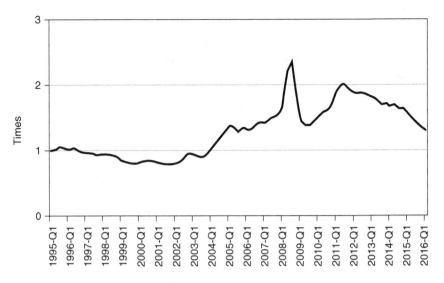

Figure 8.2 Commodity price composite for Ukraine's exports (1995 Q1 = 1), 1995–2016

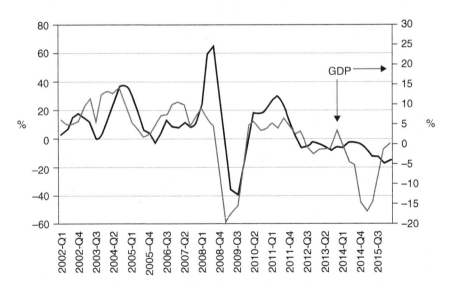

Figure 8.3 Commodity price composite and Ukraine's real GDP (annual rates), 2002–2016

The price index thus calculated allows considering its annual growth rates with quarterly breakdowns (Figure 8.3).[11] Its comparison with the corresponding rates of Ukraine's real GDP growth rates on a quarterly basis enables an insightful interpretation of the causes of Ukraine's cyclical fluctuations since the early 2000s.

Global commodity prices and Ukraine's GDP

Figure 8.3 traces almost perfectly the rises and falls of the Ukrainian economy: periods of growth clearly correlate with increases in the global prices of Ukraine's commodity exports, while periods of contraction closely follow the price decline of these same commodities. A close correlation between the cycles of international commodity markets and the Ukrainian economy could explain why the only period of sustained economic growth in Ukraine took place in 2000–2007, although corruption and political tensions at that time were no less widespread than during other periods since independence.

One of the main reasons for economic growth during this period should therefore be attributed to the rise in commodity prices rather than to "structural reforms", improved business climate or a more stable political environment. In 2002–2007, the average annual price growth for the above group of commodities exceeded 12%, contributing to a 7.5% GDP growth in Ukraine, an exceptional performance that largely exceeded the global growth rate (3.4%). In the early 2000s, Ukraine entered a "commodity Eden" period, receiving a windfall inflow of foreign currency, investments and loans, experiencing an appreciation of the Hryvnia, a record increase in net international reserves (from zero to USD 38 billion in August 2008), exceptionally high income and budget revenues, a boom in crediting and banking demands, a construction fever, irrationally-high prices in the real estate sector, and an extremely large consumption demand justifying price increases and ultimately supporting inflation.

Yet, Ukraine's "Eden growth" melted away in two or three months in the autumn of 2008, when the global financial crisis ushered in a severe drawdown in the price of international commodities.[12] Growth in annual commodity prices collapsed from +64% in the third quarter of 2008 to –11%, –36% and –39% in the first three quarters of 2009. Ukrainian GDP saw its worse year on record, plunging by 14.8% year on year. Many of the resulting problems still stand unresolved a decade later, including a strong devaluation in the national currency, foreign currency debt, external debt, endemic insolvency, domino bankruptcies, banks foreclosures, financial dependency on IFIs, falling incomes, high unemployment and, ultimately, a massive social sense of hopelessness, which only the 2014 Revolution of Dignity could partially reverse.

While in 2010 there was a new boom on the commodity market, this lasted less than two years. Its short duration together with the adoption of unsuccessful economic policies prevented a growth revival and an effective untangling of the web of problems Ukraine had accumulated by that point.

A new crisis in the Ukrainian economy began in early 2014, in association with the Russian annexation of Crimea and its military intervention in Donbass. While the military, human and financial losses that Ukraine has borne since then still need accurate estimates, there is no doubt that the 2014 and 2015 deep GDP contractions (–6.6% and –9.8% respectively) were largely due to the military aggression and the loss of national territory. At the same time, it went almost unnoticed that this phase of economic crisis coincided with a new drop in global commodity prices. In fact, the recession on world commodity markets began much earlier than 2014: most Ukrainian commodities already began giving signs of weakness as early as 2012. However, for a long time the negative consequences of the commodity prices' fall had been mitigated by keeping the Hryvnia exchange rate fixed and by the simultaneous depletion of international reserves.

By early 2014, international reserves had fallen to USD 20 billion (while at the beginning of 2012 they exceeded USD 31 billion). Taking into account the upcoming foreign exchange payments, a further defense of the Hryvnia exchange rate became unrealistic. As a consequence, the decision to devalue was taken before the Russian annexation of the Crimea. However, because the two events happened almost simultaneously, many observers became convinced that the spiral of devaluation, the fall of bank deposits and the simultaneous shrinking of Ukraine's output were the direct consequence of the military aggression. In this respect, it should be recognized that a more favourable external conjuncture in 2012–2015 would have significantly softened the 2014–2015 crisis, both in terms of currency devaluation and GDP decline.

Global commodity prices and Ukraine's budget

Given the above-mentioned cycles, it can be assumed that movements in world commodity prices should also affect the indicators of the consolidated budget of Ukraine. This is because, other things being equal, rapid growth of real GDP can be assumed to boost budget revenues at all levels, while also reducing the gap with budget expenditures. Conversely, contractions in the international commodity markets should reflect negatively in the consolidated budget – both in terms of revenue and deficit.

These assumptions are proven correct by comparing the dynamics of prices for Ukrainian exports (steel, wheat, sunflower oil and urea) and the two parameters of revenue and deficit in the Ukrainian consolidated budget during the period 2003–2015 (Figures 8.4 and 8.5). Attention should be paid to the upward phase, which took place in 2003–2008. During that period, the annual rate of budget revenues varied within a 20–60% range (on a quarter-to-quarter basis) (Figure 8.4).[13] As for the fiscal deficit, it even reversed for a while, turning into a fiscal surplus in the first half of 2007 (Figure 8.5).[14]

Remarkably, fiscal stability at that time was in striking contrast with the political situation in the country, which was besieged by permanent parliamentary elections, changes of government, challenging presidential campaigns

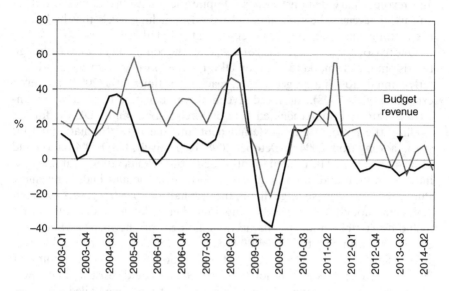

Figure 8.4 Commodity price composite and revenue of Ukraine's consolidated budget (annual rates), 2003–2014

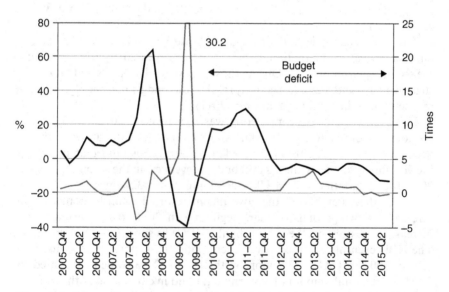

Figure 8.5 Commodity price composite and deficit of Ukraine's consolidated budget (annual rates), 2005–2015

and revolutionary demonstrations. Despite these tensions, domestic output and fiscal revenues beat all national records, reaching levels that had never been attained before and were never to be attained after.

One reason for these impressive results was the commodity boom. Although the rise in global market prices for Ukrainian exports was uneven, its quarterly annual growth averaged 17.5%, reaching at times 40% (2004), and even exceeding 60% (2008). Increased revenues from commodity exports guaranteed Ukraine an unprecedented flow of foreign loans and FDI; the former swelling the national gross external debt and the latter the national FDI stock, adding from 2004 to October 2008, respectively, USD 74.4 billion and USD 42.3 billion. The total amount of additional capital allowed an increase in consumption and imports, giving a boost to trade and budget revenues. Public revenues were so large that in the first half of 2008 the government felt confident enough to begin addressing a number of long-standing litigations, including compensation to the account holders of the former "Sberbank SSSR", promising up to UAH 1,000 to anyone who lost her savings.[15]

As mentioned, this sustained, yet fragile, boom lasted till the autumn of 2008, as neither production nor budget revenues could resist falling export prices. A rapidly degrading external environment quickly entailed a crisis in Ukraine's domestic economy and public finances: when in 2009 Ukrainian raw materials' prices collapsed by 40% in quarterly terms, they caused a 20% drop in Ukraine's real GDP and an equally severe slide in budget revenues (Figures 8.3 and 8.4). As a consequence, the budget deficit rose 30-fold (Figure 8.5).

The 2008 economic and financial collapse was somehow alleviated by another revival of international commodity prices in 2010–2011, peaking in the second quarter of 2011. During those two years, Ukraine's real GDP grew steadily (4.1% and 5.2%, respectively) and so did budget revenues (growth rate reached 55.5% in the third quarter of 2011).

However, the positive conjuncture was over by early 2012, and Ukraine's economy returned to a recession. Annual GDP growth rates in Ukraine decreased to 0.3% in 2012 and were flat by 2013. This immediately reduced the volume of financial inflows and budget revenues. In the second quarter of 2013, the 12-month deficit of Ukraine's budget grew 3.3 times.

Under these conditions, the government resorted again to domestic and foreign borrowing. In particular, beginning in 2011, the government put increasing pressure on the central bank (NBU) to support budget spending. The NBU eventuly accepted government bonds in its portfolio, moving from zero in 2007 to UAH 147 billion by the end of 2013, which accounted for 58.3% of the total amount of government bond in circulation at that time.[16]

In 2012–2015, the prices of Ukrainian raw materials fell of 30%, taking the duration of this new wave of price recession and Ukrainian GDP compression to four years. In 2015, the condition of the consolidated budget began to look more stable, although the factors of that consolidation were purely fictitious, as the balancing of the 2015 budget largely occurred because of new loans to the public sector (net financing amounted to USD 3.5 billion), writing-off part of the external debt (about USD 3.6 billion), non-repayment of a large gas loan to Russia (USD 3 billion) and a 40–50% inflation rate.

Since 2014, these developments took place against the backdrop of the Russian annexation of Crimea and the outbreak of the war in the East of the country. The latter was accompanied by a significant casualty toll as well as industrial and financial losses, which exacerbated budget problems.

Global commodity prices and the Hryvnia/US dollar exchange rate

The UAH has been pegged to the USD since its introduction into circulation on 2nd September 1996. Since then its exchange rate to the USD has fallen more than 15 fold, namely from 1.76 to 27 UAH/USD. Remarkably, almost 70% of this decline occurred during the 2014–2015 period, following the loss of Crimea, the war in Donbass, the Maidan revolution and the change of regime.

This steady devaluation trend can be explained considering the large external dependency of the Ukrainian economy, its vulnerability to commodity prices and political and military instability. A comparison of these dynamics with the corresponding fluctuations in UAH/USD exchange rates is no less indicative than the dynamics discussed in the analysis of cyclical fluctuations in Ukraine's GDP and the variables associated to the country's consolidated budget (Figure 8.6).[17] In particular, Figure 8.6 shows how, between 1996 and 2016: i) all currency crises in Ukraine followed the recessions in global commodity prices; ii) the Ukrainian economy and its currency could not resist any of the three major commodity price recessions; and iii) exchange rate stability could be achieved only under the condition of growing export prices.

While it is clear that every currency crisis had its own specificity, all of them were characterized and facilitated by the absence of full recoveries. Thus, on the eve of 1998–1999, Ukraine was still reeling from the past exchange rate shocks and from the early 1990s hyperinflation, while foreign exchange for international reserves could be only obtained in the form of debt. This situation of persistent weakness was an obvious catalyst and amplifier of the new crisis.

Similarly, the crisis of 2008–2009 was aggravated by the pyramid of loans that had been underwritten in foreign currency. Reduced income from exports entailed widespread financial insolvency and domino bankruptcies, which caused a financial collapse whose debris were still to be fully removed at the beginning of the devaluation in 2014. In addition, the government in Kiev at that time was in a state of undeclared political and financial isolation imposed by the Western community. While the unofficial ostracization was lifted with the change of the Ukrainian administration in the spring of 2014, the war in the East proved to be an equally unsupportable burden to State finances and financial stability.[18]

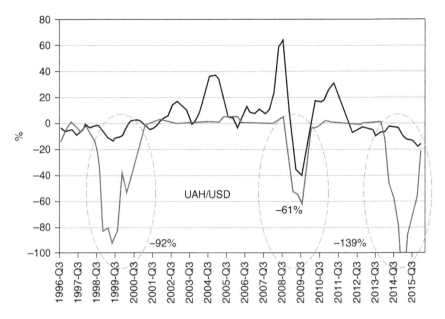

Figure 8.6 Commodity price composite and exchange rate of the UAH to the USD (annual rates), 1996–2015

On the whole, the timing of all three currency crises seems to have been defined by Ukraine's commodity export specialization and by declines in the price of key export commodities. Thus, their causal sequencing and stages were very similar: i) declining international commodity prices; ii) decreased exports and export-related incomes; iii) devaluation of the Hryvnia; iv) capital flight; v) severe aggravation of financial and budget deficits; vi) banking crisis; vi) exhaustion of the international reserves; and vii) borrowing from the IMF. Ukraine's budget gaps, which are often regarded as a root cause of its currency crisis, have in reality often been the consequence of BoP imbalances and currency weakness. Sharp increases in fiscal deficits resulted not only from poor fiscal management, but also from decreases in global demands for raw materials.

In fact, the most significant problems with the UAH exchange rate began exactly with depressed cycles in international commodity markets. After that, Ukraine initiated active contacts with the IMF in order to obtain new financial assistance. New IMF programmes began before the crisis of 1998–1999 with two Stand-By Arrangements (SBAs) in 1996 and 1997,[19] an Extended Fund Facility (EFF) in 1998,[20] a new wave of SBAs (2008, 2010[21] and 2014[22]), and yet another EFF (2015).[23] All these programmes (perhaps with the only exception of the 2010 SBA) coincided with commodity recessions: –104.3% in August 1999; –64.8% in September 2009; and –182.8% in February 2015 (on an annual basis) and were aimed at defending the UAH exchange rate while this was facing severe pressures due to deteriorations in the BoP.

Global commodity prices and Official Development Assistance (ODA)

Undoubtedly, it is easier to point at shortcomings in the financial aid system and in the ODA architecture than to eliminate them. However, these difficulties should not refrain us from such a quest.

A first necessary step is to recognize that ODA is aimed not so much at the transfer of more advanced production technologies to beneficiary countries, as it is to mitigate the negative consequences of the lack of such technologies in these countries.

This is evident from available ODA data: according to the OECD (2012), bilateral ODA from Development Assistance Committee (DAC) members is mostly channeled to social and administrative infrastructures (37.7%) and economic infrastructures (17.2%), while only 7.7% of the resources are dedicated to the development of production. Strikingly, the latter figure is only marginally above ODA administrative expenses (5.2%).

A second necessary consideration relates to the fact that, the support to the development of production itself does not mean technological modernization, as ODA donors and IFIs seldom take issue with technology transfer and the technological development of their beneficiaries at all. Instead, economic interventions are often focused on physical infrastructures. Other typical sectors of intervention include institutional capacity building, social welfare and the short-term stabilization of these countries' financial, currency and payment capacities. All these interventions are, of course, extremely important; yet, in themselves, they do not guarantee the development of the high value-adding manufacturing and service industries that low- and mid-income commodity economies need the most.

In this way, the problem of economic and financial instability in ODA recipient countries remains structurally unaddressed. This also comes as a consequence of the fact that DAC members naturally have their own interests, which do not necessarily coincide with the needs of commodity-dependent economies. For example, the industrial development policy of European countries hinges on its capacity to gain, or maintain, affordable and reliable access to energy and raw materials (European Commission 2012), a priority which is hardly compatible with the promotion of industrial development in the very same countries exporting such commodities.

Conclusion

ODA and short-term macro financial assistance provided to developing economies and emerging markets should properly assess the structural features of the economies they serve. Crucially, this assessment should include an evaluation of: i) the beneficiary country's economic specialization and comparative advantages, particularly when these rely on commodities; ii) the country's reliance upon international markets and cyclical conjunctures; iii) the country's capacity to influence these markets, with a particular attention to those cases in which the economy's small size and underdeveloped financial system make the country a pure price-taker (as opposed to a price-maker) and an unlikely candidate for economic diversification; and iv) crucially immature capacities to stand against adverse international shocks.

While IFIs mostly focus on financial equilibrium, budget discipline, moderate monetary policy, support to large caps as well as openness to foreign investments, too little is done to tackle the fundamental weaknesses of these economies. Current programmes are aimed to help transition economies to raise their market competitiveness and to improve their ability to smooth the effects of unfavourable commodity prices – yet, they fall short of the fundamental target of steering these economies towards a more stable and viable development path. Commodity dependency undermines financial resilience and leaves public finances fragmented: these limits are both systemic and cyclical, as the development literature has observed for a long time. These problems cannot be eradicated without a more structural economic diversification entailing a production movement towards more technologically-advanced industries; capital investments in the secondary and tertiary sectors and, ultimately; a resolute shift of focus towards goods and services with higher value-added content.

The recent Ukrainian experience is rather indicative in that sense, as the fiscal, monetary and currency factors seemed to be only concurrent, rather than determining, causes of the multiple economic crises the country endured since the 1990s. The most evident and direct sources of Ukraine's economy instability can be linked to its reliance upon commodity exports, its small size and the cyclical nature of prices in the international commodity markets. While adverse price conjunctures systematically caused economic and financial crises, the Ukrainian economy was able to bounce back as soon as international commodity markets underwent new expansionary phases. This suggests that the country is capable of managing responsibly windfall profits, as it is also evidenced by healthy public finances in those years.

These findings should be taken into consideration in designing and assessing ODA and macro-financial assistance programmes, whose mandate is to raise structural resilience in developing economies and emerging markets. Focus needs to be put on the manufacturing and technological development of these economies rather than on a too-narrowly focused support of their short-term fiscal, monetary and BoP equilibrium policies.

Notes

1 Ukraine: 2016 Article IV Consultation and third review under the Extended Arrangement, Requests for a Waiver of Non-Observance of a Performance Criterion, Waiver of Applicability, Rephasing of Access and Financing Assurances

Review-Press Release; Staff Report; and Statement by the Executive Director for Ukraine. IMF Country Report No 17/83, April 2017 file:///C:/Users/User/Downloads/cr1783.pdf.

2 The period 2014–2016 was excluded from this observation because of the military invasion, the war in the East of Ukraine and the dramatic economic, financial and human losses associated to these events.

3 Taking into account the results of 2015 and 2016, the real GDP fell of almost 40%.

4 Source: World Bank data. Available at: http://databank.worldbank.org/data/ unless otherwise indicated.

5 Source: National Bank of Ukraine. Available at: www.bank.gov.ua.

6 These included a set of economic policy measures mostly related to the then fashionable "shock therapy" and Washington Consensus instruments/principles, including: mass (voucher) privatization; "the quicker the better" principle; deregulation; trade liberalization; opening to any FDI (mainly from offshore zones); budget discipline; and, disinflation.

7 The annual CPI inflation exceeded 10,000% in 1993 and was obviously treated as a critical stumbling block for any further economic development.

8 The Hryvnia is the national currency of Ukraine, introduced in September 1996.

9 World Bank's statistics.

10 Author's calculation on the data of portal IndexMundi, available at: www. indexmundi.com/ commodities/.

11 Calculated on the data from Ukraine's State Statistical Service, available at: www.ukrstat. gov.ua/ and portal IndexMundi and www.indexmundi.com/ commodities/.

12 Exports of goods in Ukraine fell from USD 63.2 billion in 2008 to USD 37.1 billion in 2009, though in 2007 the proceeds amounted to USD 46.2 billion. This decline in national income deteriorated the demand for domestic goods and services, thus reiterating the vicious cycle of dependency upon boom and bust cycle, cyclically-low revenues, cyclically-low national aggregate demand and structurally low growth. National production was also undermined by FDI (net) decline in those years. This dropped from USD 9.9 billion in 2008 to USD 4.7 billion in 2009. From September 2008 to September 2009 the Hryvnia depreciated by 39%. Gross external debt grew respectively from 56.7% of GDP (2008) to 88.7% (2009). Ukraine subsequently applied for an IMF Stand-By Arrangement in September 2008. The IMF facilities extended to Ukraine amounted to USD 4.5 billion in 2008 and USD 10 billion in 2009. In addition Ukraine was provided with USD 2 billion through General and Special SDR.

13 Calculated on the data from the National Bank of Ukraine, available at www. bank.gov. ua/ and portal IndexMundi and www.indexmundi.com/commodities/.

14 Calculated on the data from the National Bank of Ukraine, available at www. bank.gov.ua/ and portal IndexMundi and www.indexmundi.com/commodities/.

15 "Sberbank SSSR" was the only household deposit bank in the former USSR. Almost all savings in the bank were annihilated by the hyperinflation in the early 1990s. Many former depositors still feel cheated as they have lost their life savings held in the bank. Since then a few politically motivated attempts have been undertaken to compensate those losses. In the first half of 2008, the government initiated the only realistic attempt at doing this thanks to the high wave of commodity prices and budget revenues. However, the attempt failed as soon as budget

resources begun suffering in the fourth quarter of 2008 against the background of falling commodity prices.

16 Equivalent of USD 18.4 billion at the official UAH exchange rate.

17 Calculated on the data from the National Bank of Ukraine, available at: www.bank.gov.ua/ and portal IndexMundi, available at: www.indexmundi.com/commodities/.

18 Both the Crimea annexation and the war in Donbass were associated not only with current losses but also with extremely negative expectations for the future. Negative financial forecasts were also fueled by the drop of the Hryvnia against the US dollar (by 70% over the first eight months of 2014) as well as by banking panic, which further deteriorated the situation in the forex market as it pushed the demand for hard currencies and weakened international reserves.

19 Both programmes were designed to support the local currency in order to bring down inflation to credible and manageable rates.

20 The programme began in September 1998 in order to cope with the BoP problems occurred after the Asian crisis and the Russian Federation's default on its debt.

21 One of the programmes was launched in October 2008, just at the beginning of the Great Recession. A second programme was agreed in mid-2010 as an immediate replacement.

22 A 24-month Stand-By Arrangement (USD 17.1 billion) involving exceptional access was agreed in April 2014 "to restore macroeconomic stability, strengthen economic governance and transparency, and lay the foundation for robust and balanced economic growth".

23 A 4-year Extended Arrangement (USD 17.5 billion) replaced a Stand-By Arrangement (2014) in March 2015 as "the conflict in the East has pushed Ukraine's BoP and adjustment needs beyond what can be achieved under the … two-year SBA-supported program." The EFF program aimed "to support economic recovery and return to external sustainability, building on the existing macroeconomic program while extending the structural reform agenda".

References

Birdsall, N., De la Torre, A. and Menezes, R. (2001), 'Washington Contentious: Economic Policies for Social Equity in Latin America', Carnegie Endowment for International Peace and Inter-American.

Ebeke, C. and Fouejieu Azangue, A. (2015), *Inflation Targeting and Exchange Rate Regimes in Emerging Markets*, IMF Working Paper, WP/15/228.

European Commission (2012), 'A Stronger European Industry for Growth and Economic Recovery Industrial Policy – Communication Update', Communication to the European Parliament, the Council, the European Economic and Social Committee and the Committee of the Regions, Brussels, 10.10.2012. COM(2012) 582 final.

Kinda, T., Mlachila, M. and Ouedraogo, R. (2016), Commodity Price Shocks and Financial Sector Fragility, IMF Working Paper, WP/16/12.

Korablin, S. (2016), 'The "lagging growth" model: economic factors and consequences for Ukraine', *Economy and Forecasting*, 2: 71–82.

Marangos, J. (2008), 'The evolution of the anti-Washington Consensus debate: from 'Post-Washington Consensus' to 'after the Washington Consensus'', *Competition & Change*, 12(3): 227–244.

Naim, M. (1999), 'Fads and Fashion in Economic Reforms: Washington Consensus or Washington Confusion?', Working Draft of a Paper Prepared for the IMF Conference on Second Generation Reforms, Washington, DC: International Monetary Fund.

OECD (2012), 'From Aid to Development: The Global Fight against Poverty', OECD Insights, OECD Publishing.

Reinert, E. (2004) (ed.), *Globalization, Economic Development and Inequality*, Cheltenham: Edward Elgar Publishing.

Reinert, E. (2007), *How Rich Countries Got Rich... and Why Poor Countries Stay Poor*, London: Constable.

Rodrik, D. (2006), 'Goodbye Washington Consensus, hello Washington Confusion? A review of the World Bank's economic growth in the 1990s: learning from a decade of reform', *Journal of Economic Literature*, 44(4): 973–987.

Stiglitz, J. (1998), 'More Instruments and Broader Goals: Moving toward the Post-Washington Consensus', WIDER Annual Lectures 2, Helsinki: UNU World Institute for Development Economics Research.

Stiglitz, J. (2004), 'The Post Washingon Consensus Consensus', Paper presented at a conference 'From the Washington Consensus towards a new Global Governance' sponsored by Foundation CIDOB and the Initiative for Policy Dialogue, The Initiative for Policy Dialogue.

Strauss-Kahn, D. (2011), 'Global Challenges, Global Solutions', Washington, DC: International Monetary Fund.

Studwell, J. (2013), *How Asia Works: Success and Failure in the World's Most Dynamic Region*, London: Profile books.

Williamson, J. (1990), 'What Washington means by policy reform', in J. Williamson (Ed.), *Latin American Adjustment: How Much Has Happened?*, Washington, DC: Institute for International Economics.

Williamson, J. (2004), 'A Short History of the Washington Consensus', Paper commissioned by Fundación CIDOB for a conference «From the Washington Consensus towards a new Global Governance», Washington, DC: Institute for International Economics.

9 Global Economic Governance, Human Security and socio-economic development in Latin America

The Colombian and Mexican experiences

Eunice Rendón Cárdenas

Introduction

According to the World Health Organization (WHO), 90% of the world's violent deaths occur in countries with low to medium GDP per capita. A continent struggling with poverty and inequality, Latin America accounts for 30% of the world's homicides, making it the most violent continent in the world. While, in 2012, homicide rates per 100,000 inhabitants were 2.7 in Asia; 2.9 in Europe; 4.4 in North America and 9.7 in Africa, this figure was as high as 23.9 in Latin America, corresponding to 400 reported homicides in every single day of the year, almost 17 homicides every hour (Chioda 2016).

The relations between violence and socio-economic development are multiple, mutually reinforcing and circular. On the one side, socio-economic disparities and lack of job opportunities in the legal economy contribute to crime and societal violence. On the other, violence and endemic insecurity have immediate repercussions on a country's Human Development Index (HDI) – measuring, among other things, life expectancy at birth – but also take a heavy toll upon long-term prospects for economic growth by negatively affecting the actual and potential value of the stock of human resources, by discouraging private investments and by wasting budget resources for security enforcement and administration. In this respect, it is worth noting that costs dedicated to crime prevention and repression are among the most criticized components of national GDPs, since they should be seen as negative externalities of dysfunctional socio-economic development models, rather than as economic sectors positively contributing to the national output/national aggregate demand.

Latin America exhibits all the features of this circular relation between poverty and violence. Most recently, the deterioration of the security situation in the 2010s is to be associated with the economic downturn entailed by the global financial crisis of 2008. At its own turn, the surge in violence costed dearly to the continent: between 2010 and 2014, the total cost of delinquency in the Latin American and Caribbean region was estimated to account for 2.41%

to 3.55% of the region's GDP, corresponding to USD 115 to 170 billion. To put this figure into perspective, the Inter-American Development Bank (IDB) suggested that crime costed Latin America a value equal to the continent's total infrastructure investment portfolio over that same period (Jaitman et al. 2017).

Taking into account the centrality of the poverty/violence nexus in understanding *Human Development*, this paper aims to: i) clarify the linkages between security and socio-economic development; ii) propose the concept of *Human Security* as a valid tool to design security policies aimed at reducing violence and its negative impact upon *Human Development*; iii) assess the effectiveness of security policies adopted by the current Global Economic Governance (GEG) system, by looking at the security strategies that major GEG shapers have adopted in Latin America, and particularly in Colombia and Mexico, where violence has come to represent the main challenge to *Human Development*; and iv) propose, on the basis of the Colombian and Mexican experiences, a model of security policy which has a proven track record in fostering *Human Development*.

The concept of violence

The *World Report on Violence and Health,* published annually by the WHO, defines violence as

> the intentional use of physical force or power, threatened or actual, against oneself, another person, or against a group or community that either results in or has a high likelihood of resulting in injury, death, psychological harm, maldevelopment or deprivation.
>
> Krug et al. 2002

The report distinguishes among three sub-types of violence, based on the relationship between victim and perpetrator: i) self-directed violence, where the perpetrator and the victim are the same individual, divided into self-abuse and suicide; ii) interpersonal violence, where the violent act occurs between different individuals and takes the shape of "family and intimate partner violence" including child maltreatment; intimate partner violence and elder abuse or "community violence", divided in acquaintance violence and stranger violence, the latter including youth violence; assault by strangers; violence related to property crimes; and violence in workplaces and other institutions; and iii) collective violence, where violence is committed by larger groups of individuals and is justified upon social, political or economic reasons.

In addition to these three sub-types, the WHO also categorizes violent actions according to the dimensions through which they may be inflicted or caused, distinguishing between: i) physical; ii) sexual; iii) psychological; and iv) deprivational (Krug et al. 2002). The overlapping of these taxonomies results in a complex classification, with different nuances in the final typologies of violence, their social effects and the recommended strategies to confront them. For all of them, the WHO recognizes how the effects of violence go beyond mortality and physical disabilities, generating severe morbidities such as psychological pathologies, of which Post-Traumatic Stress Disorder (PTSD) represents perhaps the most well-known category.

The causes of violence: the social-ecological model of violence prevention

The ultimate goal of violence prevention policies is to stop violence before it begins. Keeping this ultimate finality in mind, a number of disciplines have tried explaining the causes of violence in order to intervene upon them before they give rise to their consequences. Most sociological and public health theories agree today that no single factor alone can explain why some social groups are at higher risk of interpersonal violence than others.

The social-ecological model of violence prevention – which attempts to explain interpersonal violence by considering it as the result of interactions between individuals, relationships, communities and societal factors (World Health Organization 2007) concludes that the causes of violence are not universal and that they must be studied within the context in which they occur (Scott 2008). The theory recognizes a set of common causes as underpinning different types of interpersonal violence and distinguishes such causes into four categories (World Health Organization 2004):

1. At the individual level, the way individuals behave is influenced by personal history factors, as well as by biological factors, which also impact the likelihoods of becoming a victim or a perpetrator of violence. These factors include being a victim of child maltreatment, psychological or personality disorders, alcohol and/or substance abuse and a history of behaving aggressively or having experienced abuse.
2. Personal relationships can be a major source of risk. For instance, the relationship with family, friends, intimate partners and peers can influence the risk of becoming a victim or a perpetrator of violence. This is a remarkably important factor in degraded family and social contexts: abusive partners and violent friends have a strong influence on a person's chances of developing aggressive behaviour.
3. Community contexts in which social relationships occur, for instance, schools, neighbourhoods and workplaces, also have an impact in the likelihood of developing violent behaviour. Other risks covered by this category include unemployment, population density and mobility, as well as exposure to drug or arms trafficking.
4. Societal factors influence whether violence is encouraged or inhibited. Among these are the economic and social policies that generate and maintain inequalities between people, the possibility of obtaining weapons, cultural and social norms like those relating to gender and parental dominance, and cultural norms that endorse violence as an acceptable method to resolve conflicts (Solar and Irwin 2010).

All four risk factor categories are heavily influenced by structural inequalities in society. The socio-economic conditions in which people are born and raised and in which they eventually live and age are referred to as "social determinants". The distribution of income and its discriminations based on gender, ethnicity or disability are strong social determinants, as also are the political and governance structures that strengthen and perpetuate, rather than reduce and inhibit, inequalities in a society. That is, income distribution inequalities, which are ultimately co-responsible in shaping most of the causes underpinning social violence, are iterated and reiterated by mechanisms such as formal and informal governance structures, education systems, labour market structures and the extent and nature of redistributive policies, such as social welfare and cash transfer programmes.

Because social determinants are key determinants of violence, they often represent important entry points for public policies aimed at reducing violence and improving *Human Security*. Since the causes of violence are multiple, it is consequential that prevention policies must also tackle these risk factors in their multiplicity. Hence, the social determinants approach to violence helps understanding how crucial the integration of coherent actions across several policy areas and target groups is. It suggests the need to attend the many interlinkages and cross-cutting elements of violence at the same time, while also addressing the reality that violence is produced within specific community frameworks, characterized by specific conditions that can hardly be generalized.

Violence and conflict in international perspective

The WHO's taxonomies and the social-ecological model of violence on which they are based reflect understandings that have long prevailed in the theory and praxis of social disciplines dealing with violence in society, including psychology, sociology, urban studies and public health. Notwithstanding the fact that these conceptual categories of violence and their operationalizations have been considered valid for decades across many social contexts at national level, there has been a major detachment between these and the conceptual categories of violence and their operationalizations used at the international level.

Disciplines dealing with the international perspective, including international relations, geopolitics and strategic studies, have traditionally understood violence in a completely different conceptual framework, whereby violent conflicts represented the main instances in which violence manifested itself. That is, international disciplines have traditionally assumed that violence had most chances of erupting in traditional warfare settings – whether of a civilian or international nature. Since the State's first and foremost mandate is to defend its citizens, it was also assumed that the State's militaries and police agencies were primarily responsible for "security" and that budget lines dedicated to them were the most direct tool to foster "security".

Because the concept of "conflict" had traditionally been used in a classic State-centered and military understanding, by default the concept of "security" was also defined by referring to the universes of nation States, national armies and, ultimately, conventional and nuclear warfare. Thus, while "conflict" was strictly entangled with the military perspective, "security" and the fields of security studies and other international disciplines were also defined, hand-in-hand, in military and defense terms

This understanding was further strengthened during the Cold War era: while the prospect of a Mutual Assured Destruction (MAD) remained a realistic and tragic possibility hoovering above the future of humanity, the meaning of "security" went relatively unchallenged. During this period, anything related to "security" could claim to have ontological priority over any other policy area: because "security" was successfully portrayed as an emergency-type priority and as *the* permissive condition for life to happen, it was dealt out of the realm of normal politics. Security policies in those years came to be seen by many as the only realistic safe-nets against the prospect of a nuclear holocaust. This meant, for both governments in the NATO Alliance and in the Warsaw Pact, the primacy of military affairs over civilian affairs, and the opportunity for the militaries to claim a very large share of the national budgets for themselves.

Changes after 1989: the relevance of the Human Security paradigm

When the Cold War came to an end in 1989, the main reasoning behind State-centered security policies, and the main legitimacy sustaining national armies' claim to a leading role in the governmental affairs of OECD democracies, weakened.

A dual theoretical and normative shift could be observed in the following years. On the one side, the end of the Soviet threat and the growing nationalist and centrifugal forces in the Eastern camp, which eventually brought to the disaggregation of the former Soviet Union and former Yugoslavia, justified a re-centering of Western "security" understandings and a reform of military and strategic affairs. In particular, most of the military and security apparatus among NATO countries and their allies began focusing more on conventional (rather than nuclear), voluntary (rather than conscript-based) and highly mobile (rather than defensive) military capacity to better deal with the new international environment.

On the other side, in those very same years, it also became evident that most countries in the world were losing far more lives and missing far more growth opportunities to poverty, ignorance, poor economic policies, insufficient social-safety nets and environmental degradation than to civilian or international wars. What many international scholars in the critical tradition had maintained for decades – that, essentially, security experts were barking up the wrong insecurity tree (Human Security Centre 2005), suddenly began reasoning with mainstream views on security and international relations. Violence began to be seen as "direct, killing swiftly through war, *or* indirect, killing slowly and invisibly through poverty, hunger, disease, repression and ecocide" (Kim 1984). Similarly to what had happened to the development paradigm with the introduction of the *Human Development* concept, many began challenging traditional notions of security, arguing that a way more relevant and effective paradigm for understanding global vulnerabilities was needed, and that the proper referent for security should have been the individual rather than the State. In those same years, the UN economist Mahbub Ul Haq was theorizing on the concepts of *Human Development* and *Human Security*.

Other authors in this collection have elaborated on the concept of *Human Development*. I will focus on *Human Security*, which emphasizes the security of individuals and their communities as opposed to the security of nation States. *Human Security* implies that insecurity often derives from environmental vulnerabilities, including, among others, economic instability, natural and manmade disasters and practices of social and gender violence. Insecurity, it is argued, cannot simply be reduced to the impact of military violence, as it is also the consequence of human right violations, common crimes and material vulnerability. By overcoming the notion that the main threat to a society comes from potential external attacks or civilian wars, *Human Security* focuses instead on the most common actual threats to individuals and communities living in low- and mid-income countries, including threats to their economic livelihoods, health and personal dignity (Tadjbakhsh 2009). To a certain extent, the *Human Security* concept represents a wake-up call as to the statistical reality of what really represents a threat to the survival and wellbeing of most part of the humanity across the world.

Because *Human Security* is based on the assumption that violence cannot be understood, categorized or assessed through a single dimension, it also carries the logical conclusion that the causes of violence cannot be reduced to stand-alone, water-tight components. Indirectly, the *Human Security* concept exposes the interlinkages between peace, human rights and socio-economic development and therefore legitimizes, and to a certain extent even relies upon, the social-ecological model of violence prevention. *Human Security* also accomplishes the key and much delayed logical task of bridging the understanding and operationalization of violence in disciplines grounded in national social contexts (including psychology, sociology, urban studies and public health) with the understanding and operationalization of violence in disciplines based on the study of the international system (including international relations, development studies, geopolitics and security studies).

The added value of *Human Security* is therefore the recognition and "securitization" of new threats beyond traditional operationalizations of the concept of "violence" in the international sphere, as well as the recognition of new security actors besides nation States. It abandons the one-size-fits-it-all perspective of traditional security to embrace local necessities, focusing on how specific interventions need being adjusted to the specific context in which they operate (Tadjbakhsh 2009). *Human Security* also offers a new perspective on the ideas of "crisis" and "emergency", whereby these are created by acute threats against human rights, or against the needs and core values of a polity, formed by individuals and communities: "From a Human Security perspective, the aim is not just political stability; it encompasses a notion of justice and sustainability" (Tadjbakhsh 2009). *Human Security* crucially depends on Global Economic Governance (GEG); because it addresses multi-dimensional threats, its policies cannot be understood from the perspective of single policy areas or single national foreign policies (King and Murray 2002).

The UN has proposed a taxonomy of seven types of insecurities that need to be addressed in order to achieve *Human Security*: i) economic: caused by poverty, unemployment, difficult access to credit and other economic opportunities; ii) food: having its roots in hunger, famine and sudden rise in food prices; iii) health: originated from epidemics, sanitation habits, lack of access to basic health care and malnutrition; iv) environmental: produced by environmental degradation, resource depletion and natural disasters; v) personal: caused by physical violence in all of its forms, human trafficking and child labour; vi) community: provoked by inter-ethnic, religious and other identity-based tensions, crime and terrorism; and vii) political: expressed on lack of rule of law and justice, political repression and human rights violations (Human Security Unit 2009).

As a key component of the *Human Security* agenda, violence prevention has been growing in importance on the international development agenda. In 2002, the WHO created the Violence Prevention Alliance (VPA), a network of international agencies, civil society organizations and governments engaged in raising awareness around the problem, encouraging engagement and coordinating international responses. More specifically and more relevantly for this volume, *Human Security* is influenced by GEG via the resources, capacities and expertise available through the multiple GEG layers – including ODA, military assistance and the many international agreements regulating trade and FDI.

Violence has also been among the phenomena that have chiefly influenced *Human Development* in the global south. An excess of underprivileged young population in highly urbanized contexts has often been a pre-condition for high violence rates and low school enrollment rates (Moncada 2013). In this respect, the *Human Security* approach addresses the challenges of violence by focusing on "preventive actions that address the root causes of violence and criminality, and build on the positive contributions of at-risk community members" (United Nations Trust Fund for Human Security 2017).

As suggested in the Introduction, *Human Security* and *Human Development* are strictly interlinked concepts, as they ultimately relate socio-economic opportunities to people's wellbeing: the two are interdependent and bound in a circular relation. There can be no *Human Development* without *Human Security* and vice-versa.

Global Economic Governance and violence prevention in Latin America

Given its history of civil war conflicts, military dictatorships and drug trafficking, Latin America traditionally had a semi-military policing model to address ordinary crime, especially in poor areas. The semi-military policing model essentially supports the view that "criminals" are "enemies" that must be eliminated, and this view has long legitimized abhorrent practices by Latin American security forces. In addition to this theoretical and functional bias, Latin American security agencies generally suffer from poor funding and lack of proper training, causing poor performances and distrust among the public. As a consequence, the Latin American management of security mostly revolves around the discretionary use of coercive power, with intensity being adapted to the situation under management. This model of security has been used, among other countries, also in Colombia and Mexico, by a number of institutional actors involved in security policies: national governments, foreign governments, international organizations and dedicated programmes.

More specifically, the most active institutional actors in Latin America include, aside from the Latin American governments and US security agencies, several UN agencies and programmes, international development banks – including the IDB and the WB – the United States Agency for International Development (USAID), and the Program for Social Cohesion in Latin America (EUROsociAL). An assessment of the role of these organizations should begin by considering their investment budgets in security-related programmes.

As international development programmes addressing violence-related issues in Latin America claim to follow preemptive strategies embracing the *Human Security* concept, it would be fair to consider all resources dedicated to socio-economic development as ultimately aimed at reducing violence. While data from the national budgets of each Latin American country are not readily available, it can safely be assumed that national revenues/expenses represent the major source of financial and non-financial resources for domestic development policies. Because of the consultative nature of modern development cooperation practices, which rely on the principles of ownership, alignment, harmonization, results and accountability, it is equally safe to assume that most part of ODA is concentrated in policy areas that beneficiary governments have agreed to prioritize.

The OECD estimates that between 2002 and 2017 some USD 152 billion have been disbursed in ODA to Latin America and the Caribbean, out of which USD 72.3 billion in South America – suggesting annual averages in the region of USD 10 billion for the whole of Latin America and the Caribbean and USD 5 billion for South America alone.[1] These data are roughly compatible with the order of magnitude indicated in the financial reporting of major bilateral donors.

Between 2006 and 2016, USAID has invested USD 7.3 billion in Latin American and the Caribbean "to end extreme global poverty and enable resilient, democratic societies to realize their potential", with almost USD 900 million invested in the last reported year, 2017 (US Agency for International Development 2018). Between 2013 and 2017, the WB, through the IBRD and the IDA, has lent a total of USD 30.4 billion to Latin America and the Caribbean. This corresponds to USD 6 billion a year, out of which *at least* USD 1.5 billion can be singled out as the grant element.[2] In 2016, the Inter-American Development Bank (IADB), the largest source of development financing for Latin America and the Caribbean, has reported lending USD 9.6 billion to its members, out of which *at least* USD 2.4 billion can be singled out as the ODA component.[3] Figures from these three major donors confirm that the OECD figure of USD 10 billion a year in ODA for the whole Latin American and Caribbean region is indeed realistic.

OECD ODA figures relating to Colombia and Mexico indicate that between 2011 and 2016 the two countries received a yearly average of USD 1 billion and USD 650 million respectively. These average figures will be relevant when compared to international military and security spending in these same countries.

The Colombian experience

Before 1994, Colombia played a key role in the international trafficking of cocaine, yet only a minor role in the production of coca leaves. Cultivation and initial processing had been concentrated in Peru and Bolivia; coca base and paste were subsequently transported to Colombia, to be further processed into cocaine hydrochloride and exported to the main consumer market, North America. Two Colombian cartels – the Medellín and Cali cartels – controlled the trade. However, during the first half of the 1990's, the administration of Peruvian President Alberto Fujimori closed the routes that allowed exports of coca leaves from Peru, a measure that eventually brought to increase cultivation in Colombia. By 2000, Colombia became the lead producer of coca leaves, covering more than 70% of the world's production.

Colombia and the US had already begun cooperating on drug trafficking in 1986 by concentrating efforts on coca eradication rather than on the provision of alternative livelihoods to farmers. These measures provoked widespread protests among small farmers, which eventually led them to join the ranks of the Revolutionary Armed Forces of Colombia (FARC). As a consequence, the joint US–Colombian effort indirectly resulted in a rapid increase in the size and strength of Colombian drug cartels (Witness for Peace 2013).

During the 1990s, the capture of both Pablo Escobar, leader of the Medellín cartel, and the Rodríguez Orejuela brothers, leaders of the Cali cartel, atomized the Colombian drug trade into smaller groups, generating violent struggles to fill the voids of power and to control lucrative drug trafficking rents. Drug traffickers also began occupying increasingly powerful positions within the paramilitary groups: in that decade, the FARC became so entangled with drug trafficking organizations that it became impossible distinguishing one from the other.

In 2000, in response to increasing cocaine production and escalating violence, the Colombian government announced a joint US–Colombia strategy to fight organized crime, known as *Plan Colombia*. The strategy was originally aimed at reducing the production and trafficking of illegal drugs by 50% within a period of six years and improving security conditions by re-gaining control of areas previously ruled by illegal armed groups. Between 2000 and 2008, the US funded the military component of *Plan Colombia* in the tune of roughly USD 550 million per year, for a total of USD 4.9 billion over nine years. On the other side, the US destined USD 1.3 billion to social, economic and justice activities attached to the programme over that same period (United States Government Accountability Office 2008). This means that, out of the USD 6.2 billion that the US government invested in *Plan Colombia* between 2000 and 2008, roughly 80% of the aid package went to military and security forces. These data are compatible with the order of magnitude indicated by official ODA data and other sources (Rabasa and Chalk 2001). On its side, the Colombian government invested approximately USD 810 million per year in the plan. Taken together, the US and Colombian contributions totaled 1.2% of Colombia's average annual GDP in that period. Overall, the US–Colombian plan employed a military offensive strategy rather than a *Human Security* strategy (Mejía 2016).

Plan Colombia had mixed results on the cultivation, processing and distribution of illegal narcotics in Colombia, with particularly poor results on coca cultivation and cocaine production (United States Government Accountability Office 2008). The original plan was intended to create alternative livelihood opportunities for coca growers; yet, as for many other attempts before, the effectiveness of such activities remains questionable. Many programmes were limited to training or monetary incentives, without providing farmers with the necessary resources to produce alternative agricultural products, thus ensuring the economic self-sustainability of alternative cultivations.

At the same time, *Plan Colombia* contributed to exacerbating and justifying the Colombian national humanitarian crisis. Brutal, pro-government paramilitary groups had been used against the FARC since the 1980s, causing tens of thousands of non-combatants deaths before *Plan Colombia* began. Yet, the phenomenon assumed a massive dimension in the 2000s: with the paramilitaries playing a smaller role and the Colombian armed forces assuming far greater responsibilities in the anti-guerrilla campaign, extra-judicial killings became normal practice among State security forces. Disturbingly, armed forces were reportedly incentivized in showing "body counts" results against the guerrilla, with the Colombian Ministry of National Defense setting up a system of informal incentives for soldiers and formal incentives for civilian informants to reward body counts (Isacson 2010). In the meantime, the largest part of *Plan Colombia*'s budget was used to train and arm the very military and police forces which were shown to consistently perpetrate human right abuses.

Other statistics suggest that *Plan Colombia* contributed to worsening the human right situation. While between 1996 and 2002 Colombian human-right groups had recorded a total of roughly 3,000 arbitrary detentions, in 2004 alone that number had doubled. Throughout the early 2000s, Colombia also suffered from forced displacements at a massive scale: 1.8 million Colombians were forcibly displaced from their homes in those years, the most severe case in the world after Darfur. Women and children were the most exposed groups, since they represented 72% of displaced communities (United Nations High Commissioner for Refugees 2006). Internal displacements – basically, refugees who do not cross international borders – continued to make Colombia a humanitarian emergency case also in the following years: in 2009, as many as 300,000 people were newly forced from their homes, according to *Consultoría para los Derechos Humanos y el Desplazamiento* (CODHES), the Colombian NGO that monitors the phenomenon.

Plan Colombia incentivized human right abuses because violence eradication by coercive means typically considers only one dimension of the problem, contrary to what we know from the leading violence prevention theories – including the social-ecological model. The cultivation of illegal narcotics cannot be eradicated without providing alternative livelihoods to farmers; while this has proved a particularly elusive task across the world, the fact that both the Colombian and US governments have dedicated only marginal resources to this task, suggests that there was only a partial or instrumental understanding of the issue. By no means was such biased understanding limited to the government: in those years, media and political analysts were also ignoring the multifaceted nature of violence, indirectly contributing to legitimize traditional approaches to social insecurity, and eventually fueling more violence (United Nations High Commissioner for Refugees 2006). The Colombian experience showed that the military response can easily lead to increased segregation both in metropolitan and rural areas, negatively affecting communal identity and further marginalizing violent areas by turning them into ghettos.

Against this national example, the municipal case of Medellín likely represents the best example of the efficacy of *Human Security*-type policies based on local, inclusive, proactive and tailor-made social strategies. Mr Sergio Fajardo, who was elected mayor of Medellín (2003–2007) through the support of a heterogeneous coalition, is credited with creating the *Medellín la más educada* (Medellín, the most educated) strategy, focusing both on restraining violence through an effective policing action *and* on strengthening social policies by providing educational and cultural services as the main vectors of *Human Security* (Fábregas and Marbella 2009). Mr Fajardo's administration reached out to every sector of the society, particularly by creating new public spaces and implementing social programmes with a strong impact on the most vulnerable sectors of the society (Gutiérrez et al. 2009).

Understanding education as the key tool to achieve social transformation, Mr Fajardo dedicated 40% of the municipal budget to improve both the quality and access to education, also by building new schools in the most vulnerable neighbourhoods of the city. To improve social equality and integration, public spaces played a major role in the strategy. Social urbanism was the principle that guided the creation of *Parques biblioteca* (Library parks) built in the neighbourhoods that had the lowest Human Development Index (HDI) rates (Fábregas and Marbella 2009). Mr Fajardo's administration also contributed to reestablishing social cohesion through the programme, "Return to legality", aimed at reintegrating the paramilitaries into the socio-economic texture of the society, while also providing some social safety nets to the conflict's victims and internally displaced people, thanks to the support of local businesses and international development agencies.

The combined results of Mr Fajardo's policies have been impressive: Medellín's yearly homicide rate went from 184 murders per 100,000 inhabitants in 2002 to 28.8 in 2006 (Fábregas and Marbella 2009). The Medellín's administration showed how the proper understanding of risk factors in violence prevention can deliver results that are unconceivable through traditional policing measures. Mr Fajardo's strategy included the objective of integrating Medellín both in the national and regional context, by leveraging external assistance to increase local financial and non-financial resources dedicated to violence prevention. Accordingly, in 2002 he created the Agency for Cooperation and Investment of Medellín, the first decentralized cooperation agency of the country, which contributed to systematizing cooperation and giving sustainability to Fajardo's policies (Alcaldía de Medellín 2008).

The Mexican experience

Drug-related violence in Mexico began to increase steadily in the early 2000s, costing dearly to the country's economic growth and to the future of its youth. In 2006, a positive conjuncture deriving from changes in the Mexican administration and from the US acknowledgement that its domestic demand was fueling powerful and dangerous regional drug networks, led to the development of a bilateral cooperation project meant to meet the security needs of both countries. In 2008, the two governments eventually launched the *Mérida initiative*, a regional strategy based on four actions: i) diluting organized crime groups; ii) strengthening the rule of law in Mexico; iii) creating a stronger border between Mexico and the US, the so-called "21st Century Border Management"; and iv) developing greater social cohesion in communities at risk.

Clearly, the first three pillars of the initiative were based upon traditional security enforcement theory, tackling violence through a repressive and reactive strategy. The inclusion of the fourth pillar represented a novelty and an accomplishment in itself, since it introduced a social component, the only of the strategy focusing on prevention. This component, which had a limited budget compared to the others, allocated resources to "build stronger and more resilient communities that can withstand the effects of crime and violence" (US Agency for International Development 2015). The disequilibrium between the policing/reactive and social/preemptive components of the initiative clearly showed in the budget: out of the total USD 1.1 billion dedicated by the US budget to the initiative in 2008 and 2009, roughly USD 875 million (79.5%) went to the first component and USD 225 million (20.5%) to the second. These proportions are almost identical to those found in *Plan Colombia*. Similarly to the Colombian case, OECD figures suggest that the total value of international ODA investments in those years were only marginally superior to the value of US–Mexican military plan alone, with a total of USD 550 million disbursed in the biennium 2008/2009.[4]

In 2008, actions taken in the framework of the *Mérida initiative* enabled Mexican institutions to bring to trial some 1,000 organized crime cases. Two years later, some 7,600 Mexican police personnel were given a total of 300 trainings in one year alone, reasonably contributing to bring to the arrest of 22,000 alleged drug traffickers and kidnappers (United States Government Accountability Office 2008). Yet, while these results evidenced a strengthening of Mexico's policing capacities, they also came, just as in the Colombian case, at high social costs: the militarization of the Mexican security policy had a proved negative impact on human rights. The Mexican National Human Right Commission reported that torture and arbitrary detention skyrocketed in those same years: the number of alleged human right violations committed by the Department of Defense increased from 182 reports in 2006 to 1,230 in 2008 (Brewer 2009). Remarkably, none of the *Mérida initiative*'s funds were destined to train judicial personnel or federal police officials in human rights law (Brewer 2009).

Despite the *Mérida initiative*'s multibillion-dollar budget and bilateral efforts, the results fell short of expectations, as crime did not decline, and even showed an upward trend.[5] Eventually, the semi-military policing strategy chosen by the Mexican government with the assistance of the US government did not manage to provide Mexican citizens with the constitutional rights and the rule of law they were promised. A clear lesson learnt was the centrality of promoting a culture of crime prevention and creation of strategies capable of giving tools to the society to deal with social and economic marginalization.

When violence reached new heights in 2010, a strong popular and governmental motivation set off the political willingness necessary to experiment new policy measures. This time the government began embracing the *Human Security* approach by introducing a *Law for the Social Prevention of Violence* and creating *Security Subsidies* specifically targeted at the most insecure areas.

One of the best examples of effective violence prevention programmes was implemented in Ciudad Juarez – which, with an yearly homicide rate of 300 per 100,000 inhabitants, detained at the time the unenviable record of the most violent city in the world (Brewer 2009) – through the

Mesa de Seguridad y Justicia (MSJ) programme. The MSJ created citizen committees involving scholars, businessmen, local social leaders and authorities to devise social solutions to the problem of endemic violence. This, at its own turn, created a sense of co-responsibility among citizens, who voluntarily participated in monthly meetings with local authorities to monitor criminal indicators, favouring a common understanding of the prevalence, incidence, enabling conditions and key features of criminality in their communities, eventually leading to common violence prevention strategies.

Eventually, the participants demonstrated such a high level of commitment that they decided to self-impose a tax destined to finance security and violence prevention through the creation of a Trust Fund for Competitiveness and Security (Rendón Cárdenas 2017). Success and sustainability were undoubtedly related to the high level of ownership and the involvement of highly credible social actors; these elements allowed the initiative to continue even after multiple changes in the municipal, state and federal administrations.

Not only did the MSJ create citizen participation mechanisms on violence prevention, but it also enabled citizens to help the public administration in reforming itself. In order to reduce corruption among the police, the programme also helped in professionalizing and dignifying the work of police officers. The initiative managed to mobilize high institutional cooperation, working closely with the Attorney General and achieving a 98.5% efficacy level on the prosecution and sentencing of criminals. The MSJ also strengthened the presence of the Attorney Generals' Offices in the city by hiring 70 new agents during 2013, up from 4 in 2009. Eventually, the MSJ plaid a key role in Juarez' return to life, moving from position number 1 to position number 37 in the list of the most violent cities in the world. This successful experience was subsequently replicated in other Mexican states.

A second remarkable example of successful *Human Security*-inspired policies in Mexico is the experience of the *Palmitas* neighbourhood in the State of Hidalgo. This project focused on the reinsertion of socially marginalized youngsters and the creation of a sense of collectivity through art. The project was carried out by civil society organizations in collaboration with Federal and State authorities working on violence prevention. It illustrates how the intervention and modification of public spaces can increase security perceptions, and improve the quality of relations between residents. The physical transformation of the neighbourhood by rehabilitation works carried out by local gangs – *Los Gatos* and *Los Pichoneros* – who traditionally had rivalry and violent conflict, managed to conspicuously diminish violence and crime rates.[6] The project generated a new social identity along with a sense of belonging and pride within the neighbourhood. The case of *Palmitas* demonstrates that an active participation of the community in constructing, remodeling and recovering public spaces can be an exceptionally successful strategy in diminishing social violence. At the same time, experiences related to public space recovery show the need for continuity, as too short experiences usually fail to generate a real sense of belonging, and can even contribute in generating new sources of friction and insecurity (Geason 1989). Therefore, any social strategy must be sustainable in order to be effective, and this independently from its sector – culture, sport, art or other.

Conflict resolution through social mediation has proven a highly effective strategy in Mexico. In most of the neighbourhoods with a high number of risk factors, including conflict between criminal gangs, the recovery of public space and the strengthening of empathy have proved effective in positively impacting community dynamics, enabling the resolution of interpersonal, community and social conflicts through dialogue and co-responsibility. Still today, many urban areas in Mexico have high levels of social vulnerability due to multiple underlying risk factors; all these areas would benefit from clearly-defined social-mediation processes aimed at resolving disputes, building consensus, reaching solutions and finding damage reparation procedures that are perceived as fair by all involved parties (Rendón Cárdenas 2015).

These experiences yield important lessons for social prevention work and for the Mexican government: while trust remains the most prized social commodity and the hardest result to build, it can be achieved with persistence and a clear commitment from the authorities. Mexico understood and acknowledged that a national policy for violence prevention was needed, and the Peña Nieto administration eventually decided to create a National Program for the Social Prevention of Violence and Crime (PRONAPRED), which received financing in the tune of USD 2.5 billion in 2013, reaching over 100 cities across the country (Rendón Cárdenas 2017). PRONAPRED successfully raised awareness nationwide on violence prevention, pushing state and municipal authorities to work on integrated security strategies, which took into account not only policing actions if not also socially proactive interventions. Due to developments in the Mexican administration and the economic conjuncture, crime prevention policies suffered progressive budget cuts until 2017, when they were discontinued. Considering the objective results of crime prevention policies in Mexico, budget cuts to violence prevention undoubtedly represent a downfall in the Mexican commitment to both *Human Security* and *Human Development*.

Conclusions

On the basis of the Colombian and Mexican experiences, it could be concluded that GEG shapers – Latin American governments, the US government and major ODA donors – have continued privileging traditional security approaches to violence prevention in Latin America, and this despite claims as to the passage to the UN-defined paradigm of *Human Security*. The two most evident examples are the *Plan Colombia* and the *Mérida initiative*, representing hybrid security cooperation programmes with military and social components, in which the former had however a far stronger weight (80%) than the latter (20%). A similar conclusion could be reached even after taking into consideration the broader picture of local and international policies and investments, e.g. local budget allocations and Western ODA channeled to security in Latin America.

Possible explanations for this have pointed at traditional criticisms of OECD foreign and development cooperation policies, underlying the direct interests of donor countries, including through the "tied aid" mechanisms. Lucatello, in particular, suggested that

> US bilateralism in the form of tied aid and its security area is the inevitable result of the "securitization" of the drug trafficking and drug-trafficking-related terrorism agenda, which easily positions itself in a regional Latin American context in which there is no strong, consolidated cooperative security regime. This means that the US agenda of militarization in the fight against the drug cartels is imposed despite its clear failure over the last 20 years.
>
> Lucatello 2009

While both the *Plan Colombia* and the *Mérida initiative* had some positive results in stemming the cultivation, processing and distribution of illegal narcotics, these results were temporary, costly, discontinuous and, ultimately, unsustainable. Crucially, they also came with unacceptable human rights costs. Contrary to these mixed achievements, some local violence prevention projects based on a strong knowledge of the territory and the implementation of activities inspired by the *Human Security* approach, managed to address the root causes of violence by empowering communities, suggesting the potential for alternative life opportunities and, ultimately, reinforcing the capacity of local and national institutions. Contrary to the current state of affairs in international cooperation on security issues, which often offers one-size-fits-it-all solutions to violence and replicates projects without adapting them to the contingencies of countries sharing common challenges but also obvious differences, violence prevention requires willingness from GEG shapers to carve country-specific grassroots strategies, and abandoning for good traditional understandings of "security" to embrace the concept and practice of *Human Security*. How to do this in a scalable and economically sustainable fashion remains a major challenge ahead.

Notes

1 Data from OECD Query Wizard for International Development Statistics.
2 In order to be defined as ODA, concessional lending needs to convey a grant element of at least 25%. Compilation based on WB annual report 2017, lending data.
3 Compilation based on Inter-American Development Bank Data. Available at: https://publications.iadb.org/bitstream/handle/11319/8221/Inter-American-Development-Bank-Annual-Report-2016-Financial-Statements.pdf?sequence=10 (last accessed: 15 March 2018).
4 Data from OECD Query Wizard for International Development Statistics.

5 Yearly homicide rates, kidnaping rates and extortion rates per 100,000 inhabitants went from 11.82; 0.81 and; 4.37 in 2008 to 20.51; 0.93; and; 4.57 respectively in 2017. Available at: http://secretariadoejecutivo.gob.mx/docs/pdfs/tasas%20por%20 cada%20100%20mil%20habitantes/Tasas122017.pdf (last accessed: 15 March 2018).
6 According to the National Public Security System, the number of registered incidents in the community diminished from 56 in 2012, to 34 in 2014, and 12 in 2015. Administrative infractions went from 48 in 2012, to 40 in 2013, 28 in 2014, and 7 in 2015. Available at: https://www.gob.mx/presidencia/prensa/palabras-presidente-de-los-estados-unidos-mexicanos-enrique-pena-nieto-durante-la-inauguracion-del-macromural-pachuca-se-pinta?idiom=kpjmnnii (last accessed: 15 March 2018).

References

Alcaldía de Medellín (2008), 'Del miedo a la esperanza'. Available at: http://acimedellin. org/wp-content/uploads/publicaciones/del-miedo-a-la-esperanza-2014.pdf (last accessed: 15 March 2018).
Brewer, S. (2009), 'Structural Human Rights Violations: The True Face of Mexico's War on Crime', Inter-American Court of Human Rights. Available at: www. corteidh.or.cr/tablas/R22180.pdf (last accessed: 15 March 2018).
Chioda, L. (2016), *Fin a la Violencia en América Latina. Una mirada a la prevención desde la infancia a la edad adulta*, 1st ed. Washington, DC: World Bank.
Fábregas, J. and Marbella, B. (2009), *Medellín, la más Educada. Aprendiendo de Colombia*. Fundación Kreanta. Available at: www.catedramedellinbarcelona. org/archivos/pdf/20-Intoduccion- MedellinlamasEducada.pdf (last accessed: 15 March 2018).
Geason, S. (1989), *Designing Out Crime. Crime Prevention Through Environmental Design*. Canberra: Australian Institute of Criminology.
Gutiérrez, F., Pinto, M., Arenas, J., Guzmán, T. and Gutiérrez, M. (2009), *Politics and Security in Three Colombian Cities*, Bogotá: Instituto de Estudios Politicos y Relaciones Internacionales.
Human Security Centre (2005), *Human Security Report 2005: War and Peace in the 21st Century*, Oxford: Oxford University Press.
Human Security Unit (2009), *Human Security in Theory and Practice*, United Nations. Available at: www.un.org/humansecurity/sites/www.un.org.humansecurity/files/ human_security_in_theory_and_practice_english.pdf (last accessed: 15 March 2018).
Isacson, A. (2010), *Colombia: Don't Call it a Model*, Washington, DC: Washington Office on Latin America.
Jaitman, L., Caprirolo, D., Granguillhome Ochoa, R., Keefer, P., Legget, T., Lewis, J., Mejía-Guerra, J., Mello, M., Sutton, H. and Torre, I. (2017), *The Costs of Crime and Violence, New Evidence and Insights in Latin America and the Caribbean*, Washington, DC: Inter-American Development Bank.
Kim, S. (1984), 'Global violence and a just world order', *Journal of Peace Research*, 21(2): 92–181.
King, G. and Murray, C. (2002), 'Rethinking human security', *Political Science Quarterly*, 116(4): 585–610.
Krug, E., Dahlberg, L., Mercy, J., Zwi, A. and Lozano, R. (Eds.) (2002), *World Report on Violence and Health*, Geneva: World Health Organization.

Lucatello, S. (2009), 'International cooperation and security Mexico and the challenges of the Mérida Initiative', *Voices of Mexico*, 86: 17–20.

Mejía, D. (2016), *Plan Colombia: An Analysis of Effectiveness and Costs,* Brookings: Center for 21st Century Security and Intelligence.

Moncada, E. (2013), 'The politics of urban violence: challenges for development in the global south', *Studies in Comparative International Development*, 48(3): 217–239.

Rabasa, A. and Chalk, P. (2001), 'Colombian government strategy', in A. Rabasa and P. Chalk (Eds.), *Colombian Labyrinth: The Synergy of Drugs and Insurgency and Its Implications for Regional Stability* (pp. 61–70), Arlington: RAND Corporation.

Rendón Cárdenas, E. (2015), 'Justicia cotidiana y mediación comunitaria', *La Crónica*. Available at: www.cronica.com.mx/notas/2015/900022.html (last accessed: 15 March 2018).

Rendón Cárdenas, E. (2017), 'La prevención social del delito en diez reto', in *20 Voces para prevenir el delito*, INACIPE.

Scott, K. (2008), *Violence Prevention in Low and Middle Income Countries: Finding a Place on the Global Agenda: Workshop Summary*, Washington, DC: National Academies Press.

Solar, O. and Irwin, A. (2010), 'A Conceptual Framework for Action on the Social Determinants of Health, Social Determinants of Health', Discussion Paper 2, Geneva: World Health Organization.

Tadjbakhsh, S. (2009), 'Human Security: Looking Back Before Looking Forward', Proceedings of the International Conference on Human Security in West Asia. Available at: www.birjand.ac.ir/ichswa/downloads/Dr%20Tajbakhsh% 27s%20 Paper%20in%20ICHSWA.pdf (last accessed: 15 March 2018).

United Nations High Commissioner for Refugees (2006), *The State of The World's Refugees 2006: Human Displacement in the New Millennium*, UNHCR.

United Nations Trust Fund for Human Security (2017), *To What Issues Can Human Security be Applied? Urban Violence*, United Nations. Available at: www.un.org/ humansecurity/human-security-unit/human-security-approach (last accessed: 15 March 2018).

United States Government Accountability Office (2008), 'Plan Colombia Drug Reduction Goals Were Not Fully Met, but Security Has Improved; U.S. Agencies Need More Detailed Plans for Reducing Assistance', United States Government Accountability Office. Available at: https://www.gao.gov/assets/290/282511.pdf (last accessed: 15 March 2018).

US Agency for International Development (2015), 'Mexico: Country Development Cooperation Strategy', USAID. Available at: https://www.usaid.gov/sites/default/ files/documents/1869/Mexico%20CDCS%202014%202018.pdf (last accessed: 15 March 2018).

US Agency for International Development (2018), 'What We Do'. Available at: https:// www.usaid.gov/what-we-do (last accessed: 15 March 2018).

Witness for Peace (2013), 'Report on the Impact of the U.S War on Drugs in Colombia'. Available at: http://witnessforpeace.org/wp-content/uploads/2017/08/ReportontheI mpactoftheU.S.WaronDrugsinColombiaFINAL (last accessed: 15 March 2018).

World Health Organization (2004), *The Global Burden of Disease: 2004 Update*, Geneva: World Health Organization.

World Health Organization (2007), *The World Health Report 2007: A Safer Future: Global Public Health Security in the 21st Century*, Geneva: World Health Organization.

10 Global Economic Governance and the challenge of economic sustainability in Afghanistan

Emily Bakos and Paul Fishstein

Introduction

This chapter looks at Afghanistan as a case study for whether following macroeconomic orthodoxy and integrating into the world economy necessarily leads to economic growth, job creation and social betterment. Afghanistan is an interesting case study, as an imploded state, a perceived "blank slate", and lack of its own resources gave the US and its allies a relatively free hand in designing policy. On the other hand, given the conditions particular to Afghanistan, the country may be considered *sui generis*, with limited implications for other post-conflict and developing economies.

Afghanistan's economy before 2001

Even before the onset of conflict in 1978 and the subsequent Soviet invasion at the end of 1979, Afghanistan was one of the world's poorest and least developed countries. In 1975, which is considered the height of the country's development, Afghanistan's per capita GDP was the 13th lowest in the world.[1] The country's pre-war economic system has been called "mixed-guided", with elements of both a market economy and a command or socialist one (Fishstein and Amiryar 2015). While the mostly informal agriculture, small-scale production and trading sectors were private, the limited medium- and large-scale manufacturing sector, was, with some periodic vacillation between state and private ownership, almost completely in the hands of the state, or in the *shirkat* system in which company ownership was shared between the government and private individuals. Moreover, the government attempted to guide the economy through price controls and monopsony purchases of important agricultural outputs such as cotton and sugar beets.

Until 1978, Afghanistan steered an uneasy path between Cold War rivals the US and the Soviet Union, seeking and accepting foreign aid and technical assistance from both sides while remaining ostensibly non-aligned. In 1977, the last full "normal" year, 39% of government expenditures were covered by foreign assistance (Rubin 2002).[2] Due to its reliance on foreign sources of finance, Afghanistan has been called the quintessential "rentier" state (Suhrke 2006).

With the collapse of the Soviet Union in 1991 and the discrediting of the socialist path to development in favour of what came to be known as the "Washington Consensus", after the fall of the Taliban in 2001 a return to such a mixed system was impossible, especially as without its own resources the new government had to rely on external funding – and the directives of those who were providing that funding. Moreover, much of the basis of Afghanistan's limited export economy had undergone either external changes (consumer tastes, trade patterns, new competing producers in the region) or was less competitive due to degradation of irrigation and other infrastructure.

Between the fateful year of 1978 and 2001, with fighting destroying agricultural and transport infrastructure, displacing up to one-half of the population either internally or externally (Girardet 2011), and breaking internal and external trading links, overall GDP contracted by 25% (from USD 3.3 billion to USD 2.5 billion) (Guimbert 2004). According to figures released by UNDP in 2001, 70% of Afghanistan's population was estimated to be undernourished, only 13% had access to improved drinking water, and at 26%, Afghanistan had one of the highest rates for child mortality in the world (UNDP 2001). At the end of 2001, after 23 years of war and conflict, the new Interim Administration of Afghanistan faced the future with a shattered economy, degraded infrastructure and decimated institutions.

What was done to revive Afghanistan's economy

After the capture of Kabul and Kandahar by Coalition forces in early November 2001, it was generally assumed that the Taliban were a spent force and that Afghanistan was therefore a "post-conflict" country. The Bonn Conference in December set the political and security directions, while the economic policy directions were set starting with the January–February 2002 donor pledging meeting in Tokyo. Most of the policies and instruments introduced into Afghanistan were similar to those put in place in the most recent post-conflict countries, Kosovo and East Timor. These reflected the macroeconomic orthodoxy of an open, outward-looking, trade-oriented economy. The division of labour between international institutions was likewise similar to the other post-conflict reconstructions, with the WB taking the lead in conducting initial assessments and the IMF taking the lead in developing frameworks for macroeconomic stability and the financial system. The international community, especially the US, insisted on a so-called "light footprint", with a limited foreign presence. This was due in part to an interpretation of history in which Afghans were seen as rejecting anything or anyone that could be called occupiers, but also due to the US wariness about becoming involved in "nation-building."

With 25 nations involved militarily, and more than 60 nations contributing to the reconstruction of Afghanistan, reconstruction has to be seen in the context of the US-led coalition's Operation Enduring Freedom, first and foremost a security endeavour, and part of the US "global war on terror".

Troop-contributing nations mostly viewed reconstruction as part of a larger "whole of government" approach (Fishstein and Wilder 2012).

The US was largely in the lead partly because of its allies' deference in the aftermath of 9/11, but also simply because it mobilized by far the most military power and financial resources. The other Western nations (e.g., the UK, Germany) were largely aligned with the US when it came to policy prescriptions and their implementation. The few minor policy divergences between the US and Europe were precisely on what sort of state Afghanistan should have, and the extent of its role in the economy. In the political realm, most European nations favoured a parliamentary form of government rather than the winner-takes-all presidential one that emerged, while in the economic realm Europe largely favoured a government that would take a more active role in the economy.

Western donors set out to create an enabling environment to promote private sector investment and other economic activity through a wide range of activities: holding investment conferences, establishing legal frameworks and property rights, encouraging privatization of state-owned enterprises, building industrial parks and providing technical assistance for capacity building. Finally, the macroeconomic orthodoxy and the market economy fit into the larger comprehensive package of Western liberal values, including electoral democracy, individual freedoms, free media, and women's rights.

At the *Human Development* level, exceptionally large influxes of ODA that flowed into Afghanistan took its standard form of grants, humanitarian aid and welfare enhancing programmes in government and private service delivery and the building of roads, schools and other infrastructure. The influx of financial resources raised incomes and led to increased availability of consumer goods such as mobile phones, radios, televisions and personal motor vehicles.

With Afghanistan making the transition from a mixed economy, with socialist elements to an open market economy, above all else the focus was on creating the policy and institutional enabling environment in which the private sector could thrive. The immediate focus was on fiscal policy and tax reform, including placing limits on the government's ability to undertake deficit spending. Fiscal policy was a focus from the start because of the international community's interest in setting the stage for self-sufficiency so that Afghanistan would not become a "ward of the international community" (Dowdy and Erdmann 2011). For similar reasons, tax reform and customs performance were also priorities. An important piece was the introduction of a new currency, which was rolled out between September 2002 and January 2003.

Also from the start, regional integration was included in strategies of the US and its international partners, with the push to bring down formal barriers to trade. Afghanistan gained WTO observer status in 2004, and within a few years Afghanistan had become one of the most open economies in the region (Byrd 2007). Meanwhile, Afghanistan signed a number of regional trade agreements, including the South Asian Free Trade Area (SAFTA) agreement in January 2004 and the Afghanistan–Pakistan Trade and Transit Agreement (APTTA) in June 2010, the latter essentially an updated version of a 1965 agreement. APTTA was specifically prioritized as Pakistan remains Afghanistan's most important trading partner and neighbour.[3]

In 2004, after Afghanistan's long-standing debts were cleared with the help of grants from bilateral donors, Afghan authorities began the implementation of a Staff Monitored Program (SMP) in coordination with the IMF.[4] Despite ambivalence and skepticism among the Afghan population and government officials (Fishstein and Amiryar 2015), these standard policy prescriptions were reflected in the government's strategy documents, starting with the initial National Development Framework in April 2002, and subsequently in Securing Afghanistan's Future in 2004 and successive iterations of the Afghanistan National Development Strategy. The market economy, with some caveats, was confirmed in Article 10 of the 2004 Constitution. In April 2006, the Afghan government issued its Interim Afghanistan National Development Strategy (I-ANDS), followed in 2008 by the full ANDS, which was presented as the government's own spontaneous development plan, but which fulfilled the role of a Poverty Reduction Strategy Paper (PRSP) in qualifying the country to participate in the IMF and World Bank Heavily Indebted Poor Country initiative.

Outcomes and results

The economic and social impacts of the outside interventions and formation of the Afghan economy were mixed. While early efforts at economic stabilization and support to the ministries were mostly successful, some outcomes were only short-lived successes, and in certain cases policies, inflexible implementation, and unrealistic expectations hindered economic progress, as did other external political and social factors, most significantly pervasive uncertainty.

Macroeconomic and Balance of Payments (BoP) variables

Growth and economic structure

Consistent with other post-conflict economies, the initial infusion of international civilian and military funds produced a sharp increase in economic activity. Afghanistan was also fortunate that the lingering drought that began in the late 1990s partially abated in 2003–2004, leading to a significant uptick in the agriculture sector, an important component of the economy. This growth was reflected in an increase in real GDP of an average of 9.1% per year between 2003/2004 and 2010/2011. Per capita income increased from USD 120 in 2001 to USD 691 in 2012, a more than five-fold jump (World Bank 2018b). After the first few years, however, corruption, unmet expectations, insecurity and uncertainty began to set in, putting the brakes on the economy's growth. As

Afghanistan anticipated the 2014 drawdown of NATO forces, growth slowed to 1.96% in 2013 and has remained below 2.5% annually ever since (World Bank 2018b). The reduction in the growth rate coinciding with the drawdown of the international presence confirmed the notion that the massive increases in GDP during the first decade of reconstruction, resulting from the influx of external financing and the demand created by a strong international presence in Kabul, were largely unsustainable.

US and NATO troops, as well as international civilian operations, made up a massive economic presence in Afghanistan through 2013, acting as a stimulus in increasing aggregate demand and inflating prices (Aslam et al. 2013). The fastest growing sectors were construction and services, especially communications, financial and business services, government services and transport, which were to a great extent driven by the international presence (World Bank 2018b). Telecommunications and government services were the only ones definitively driven by domestic demand, and much of the government services were financed by foreign aid. It is therefore unlikely that these sectors, outside of telecommunications, will remain drivers of future growth.

Macroeconomic stability

Macroeconomic stabilization was the first priority in implementing orthodoxy in the money market. In 2001, multiple printings of the national currency were in circulation, as were counterfeit versions issued by warlords which traded at slightly less than the value of the official afghani. Various international currencies were also in use. While the IMF wanted to pursue a policy of partial dollarization to swiftly reinstate stability, Afghan authorities pushed for the introduction of a new currency in order to gain trust and confidence in the government and the central bank. The Afghan plan was adopted, and the currency overhaul was successfully completed in less than four months, between September 2002 and January 2003.

Given the absence of a functioning banking system, employing standard monetary policy tools was not an option. During the years of conflict and instability, the central bank's role had been reduced to subsidizing government deficits, and therefore lacked the capacity to perform the functions required by a modern market economy. Two state-owned commercial banks and four state-owned development banks, all of which were largely moribund, made up the rest of the financial sector (IMF 2003; SIGAR 2018).

The international community instead created a mechanism of foreign exchange auctions using large money traders. These foreign exchange auctions have been quite successful and continue on a semi-weekly basis. At the same time, the international community actively worked to build and formalize the commercial banking system, which was regulated by the revitalized central bank (da Afghanistan Bank (DAB)). A major motivator for formalization was the desire to monitor and regulate the informal *hawala* system, which played a major role in financial transactions but also was used in the financing of terror networks. The establishment of stability did generate a level of confidence in the currency, the new Afghani, as well as in DAB; no inflows of money from donor countries, or any formal investment would have been possible without it.

The restricted monetary policy tools and use of foreign exchange as the sole means to influence the money supply forced the linkages between the exchange rate and domestic price levels closer than would be expected in a country with a functioning banking system and standard policy tools. This forced the imposition of a tight range within which the exchange rate was allowed to float. The Afghan Government's Central Statistics Organization (CSO) Consumer Price Index (CPI) estimates suggest that inflation remained relatively stable through 2006.[5] This was viewed as an important success for monetary policy, especially after the massive hyperinflation experienced during the *mujahedeen* and Taliban governments of the 1990s (Byrd 2016; World Bank 2005).

International trade

As early as 2003, reforms were being made to influence BoP accounts and variables. The reforms had two intended results: to lower barriers in order to improve Afghanistan's ability to engage in trade, and to increase customs collection in order to generate government revenues. While substantial quantities of goods were crossing Afghan borders, local warlords in important border provinces, such as Balkh and Herat, retained significant amounts of customs revenues rather than sending them to Kabul. At the time, there were 25 tariff bands and 888 tariff headings; rates ranged from 7% to 150% (IMF 2003). Following the introduction of the new currency in January 2003, customs duties were still being calculated on the value of goods using an artificially low exchange rate of between AFN 2 to AFN 4.5 per US dollar, a fraction of the market rate of approximately AFN 48. In 2004, the Afghan government adopted a new customs reform package and authorities rationalized many tariffs, reducing the number of tariff bands from 25 to 4, at 0, 5, 10 and 25% of value. The lowered rates made Afghanistan one of the region's most open economies (Byrd 2007; IMF 2003).

Afghanistan's trade imbalance has continued to grow since 2002: the value of imports has more than tripled, while the value of exports has been essentially constant. The stark trade imbalance largely reflects the state of Afghan production capabilities as well as the continued difficulties in getting products to market and across borders. Some of the trade imbalance is predictable in a post-conflict economy, with a sudden influx of money and little domestic production of goods, especially luxury consumer items. The international community continued to support agricultural goods as potential exports (e.g. pomegranates, saffron), but even those farmers that could produce goods efficiently still lacked the infrastructure necessary to store and transport those goods across the border, or a clear pathway into regional or global markets in which they may have been competitive, especially with uncooperative neighbours.

Similarly, since 2001, Afghanistan has signed over 30 trade agreements, with varying levels of relevance, actual implementation and effect on trade. In 2004, Afghanistan signed a Trade and Investment Framework Agreement with the US and gained WTO observer status. Three years later it became a full member of the South Asian Association for Regional Cooperation (SAARC), and subsequently signed the South Asian Free Trade Agreement (SAFTA) and the Afghanistan-Pakistan Trade and Transit Agreement (APTTA) in 2011. Afghanistan became a full member of the WTO in 2016, partly in hopes that membership would help negotiation with historically uncooperative trading partners, but also because it would force Afghanistan to come up to international best practices in certification, inspection, and other standards. While Afghanistan rapidly lowered trade barriers across the board, the wider region has remained relatively closed.

As a least developed economy, with already limited human capital which was further depleted by the flight of much of the educated class during the conflict, Afghanistan also lacked the capacity necessary to independently negotiate and implement these trade agreements (Hunter-Wade 2005). Although substantial technical assistance and international consultants were provided to facilitate negotiations, institutional knowledge was not necessarily inculcated or retained. The notion of "renting" rather than building capacity was a recurrent complaint across much of the reconstruction programme, but the complexity of the trade technical area made it especially challenging. High turnover rates and donor organizations hiring the most qualified employees to join their own institutions also played an unhelpful role.

Despite the signing of the various trade agreements, oftentimes trading partners failed to implement the agreement fairly, further disadvantaging domestic producers. Political disputes with Pakistan, for example, have made implementing APTTA, as well as furthering trade with other nations requiring transit through Pakistan, difficult. Smuggling, trade controls and shipping restrictions remained points of tension (Paterson 2006). Trade levels between the two economies dropped by nearly a third in the second half of 2017, in large part due to the deteriorating relationship between the two countries, and India has been forced to bypass Pakistan in order to export to, or import from, Afghan markets. In 2016, India signed a deal with Iran to invest USD 8 billion in the expansion of the Chabahar port, officially inaugurated in December 2017. In large part due to regional disputes and political discord, the anticipated benefits of regional agreements and opening to trade have not been realized. Negotiations on various regional trade and transit initiatives, including with Pakistan, continue, but the process appears more driven by political optics than an actual will to cooperate.

Poverty, employment and human capital indicators

In 2015, the Afghanistan Central Statistics Office released the fourth Afghanistan Living Conditions Survey (ALCS), the most comprehensive compilation of socio-economic indicators available for Afghanistan.[6] The ALCS reports compile data based on surveys of over 150,000 Afghans across all provinces. The 2015 report notes significant progress in certain HDIs since the 2007/2008 survey including: improvements in the adult and youth literacy rates to 34.3% and 51.7% respectively, up from 26.2% and 39%; net attendance ratio in secondary education at 37.2% up from just 16.2%; access to reproductive health services increasing, with 45.2% of women giving birth attended by skilled health personnel compared to 23.9%; access to electricity more than doubling from 42.2% to 89.5%; and the percentage of the population using an improved drinking water source at 64.8% compared to 27.2%. Overall, these statistics indicate positive results in basic *Human Development* overall.

Still, while these indicators show progress, measured national poverty rates have seen no significant change over the last fifteen years. According to the ALCS surveys, around one-third of the population remained below the poverty line throughout the decade, the percentage of the population considered food insecure increased from 28.2% to 33%, and the migration rate shows more people leaving Afghanistan than returning. The National Risk and Vulnerability Assessment (NRVA) surveys, however, only make up a few data points, and are unable to take into account other dimensions of poverty, including factors that lead to a poverty trap or cycle (Kantor and Paine 2009).

While these data are incomplete, reputable, if sometimes anecdotal, evidence continues to indicate that unemployment, underemployment and poverty remain high. The 2017 World Bank Poverty Status Update noted that national poverty levels were increasing due to deteriorating security and labour market conditions (World Bank 2017). At a micro level, a number of small scale studies reinforce this conclusion. For example, a 2016 study on poverty in three villages in Herat also found unchanging levels of poverty, and that village life remained a poverty trap with few options for economic progress (Huot et al. 2016). The urban rural divide was exacerbated by the urban enclave economy. With the inflated urban salaries from internationally financed construction and infrastructure projects, those located in urban centers had better access to opportunities for higher incomes. The large GDP gains throughout the first decade of reconstruction, therefore, were not distributed evenly, and did not accrue to the most poor. This ballooned an already wide inequality gap. The NRVA data-derived estimate of a Gini coefficient, a statistical measure of the degree of inequality between incomes in an economy, increased from 0.297 to 0.316 between 2007/2008 and 2011/2012, further evidencing this claim (UNDP 2016). That poverty has remained persistent despite the significant amount of aid inflows that have boosted the Afghan economy is troubling, but not necessarily surprising given the Afghan context as well as the structure of aid.

Strategy papers from both the Afghan government and international donors stressed job creation and poverty reduction, yet in practice most jobs created were measured by counting the number of persons employed by specific projects (Government of Afghanistan 2008; IMF 2008). These were mostly short-term project-based jobs that did not represent sustainable employment opportunities, and often resulted in underemployment. Furthermore, over 60% of the country remained employed in agriculture, often in the subsistence economy (World Bank 2018b). The jobs created by these projects, therefore, were exacerbating this second, parallel, urban economy detached from most of the population. The International Labor Organization (ILO) noted in 2012 that 90% of jobs in Afghanistan should be classified as vulnerable employment (ILO 2012).

Part of this inequality can be explained by the low *Human Development* progress that has been made for the rural poor. In its 2015 report, the UN ranked Afghanistan among the lowest in the world for *Human Development* with an HDI score of 0.479 (out of a possible high of 1.0) (UNDP 2016). Adjusting for inequality, the index value is even lower at 0.327. While this constitutes an improvement over the UN's 2000 *Human Development* report with an HDI score of 0.340, improvement has been incremental at best (UNDP 2016). However, as discussed in the following section, an even larger problem lies in the structure of markets in many Afghan sectors, which are skewed such that rents accrue to those who are in well-connected positions, and with little income accruing to the poor.

Moreover, Afghanistan's population growth rate is among the highest in the world, meaning a staggering number of jobs that need to be created to sustain the growing labour force. According to the same ILO report, meeting the needs of labour force entrants would require an additional 400,000 jobs to be created annually (ILO 2012). The high population growth also contributes to a skewed age structure, where per every 100 persons of working age, there are 95 children under 15 and five seniors over 65. With such a high dependency ratio and an average household size of 7.4, any increases in income may not show statistically (CSO 2016). This, combined with the continued reliance on agricultural jobs, means that benefits to GDP from the donor-fueled urban economy are unable to reach a large portion of the population.

At the same time, there is no doubt that the level of human capital in 2018 is vastly greater than in 2001, even if it is concentrated in urban areas. Job opportunities derived from the infusion of aid and other foreign spending created an intense demand for education and training, leading to the emergence of large numbers of private schools and training institutions, albeit of varying quality. Significant numbers of Afghans have been trained and given experience by the myriad agencies and companies which have been operating in the country. Foreign educational opportunities have led to a vast increase in the number of Afghans with advanced degrees. As an indicator, in 2001, Afghanistan had 7,900 public university enrollments, while by 2017 there were 174,425 (World Education Services 2016). Many of these gains are the positive consequence of investments in human capital made by donors and by the motivation of Afghans themselves, and may yield benefits to the country in the future if peace and security can be achieved.

Impacts on development and societal welfare

On whether macroeconomic orthodoxy and integrating into the world economy lead to economic growth, job creation and social betterment, it is difficult to draw conclusions. Above all else, the country is not "post-conflict", but rather a country still at war, suffering from uncertainty, insecurity, political instability, human dislocation and migration and capital flight. We can say, however, that early macroeconomic stability efforts and movements towards macroeconomic orthodoxy had largely positive outcomes, as noted above. Reforms in the fiscal sector including the currency overhaul and capacity building of DAB, for example, were necessary to absorb donor inflows and support the rapid GDP growth. This created confidence that was necessary for firms to operate, invest and expand in the formal economy, although domestic and foreign investment have remained low. Other successes may prove less sustainable in the long run. While the sharp decline in GDP growth rates beginning in 2014 is largely attributable to the international military and donor spending drawdown, the simultaneous political transition, and general uncertainty, it also indicates that the economy remains quite susceptible to external shocks. Unfortunately, this means that a prolonged drought, deteriorating security or political turmoil could begin to unravel some GDP gains made over the past decade and a half (Byrd 2016).

Furthermore, while monetary policy tools have been successful in maintaining low-levels of inflation, Afghanistan remains vulnerable to international food and energy prices (Byrd 2016). Anecdotal evidence from market studies beginning as early as 2004, reinforced by recurrent complaints registered in the media, also indicates that the actual price levels experienced in the markets were fluctuating at levels much larger than the official CPI estimates claimed. This likely means that the data sources for the CPI measures were not wholly accurate. It is possible, therefore, that consumers were in fact facing price hikes, further limiting the standard of living for many Afghans. According to the annual public opinion survey conducted by The Asia Foundation, those Afghans surveyed focused on significant price increases in the housing market, which has become unaffordable to many Afghans, especially in urban areas (Asia Foundation 2017).

Conversely, rapid integration into regional and global markets led to a massive BoP deficit, and has had negative impacts on local producers in certain markets. Afghanistan's economy in 2002 was so beset by high energy costs, low human capital, unreliability of intermediate goods and high "informal" transaction costs that firms were not operating productively enough to reach economies of scale and compete regionally. In some cases, opening up to trade so quickly with no clear path to increase exports, especially in potentially competitive sectors and infant industries, led to imports flooding the markets. This became especially salient as hostile and uncooperative neighbours engaged in unfair trade practices–or at a minimum enjoyed a competitive advantage due to their own government's practices – and pushed potentially productive Afghan firms out of business.

Accounts from factory owners and market shops owners in Herat, for example, consistently noted the low-priced imports in manufactured goods and processed foods coming in from Iran. The industrial park that opened in 2005 has seen over 200 businesses close as they were unable to compete with the prices of Iranian products, taxed at the border at only 2–4% (Saber 2014). At the same time, the cheap imports from neighbouring countries and beyond did make some commodities less expensive, positively benefitting some consumers.[7] These benefits did not necessarily accrue evenly, given the disparities in income between the urban areas and the rural poor, often cut off from distribution of products available in the cities.

Additional factors to consider

Outcomes and results of both macroeconomic and trade variables were notably impacted by other factors, either external or inherent to the Afghan economy.

First and foremost, poor economic and overall governance discouraged formalization, expansion and investment, in addition to creating unnecessary barriers for traders. Corruption in both the public and private sectors remains the largest obstacle for economic progress and wellbeing, as corruption is rampant at all levels of administration. Evidence is extensive. The United Nations Office on Drugs and Crime (UNODC) has reported that over 50% of Afghans are forced to resort to bribery when dealing with a public official (UNODC 2012). In its 2017 Ease of Doing Business (EODB) report, the WB ranked Afghanistan number 175 out of 190 countries, one place lower than its 2016 place. The EODB report notes that interpretations of laws differ across different geographic areas, meaning businesses in some locations face even more unnecessary regulatory hurdles for permits, electricity and registering property. For example, in 2017 obtaining a construction permit in Kabul required 13 procedures, an average of 356 days, and 82.7% of the warehouse value. Meanwhile, in Herat, obtaining the same type of permit required 23 procedures, but 133 days and 32.1% of the warehouse value (World Bank 2018a).

Because generating tax revenue is such an integral part of creating fiscal sustainability, the tax system has been under almost continuous reform and modification since 2003. Afghanistan passed a new income tax law in 2005, revising tax legislation on individuals, corporations, companies, and other legal entities. This law showed major efficiency improvements, including the reduction of the top marginal tax rate.[8] Still, Afghans were unaccustomed to paying taxes, and the prospect of the government taking a share of already uncertain profits (not to mention the additional costs of time and illegal "fees" involved in actually making the payments) has prompted many firms to continue to operate informally (Fishstein and Amiryar 2015).

In a similar vein, customs reform was emphasized primarily as a mean for increasing revenues and encouraging trade. Still, despite systems being put in place, Afghanistan's continued poor performance in the EODB indicators is in large part due to poor performance in ease of cross border trade. In 2016, Afghanistan ranked 174 out of 189 in ease of trading across borders due to long and costly documentary compliance, border compliance and domestic transport (World Bank 2018a). A cross-country analysis shows that requiring signatures and excessive registration procedures lower the overall export volume for those countries where bureaucratic procedures are more complex. The bureaucratic process of requiring signatures can reduce overall exports by the same amount as an additional 5% tariff (Sadikov 2007). Considering that exporting in Afghanistan requires on average ten separate documents and documentary compliance has an associated cost of USD 900 according to the EODB indicators, the trade costs regarding bureaucratic processes remain high (World Bank 2018a).

Poor infrastructure (e.g. roads, access to and availability of storage) and physical insecurity have also discouraged trade. These informal, behind the border barriers to trade make it more difficult for any Afghan products to have a chance at getting to the border to sell and being competitive if they get there. Possibly more importantly, the entire process continues to be mired in corruption. As an indicator of corruption, poor governance at border crossings, the percentage of items that remain unspecified coming into and leaving the country remains high. In 2014, more than 70% of exports and nearly 63% of imports in Afghanistan were classified as "goods not elsewhere specified" according to the Classification by Broad Economic Categories (BEC) commodity classifications (Sadikov 2007). According to some Afghan customs officials, information about contents, weight and the country of origin can be altered such that the customs bill can be undervalued by up to 70% (Walsh 2014). A 2017 audit found that as much as half of the potential government revenue from customs from 2014 was lost to corruption at the border (SIGAR 2015).

Moreover, substantial barriers and informal market regulations prevent certain groups or individuals from entering certain markets. In trade, larger trading companies with more capital were the only firms able to trade profitably, mainly due to their personal networks within and outside Afghanistan. Almost all trading companies had ties to regional warlords who provided them security and often allowed them to skirt border taxes (Lister and Karaev 2004). Smaller entities, or those with fewer or weaker connections, were often strongly disadvantaged, as they suffered from unequal treatment at borders, were often subject to informal payments to local power-holders, and were unable to negotiate better terms for themselves making trade less profitable (Lister and Karaev 2004).

Some firms faced similar difficulties with market access in domestic markets. For example, in the booming construction sector, only a small number of large contractors and sub-contractors were awarded contracts for large construction projects, making it difficult for smaller firms to compete (Lister and Karaev 2004). This occurred in other sectors as well. In Jalalabad, the terms of market participation of vegetable traders remain dependent on their relationships to a small group of elites who dictate market access, supply and pricing (AREU 2016). Connection to networks of access are mandatory in many cases for ability to import and export goods, sell products at local markets, and sometimes even maintain physical safety (AREU 2016). It is evident how the well-connected have acted, sometimes using violence, to suppress competition and gain benefits for themselves. These dynamics discourage investment, and the criminal patronage system creates yet another obstacle for businesses. According to one analysis, this has limited the spread of wealth such that it has inhibited the creation of a business class (Giustozzi 2007).

Second, when discussing economic outcomes in Afghanistan, it is necessary to note that the majority of growth was due to the Kabul-centered, donor-fueled economy and a massive inflow of exogenous financial injections. In any post-conflict economy, it is common to observe high growth rates as initial investments to restore infrastructure and human capital generate a high multiplier effect. Reconstruction spending translates into local market demand for goods and services, especially construction, transport and other logistics services. In Afghanistan, this was primarily funded by foreign aid and international presence.

The main structural change to Afghanistan's economy was the sharp increase in the service sector, driven largely by the international presence, as noted above. The largest component of industry growth, meanwhile, was construction (Hogg et al. 2013). Based on international experience, strong growth in these subsectors is common following conflict, as demand is driven by the international aid flows; this growth is not sustainable following withdrawal of personnel and donor money. In Afghanistan, these sectors saw even higher growth due to the large military and civilian presence in the economy. Initially, international firms dominated the construction market, but over time Afghan firms were contracted or sub-contracted to build infrastructure for military bases and other international structures. Still, despite the construction boom, the jobs created in this sector were mostly short term, project-based employment. The international and military presence did create job growth, but it was mostly temporary employment and centered in the cities. This donor-fueled economy had limited direct effect on agriculture, which as employer of approximately 44% of the population remains the most important sector (CSO 2016). Therefore, this did little for long-term growth in GDP, employment, investment, and consumption once the international presence began to diminish.

Although much of the employment was short-term, wage rates and salaries for all types of work rose substantially from 2002 to around 2012. Although no systematic measures are readily available, international agencies and contractors paid salaries up to 11 times the established civil service wage rate (Sud 2013). This led to substantial wage inflation across the board (IMF 2016). The over-heated economy, especially in construction, also positively affected the wages for skilled and even unskilled casual labour. Increased wage rates also had some negative consequences, as it meant that Afghanistan's labour costs were less competitive regionally, and that some projects would prefer sourcing labour from neighbouring Pakistan. However, as the 2014 drawdown in military forces approached, the availability of employment along with the salaries and wages of office workers and labourers levelled off or declined, reflecting both the reduced international spending and, relatedly, the increasing uncertainty about the post-2014 economic, political and security environment.

Interestingly, provincial differences in aid spending show that more conflict-prone areas actually saw a larger increase in household consumption than more peaceful areas. These areas received substantially more international aid and military presence, and therefore saw increases in employment, albeit much of it temporary (World Bank 2016).

Third, it is impossible to discuss Afghanistan's economy without discussing the implications of its most significant cash crop, opium poppy. With the net value of opiates estimated at 16% of GDP in 2016, opium persists as Afghanistan's most significant cash-generating industry, albeit proportionately less so than in 2004, when it was equivalent to one-third of GDP (Byrd and Ward 2004; Byrd and Mansfield 2014). The opium economy provides Afghanistan with a very mixed bag of benefits and threats.

At the macroeconomic level, it has helped to generate aggregate demand for goods and services and has helped with BoP. Although, as an illicit product it is not taxed by the state, the government acquires customs and other revenue on goods purchased with ill-gotten gains. At the microeconomic level, in many areas of Afghanistan, high returns to opium poppy cultivation and trade produce a multiplier effect in creating secondary jobs, as farmers have money to spend on food, medical care and other consumer products (Byrd and Mansfield 2014). As a labour-intensive crop, it creates employment, especially for the landless. For the rural poor, opium often represents the only available means of stored value and savings, and provides a source of capital to improve livelihoods. This also allows households to send children to school and to accumulate money to liquidate debt and for financing larger capital purchases such as cars and other forms of transport, which enabled them to leave opium poppy cultivation in favour of licit transport activity. For the rural landless and land-poor, cultivation of opium poppy can be the only means by which they can access land and credit.

Ultimately, however, the opium economy remains a threat to sustainable, licit development. By reinforcing corruption, it has clearly had a corrosive effect on governance, which in turn has discouraged licit economic activity, not to mention lack of support for the State. As an agricultural commodity which is susceptible to both weather and plant diseases, resultant sharp price swings have the potential to create opium-denominated debt from which farmers cannot get out from under. By generating large amounts of cash, opium poppy has led to elevated prices and has thereby been "capitalized" in many aspects of the economy, including agricultural landowner-tenant relations, rural and urban land prices and bride prices (Byrd and Ward 2004).

Opium poppy thrives in insecurity, which provides incentives to maintain insecurity and an environment without the rule of law. Viable rural enterprises require well-functioning markets and good governance; without accessible, well-functioning markets, rural opportunities will be limited, and economic incentives will continue to run in the direction of opium poppy cultivation, processing and trade (Byrd and Ward 2004).

Conclusions and implications

In the case of Afghanistan, the answer to whether following international standards on macroeconomic policy and opening up to trade has had positive impacts on economic growth, job creation and *Human Development* is not clear cut. Early macroeconomic stabilization created confidence in the currency that was necessary to support what limited investment did occur and made it possible for the international community and military presence to contract jobs to Afghan firms. Because the Kabul-centered donor-fueled economy was the biggest contributor to growth and job creation throughout the intervention, macroeconomic stabilization directly led to economic growth and indirectly fostered employment, at least in the short term.

The BoP variables and regional integration, however, paint a less positive picture. Although there may be some longer-term benefits from WTO accession in terms of applying international best practices and a legal framework for trade disputes, in the short term rapid and sweeping lowering of trade barriers hurt many firms who may have otherwise become competitive. A policy of slower, more deliberate opening of markets, focused on increasing productivity and efficiency, facilitating transport to and across the border, and providing support to compete in regional and international markets, could have helped firms expand and provide more employment opportunities in those sectors.

While the linkages between economic interventions, growth and *Human Development* in Afghanistan vary in strength, this cannot necessarily be taken as a policy prescription for other developing countries. The short and long-term impacts of the donor driven economy make Afghanistan an abnormal case. This is not only because it was a country at war, but it is also impossible to determine the extent to which these interventions impacted growth and development separate from international spending and military presence.

Notes

1 GDP per capita figures from the WB, "World Development Indicators". Available at: http://databank.worldbank.org/data/reports.aspx?source=world-development-indicators (last accessed: 15 March 2018). Figures from Afghanistan are notoriously unreliable, even without considering the discontinuities from the war years. It is notable that for a variety of reasons (including political sensitivity), Afghanistan has never had an official census and therefore lacks a population baseline.

2 An additional 8% of expenditures were covered by natural gas sales, which is typically also considered rentier income. The reliance on foreign sources goes back to at least the nineteenth century, when the British provided "subsidies".

3 Though Pakistan remains Afghanistan's largest trading partner, political tension and transit issues have led to a substantial decrease in trade between the two countries from 2016–2017, while trade with India and Iran both grew.

4 IMF staff publishes a Country Report every few months reviewing the status of the ongoing or renewed SMP as well as the Extended Credit Facility. These reports can be accessed at www.imf.org/en/Countries/ResRep/AFG.

5 The CSO publishes CPI statistics online at: http://cso.gov.af/en/page/ict/5555/5353.

6 Previous reports were released for 2005, 2007/2008 and 2011/2012, though changes in methodology post-2005 render those data point incomparable to the later three. The ALCS reports were formerly titled the National Risk and Vulnerability Assessment.

7 For several years, chickens from Brazil were the preference of the international community and many well-off Afghans.

8 An unofficial translation of Afghanistan's 2005 Income Tax Law prepared by the Ministry of Finance can be found at: www.afghan-web.com/economy/afghan_income_tax_law.pdf.

References

AREU (2016), 'The Rules of the Game: Towards a theory of networks of access'. Available at: https://securelivelihoods.org/wp-content/uploads/BP19-The-rules-of-the-game_Towards-a-theory-of-networks-of-access.pdf (last accessed: 15 March 2018).

Asia Foundation (2017), 'A Survey of the Afghan People'. Available at: http://surveys.asiafoundation.org/Dashboard?SurveyCode=AGSAP&SampleName=GP&SectionName=Default&LanguageName=English#tptab15 (last accessed: 15 March 2018).

Aslam, A., Berkes, E. G., Fukac, M., Menkulasi, J. And Schimmlepfennig, A. (Eds.) (2013), 'Afghanistan: Balancing Social and Security Spending in the Context of Shrinking Resource Envelope', IMF Working Paper, May.

Byrd, W. (2007), 'Responding To Afghanistan's Development Challenge: an assessment of experience during 2002–2007 and issues and priorities for the future', World Bank, October 10.

Byrd, W. (2016), 'Macroeconomic and public financial management in Afghanistan', in S. Smith and C. Cookman (Eds.), *State Strengthening in Afghanistan: Lessons Learned 2001–2014* (pp. 81–99), Washington, DC: United States Institute for Peace.

Byrd, W. and Mansfield, D. (2014), 'Afghanistan's Opium Economy: An Agricultural, Livelihoods, and Governance Perspective', The World Bank, June 23.

Byrd, W. and Ward, C. (2004), 'Afghanistan's Opium Drug Economy', World Bank, 1 December 2004.

CSO (2016), 'Afghanistan Living Conditions Survey (ALCS): Key Indicators'.

Dowdy, J., and Erdmann, A. (2011), 'Private sector development in Afghanistan: the doubly missing middle', in J. S. Nye, B. Scowcroft, N. Burns and J. Price (Eds.), *American Interests in South Asia: Building a Grand Strategy in Afghanistan, Pakistan, and India* (pp. 109–127), Aspen: Aspen Strategy Group.

Fishstein, P. and Amiryar, M. E. (2015), 'Afghan Economic Policy, Institutions, and Society Since 2001', United States Institute of Peace (USIP), October.

Fishstein, P. and Wilder, A. (2012), 'Winning Hearts and Minds? Examining the Relationship between Aid and Security in Afghanistan', Feinstein International Center, Tufts University.

Girardet E. (2011), *Killing the Cranes: A Reporter's Journey Through Three Decades of War in Afghanistan*, White River Junction, VT: Chelsea Green Publishing.

Giustozzi, A. (2007), 'War and Peace Economies of Afghanistan's Strongmen," *International Peacekeeping*, 14(1), January 2007, 75–89, 109.

Guimbert, S. (2004), 'Structure and Performance of the Afghan Economy', SASPR Working Paper no. 30861, World Bank, May.

Hogg, R., Nassif, C., Gomez, O. C., Byrd, W. and Beath, A. (2013), *Afghanistan in Transition: Looking Beyond 2014. Directions in Development; Countries and Regions*. Washington, DC: World Bank.

Hunter-Wade, R. (2005), 'Why Free Trade Has Costs for Developing Countries', *Financial Times*, 10 August.

Huot, D., Pain, A. and Ghafoori, I. (2016), 'Livelihood trajectories in Afghanistan: evidence from three villages in Herat Province', AREU, December.

ILO (2012), 'Afghanistan: Time to Move to Sustainable Jobs, Study on the State of Employment in Afghanistan', May.

IMF (2003), 'Rebuilding a Macroeconomic Framework for Reconstruction and Growth', Country Report No. 03/299, September.

IMF (2008), 'Islamic Republic of Afghanistan: Poverty Reduction Strategy Paper', 9 May.

IMF (2016), *Ex-Post Assessment of Longer Term Program Engagement*, 8 February.

Kantor, P. and Pain, A. (2009), 'Delivering on Poverty Reduction: Focusing ANDS Implementation on Pro-poor outcomes', AREU Discussion Paper, January.

Lister, S. and Karaev, S. (2004), 'Markets in Afghanistan: A Case Study of the Construction Materials Market', AREU, June.

Paterson, A. (2006), 'Going to Market: Trade and Traders in Six Afghan Sectors', AREU, June.

Rubin, B. R. (2002), *The Fragmentation of Afghanistan: State Formation and Collapse in the International System*, Second Edition, New Haven: Yale University Press.

Saber, S. (2014), 'Foreign Imports Killing Afghan Industry', Institute for War and Peace Reporting, 14 June.

Sadikov, A. (2007), 'Border and Behind-the-Border Trade Barriers and Country Exports', IMF Working Paper no. 07/292, December.

SIGAR (2017), 'USAID's ATAR Program has Failed to Achieve Goals for Implementation of E-Payment System to Collect Customs Revenues', SIGAR 17-61-SP, August.

Sud, I. (2013), Afghanistan: A Synthesis Paper of Lessons from Ten Years of Aid', Washington, DC: World Bank.

Suhrke, A. (2006), 'When More is Less: Aiding Statebuilding in Afghanistan, FRIDE Working Paper no. 26, September.

UNDP (2001), 'Level of Human Development in Afghanistan Among Lowest in World: UN Figures', 8 October. Available at: https://news.un.org/en/story/2001/10/16732-level-human-development-afghanistan-among-lowest-world-un-figures (last accessed: 15 March 2018).

UNDP (2016), 'Human Development Data (1990–2015)'. Available at: http://hdr. undp.org/en/indicators/137506# (last accessed: 15 March 2018).

UNODC (2012), 'Corruption in Afghanistan: Recent Patterns And Trends', December.

Walsh, D. (2014), 'At Afghan Border, Graft is Part of the Bargain' *NY Times*, 11 November.

World Bank (2005), 'The Investment Climate in Afghanistan: Exploiting Opportunities in an Uncertain Environment'. Available at: https://openknowledge.worldbank. org/handle/10986/8484 (License: CC BY 3.0 IGO).

World Bank (2016), 'Conflict and Poverty in Afghanistan's Transition', A. V. Floreani, G. Lopez-Acevedo and M. Rama, Policy Research Working Paper 7864, October.

World Bank (2017), 'Afghanistan Poverty Status Update – Progress at Risk'. Available at: www.worldbank.org/en/country/afghanistan/publication/afghanistan-poverty-status-update-report-2017 (last accessed: 15 March 2018).

World Bank (2018a), 'Doing Business in Afghanistan in 2017'. Available at: www. doingbusiness.org/data/exploreeconomies/afghanistan (last accessed: 15 March 2018).

World Bank (2018b), 'World Development Indicators'. Available at: https://data. worldbank.org/indicator (last accessed: 15 March 2018).

World Education Services (2016), 'Education System profiles: Education in Afghanistan', World Education News and Review.

Index

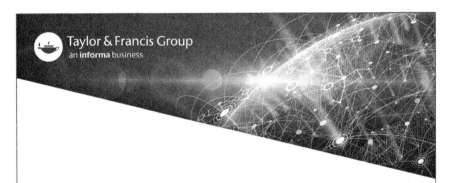

Printed in the United States
by Baker & Taylor Publisher Services